Between You And Me

LOUIS NIZER

Between You And Me

Revised Edition

THOMAS YOSELOFF, PUBLISHER
NEW YORK • LONDON

Thomas Yoseloff, *Publisher*
8 East 36th Street
New York 16, N. Y.

Thomas Yoseloff Ltd
18 Charing Cross Road
London W. C. 2, England

First printing April 1963
Second printing August 1963

9889
Printed in the United States of America

Contents

Part IV—LOOKING OUT THE WINDOW

Part V—CLOSING THE DOOR

DEDICATED
To My Mother and Father

PART I

At the Gate

CHAPTER 1

The Author's Jacket

IT IS CUSTOMARY for a publisher to describe the contents of a book in a brief summary printed on its paper jacket. This is an unenviable task. If he is lavish in his estimate, he may well be accused of bias. If he is conservative and practices understatement, then he is open to the charge that he lacks appreciation for his own presentation. Caught in the conflict between self-interest and objective appraisal, he is in no better position to write a promissory note on the work he presents than—well, to come right out with it, the author himself.

To preserve his dignity, an author often writes *his* blurb in a preface. Since the preface is read only after the book has been elected for bed-table use, no commercial stigma attaches to it. Furthermore, the author's self-interest is offset by many factors. Even if he nursed the private conviction that he was a genius, he would not dare incite the reader's defiance by sharing such a confidence. Shaw and several others have whispered (should I have said shouted?) confessions of their genius to their readers. It has been pointed out that Shaw's belief in himself is refreshing in these atheistic days when so many believe in no God at all. He and a few like him are exceptions who have become heady because of the recognition of their extraordinary gifts and who have repaid such flattery with their unorthodox vagaries. But, in the ordinary case, the reader can depend upon the modesty of an author in describing his work. Most writers are neurotically unappreciative of their own efforts anyway.

I assume for myself a happy norm which recognizes that the fires of an inflamed ego do not give genuine heat and, also, that the chill winds of an inferiority complex will freeze only one's inner sense of values. Thus equipped with a badge of balance gallantly conferred upon myself, I venture forth to write my own jacket.

To this much conceit I cling: I claim I know best the contents of this book and the objective of the author in presenting it. I may even be as able as anyone else to fore-warn the reader and create a sense of anticipation which will aid him in evaluating the book (as likely to my chagrin as otherwise).

The key word is *awareness.*

If an infant could record its first impressions, a great writer would be acclaimed. It is the freshness of original observa-tion which creates imagery and meaningfulness. Unfortu-nately, life dulls the senses with repetition. It is impossible to react rawly to a stimulus once before experienced. Always the succeeding sensation produces less "shock" until a point is reached when our reaction, whether emotional or intel-lectual, to oft-repeated events, is imperceptible. We take them for granted. Soon we do not see, hear or understand things assailing our senses. Like the patient who no longer obtains relief from a drug because his body is inured to its stimulation, so healthy people can no longer be relieved from boredom by the normal occurrences which are teeming around them.

A child, throwing a pebble for the first time into a still lake, says, "The lake smiled back at me." An adult throws a pebble into the water aimlessly and does not even see the ripples. If, by some miracle, the lake remained glasslike despite the pebble, the adult, startled by the unaccustomed phenomenon, would instantly observe the incident and per-haps conjure up the image that the lake is "dead."

A child who, for the first time, sees his father take a white cylindrical object from a package, place it in his mouth, set fire to it so that it floods his mouth with smoke which he expels, must be bewildered to find that the fuming stick which is befouling the air is not thrown away or doused with water, but put back into the mouth so that its smoke fills his father's lungs. After a number of such silly exhibitions, the child accepts this extraordinary procedure without further reaction. Although it makes his eyes smart and he recognizes the evil smell in the house, he no longer sees these things. It simply registers on his mind as "Father is smoking."

Awareness, then, is the precious faculty through which we enjoy or suffer. It is to be noted, however, that cults practicing "higher consciousness" assume it is something to be acquired rather than something to be preserved. We start with keen awareness. It is the process of erosion which permits the soil of our concentration to be washed away in the flowing waters of repeated experience.

It is interesting to trace this process in the arts. A child given a paint brush paints crudely but imaginatively, and without the standard clichés of proper form. He grows up and devotes a lifetime to study. He acquires the equipment of a good academician. Likeness and perspective flow from his brush, but he is unhappy. He fears being a "photographer" with an easel. So he deserts his classical training, painstakingly acquired. He strives to see freshly and uninhibitedly. His paintings become more and more crude and untrained. Soon they resemble those of a child. The cycle is completed. The detractors of modern art defy the uninitiated to distinguish between the first paintings of ten-year-olds in the public schools and those of a master in his new period. Is this not an approximation of some of the changes in Picasso's style?

In writing, too, the struggle for "higher consciousness" is unending. Here, too, the clarity and insight of first reaction is not to be recaptured by techniques. Too often familiar clichés are slightly distorted and then called invention. Plots, which are only the reflection of standardized formulas, bear less and less resemblance to reality. Feelings begin to fit bromidic conceptions. Thoughts conform to accepted notions of right or wrong. The story becomes stilted. It is a series of postures, no more valuable as an interpretation of American life than an escapist Hollywood picture. The writer finds that his training in the use of words cannot compensate for the blindness of his eye or the failure of his other senses. That is why eloquence of tongue or pen is frequently associated with lack of content. Progress in the art of expression is far ahead of progress in the art of fresh thinking. It is more than a coincidence that the same disparity exists between scientific progress and civilized thinking.

The result is a revolt. Some writers, like Saroyan, abandon form to concentrate on feeling, as if the shell were to blame for the lack of a kernel inside. Others, like Thomas Wolfe, are so anxious to get to the essence of things that they not only ignore form, but tear it out by the roots and, together with it, all self-discipline and organization. Then thoughts and feelings flow like a torrent, undammed. Others, like James Joyce, attack form by mutilating language and breeding new word spores. Others, like Gertrude Stein, indulge in the illusion that they have never been contaminated by form, and revert to the stammering, repetitive simplicity of children.

The phenomenon of recapturing awareness has myriad other expressions—to mention only some, deliberate resort to shock, irreverence, insult, slang, self-depreciation, confession, morbidity and perversion. The reader can fit many books (like *The Lost Weekend, The Snake Pit* and *Memoirs of Hecate County*) into their appropriate categories.

The point is that writers, like painters, fear the heavy layers of paint. They dread the techniques of the caressing word and the subtleties of style. They are horrified lest they cease to see and feel because they have sublimated their intellectual and emotional energies into mere formalism. In their effort to remove the chains which they acquire with their writing equipment, they look longingly to the style-lessness of infancy. Thus the cycle is completed.

There is an unending struggle in the arts. It is between thought and form, freshness and callousness, first reaction and experience, naïveté and sophistication, originality and stereotypery, the natural sense and culture. It is a struggle to preserve consciousness and sensitivity.

There are a few rare poets (whether they work in clay, words, paint or music) who can project their instinctive and sensitive reactions in felicitious form. They combine sub-stance and form, creating thereby an artistic whole. They do not feel that their faculties are drained by their attention to the beauties of expression. On the contrary, they find that substance is enriched and given greater meaning through form. They are the gifted few who can preserve the purity of infancy with the training of maturity. All who transcribe thought with ink aspire to these heights, though we know full well how impossible the climb is for most of us.

Since what I have called awareness is the key to at least partial success for every writer, the subject matter of his work is often less important than the sensitive reaction he brings to bear upon it. Even a central theme may be unnecessary, for events and impressions are not carefully ordered. They are quite haphazard and accidental. It is our response to their stimuli which make them subjectively a unity.

Often one's awareness gives rise to a series of impressions without any cementing unity. The central theme is merely the varied reactions of an observer to a moving belt of people and things. The following pages offer only such a unity. If a more traditional single subject matter is sought, it will not be found.

A preface affords an author an opportunity to comment on his purpose and hopes, without encroaching on the domain of more objective appraisers. In this spirit I have made an explanation which may be interpreted to be antic-ipatory defense or even apology. But I prefer it to a ruse which I once practiced and which, in the momentum of self-revelation, I am ready to confess.

My dereliction involved a book called *Thinking on Your Feet*. It was a collection of introductions of significant people and addresses on a wide variety of subjects. A vociferous few had been impressed by the original talks and word of their enthusiasm had reached the ear of a publisher. I was invited to reconstruct these talks from radio recordings and from memory so that they could be collected in a book. I did so. The material had no central theme or unity.

The resourceful publisher then made a suggestion. Perhaps he had known from the beginning that he was going to make it, but merely bided his time to assure himself that the major work would be done; or perhaps it was a last minute inspiration arising from the necessities of the occasion. I shall never know. In any event he said, "Why don't you tie together this material by writing a chapter or two on the art of public speaking? Then comment on each introduction and speech to demonstrate how it was constructed and how it applies the principles you have set forth." Reluctantly I undertook the task. The book was transformed into a "how to" work.

The experiment was interesting. It was like literary grafting from which a new fruit came into being. I am happy to say that many found it not undelectable. Surely it justified the publisher's shrewdness, for the work attracted an audience which would otherwise have paid scant attention to it. Indeed, to this day it continues in steady circulation, as a textbook and among those who ask, not for this book nor certainly for the author, but for any work on how to speak. The book is then foisted upon them. The reputation of a subject is more dependable than the reputation of an author.

Although the transposition from discourse to instruction satisfied the publisher, it left a void in me. What I had intended to be artful evaluations of significant people and stimulating thinking on difficult subjects became mere illustrations of the art of speaking. It was as if a footnote had been elevated to prime position while the text had become simply an annotation. Or at least so I felt. In a concluding chapter of that book (I dared not put it into the preface and frighten away the student bent on learning public speaking) I hinted slyly that perhaps the content of the "illustrations" was more valuable than the principles of speech construction which they demonstrated.

This previous experience in creating a central thread upon which to string together varied subjects has encouraged me, not to emulation, but to independence. I therefore present this book for what it is, without the appurtenances of unifiers, central themes, organizational devices and the like.

Since there will not be lacking those whose duty it will be to point out the disadvantage of a disconnected discourse, I hasten to list a few of its advantages. In the first place, this is definitely not a book which you will be unable to put down once you have begun reading. You will not neglect your business or your family because you have become enmeshed in the succeeding pages. There is no high-voltage attraction which, though you scream with pain, prevents you from loosening your grip.

I know that in writing the lure of suspense has been proved to be as irresistible as the lure of sex. From the lowliest cartoon to the most artful Maugham story, the reader's interest is coaxed and teased until he hungers for satisfaction. Then he is playfully pushed aside and invited to read the next installment. He may have to wait for the succeeding newspaper while uncertainty gnaws at him or he may, as in a book, pounce upon the next chapter. Here his curiosity is sufficiently gratified to reduce his fever, but only temporarily. Inevitable is a new incitation which tempts him farther, so that by the end of the chapter his craving has been renewed and, if possible, whetted to an even sharper edge. So the process continues until, at the end of the book, he is either disillusioned or exhausted. Though readers are quite familiar with this technique, they do not seem to shy away from it any more than most men do from the blandishments of a pretty woman simply because they recognize her wiles.

Well, this book eschews such methods. By virtue of circumstance rather than principle, the bait of suspense has been omitted and there is no line of continuity upon which the reader is reeled in and gaffed. On the contrary, the very fact that one chapter has no association with the next serves as a notice of recess and invites you to observe a decent interval for reflection before proceeding with what I should like to call the next adventure.

Another advantage of loose-jointed structure is that the reader need not maintain a continuous thought. He can open the book at any chapter and fare as well reading backward as forward.

I might refer to the analogy between this book and collections of short stories which permit similar segmented interest. True, the mood is broken frequently, but this can be an advantage to the author as well as to the reader, for he can always discount a failure by the bright promise of a fresh start.

Above all (and here tongue is no longer in cheek) a kaleidoscopic variety of subjects reflects most nearly the profusion of events as they register on our consciousness. One need only observe the mind's process in the reading of a daily newspaper to recognize that normally our interests are varied and chaotic. In quick succession we respond to the stimuli of international tug and pull; a morsel of divorce gossip; the latest labor-capital truculence; the awesome predictions of the contestants in next Friday's boxing match, or the lachrymose forecasts of the coaches concerning next Saturday's football contests; the economic high blood-pressure of American business expected in 1948; the perpetual civil war in bridge in which North replies to South; the profundities of columnists, expressed anonymously in editorials and under photograph and name on adjoining pages; the human interest news, which is as prolix and inconsistent as humanity; the religious appeals for faith expressed in thundering accents revealing lack of faith in man's conversion; the latest didoes of cartoon characters appealing to our infantilism and fantasies; Russia's suspicions of our suspicions and our fears of Russia's suspicions; the newest dreadful darling, the cosmic ray; the legal maneuvers in a murder trial, and a host of other miscellany.

This book casts a roaming eye on the panorama of rushing, disorderly events and records certain impressions about them. From chapters on What To Do With Russia to Gin Rummy,—The National Illusion, this book deals with the profound and the trivial, because life is not selective and one's awareness must encompass a wide area or cease to be awareness at all. I have always had sympathy, if not contempt, for the specialist whose energies are so canalized that all but one faculty becomes atrophied. Who of us does not know a doctor who is ill at ease in any discussion but medicine? As familiar is the businessman whose interests are so limited that retirement means mental and physical inertia, deterioration and death.

Versatility should not be looked upon as a unique gift, but rather as an inevitable result of practicing a full life. The degree of our varied skills will, of course, differ according to the extent to which we develop our inherent qualities. But to surrender our faculties by disinterest and disuse seems to me to be a default of life itself. That is why it is no mere figure of speech to say that some people are partly dead. To be tone deaf is to be dead to a sublime phase of life. To be unaware of the exhilaration of playing tennis, golf or other exercise is to be partly dead. To ignore the theatre or motion pictures is to be deprived of the joys of fantasy, no less genuine because they are man-made. The wider our enthusiasms, the richer our lives. In measuring the scope of our interests, there is no law of diminishing returns because those interests tend toward trivial rather than universal subjects, or toward physical rather than cerebral pursuits. Happiness is not snobbish. It can come equally to the savage because he is dangling shining beads, the rider because he is mastering his horse, the statesman because he is achieving a cohesive compromise, or the scientist because he is unravelling a chemical knot. No, ignorance is not bliss. The cynic who coined that phrase was weak on semantics. Ignorance, by itself, is nothingness, and nothingness is boredom, another form of death. To know may sometimes be painful, but pain is also life. There is none in death. The cynic probably meant to use the word "simplicity" instead of "ignorance," and even then he told only a half-truth, for a simple life can be bliss only if fully lived.

This is the reason for the unevenness of the subject matter selected for eyeing in the succeeding pages. Mountain peaks and molehills are within the focus of the eye. Shallow yearnings as well as deep feelings are recorded on our psyche. Temperamental flurries as well as basic motivations affect not only personal but also mass history. The caressing jest, as well as the profound principle, colors our lives.

So much for the diversification of the subject matter. The forewarning now turns to the other half of the book: people.

The only things that do not get out of date are people. This is a tragic fact. It means that centuries of progress have left the basic nature of man substantially untouched. The following pages are devoted to mankind by glimpsing special samples of it. The significant contributions of certain men to events are often chronicled. But this is not the main emphasis because events which loom large and historic have a way of shrinking into corners where only researchers will some day find them. The vast roll of time seems to swallow up each generation of struggling man and make his advent on the scene a trivial incident in a cosmic process.

What a man has done, described seriatim, may not reveal him as much as describing the personality pattern into which he falls. Portraitists aspire not merely to literal likeness but to painting which will survive any disinterest in its accuracy. Writers can aim at the same target. That is why some of the word portraits in the following pages may rightly be deemed descriptive not of just one particular person, be he senator, actor or writer, but of the class of such persons. In other words, many of the sketches are archetypical rather than specific. Yet we cannot ignore the fact that each man differs from the hundreds of millions around him in face and in inner face. The way in which he differs is one of the most fascinating of all studies. What motivates him, what talents he develops and how he uses them constitute the living drama continuously enacted all about us.

While remarkable men may exist here and there who conceal the special gifts which would bring them recognition, the converse is not true. Those who have achieved attention possess some unique claim to it. It may not be admirable, but it is sure to be distinguishable. It is useful to isolate and examine unusual characteristics, for sometimes a directional impulse can change the force behind a vice into the power behind a virtue.

Famous people are frequently disappointing. This is because their distinctions have been embellished with publicity's gold tinting, concealing equally the hard steel and the fragile glass which may lie underneath. When the discerning observer has the opportunity of personal examination, he is oft-times disillusioned by the discovery of the fraud. This reaction sometimes obscures appreciation of the original product. The hero may not be what he pretended to be, but he may be more interesting for what he is.

This is one of the reasons why I have frequently resorted in this book to historical analogy. A man's relationship to his times is often best perceived by references to his predecessors in achievement. History gives us known poles from which our reckonings can be best computed. It is a simple trick which every historian practices. A man's status having been established from the vantage point of historical perspective, we can place him more accurately in our modern firmament.

The risk of confusion from such an exercise is not to be

denied. Whenever one looks at past centuries alternately through the small and the large end of a telescope, distance and time become somewhat blurred. I have tried to avoid the error of the amateur playwright whose rush into past centuries was so headlong that he lost his time balance. In a gripping scene he portrayed an obstetrician returning home in the early hours of the morning from his labor and that of his patient. His wife solicitously inquired, "Are you very tired, dear?" "Ah, I am exhausted, utterly exhausted," he replied. And then with a sudden burst of enthusiasm, "But it was worth it, the baby's name was Victor Hugo!"

Our bearings can be checked not merely against the misplacement of a century but for the accuracy of our direction. Does the comparison dwarf our subject so that we are shamefaced at making it? Does it suggest a whole series of plausible comparisons which suddenly reveal a progressive line from past generations to our own, in which the latest bearer of the torch is the man we are weighing? I hope this method of looking backward for spiritual ancestry proves as rewarding to the reader as it has been to me in making evaluations.

The biographer is a critic and his sense of values can either reveal or distort. If he devotes a whole book to one man, he depends upon minute detail to give insight into his subject. I have not indulged in the luxury of protracted recital nor, as already noted, have I followed the biographical pattern. This has been a task of condensation and severe selectivity, the avoidance of literalness and the substitution of other values in an effort to indicate the significance of the man. Brevity has not simplified the task of lucid revelation and discriminating interpretation. "My novel would have been much shorter," said a knowing author, "had I had more time." Pruning is always more painstaking than sowing. To say more in fewer words is not only a feat of conservation, but also of clarity. In treating with people in this book I have endeavored to relieve the reader of unnecessary burdens. My aim has been to have surgical courage, so that the message will be unencumbered by prolixity and purified by self-examination. All of this is to revert once more to awareness, this time of people rather than things.

The sub-title of this book, *A Biography of Spare Time,* will serve to explain the haphazard method by which the people in this book were selected for review. They were all honored at public functions at which I happened to preside. The ancient custom of conferring academic degrees upon people of distinction has been informalized and democratized, so that now institutions other than universities make free use of the privilege. Pulitzer Prizes, Motion Picture Academy awards, Freedom House awards and many others dot the horizon of the daily newspapers. Philanthropic and other public causes utilize the distinction of a leading citizen by tendering a dinner in his honor and obtaining financial support from the large assemblage which gathers to pay tribute to him. These occasions seem to me to be useful in every way. The guest of honor knows full well that his popularity is being exploited for a worthy cause. He is under no illusion as to the real purpose of the dinner and his willingness to lend his name and presence to a humanitarian undertaking reflects more credit to him than if he were simply receiving a prize or honorary degree for his past achievements. The plaque and scroll, which are supplementing the diploma as a mark of distinction, hang on many a wall as a symbol of a service rendered rather than an honor received.

The selective process for choosing a guest of honor has a much wider base than that for choosing a recipient of a degree or award. While the two overlap in paying tribute to outstanding leaders in science, the arts and government, a guest of honor may be a popular entertainer, a sports figure, a labor leader, a judge, or a businessman. The test is whether there is such public esteem and affection for the candidate that the community will be anxious to honor him. I do not frown upon this standard of popularity. I believe it is instinctively sound and democratic and I respect mass judgment (which anomalously is sneered at in our democracy, something about which I have written more). So it comes about that the people about whom I have written are not all of the select caste to which the more formal prizes of recognition are customarily extended. This, I hope, will lend some natural warmth and color to the subject matter, for variety of personality, like variety of ideas and things, is true to life, and stimulates awareness.

Furthermore, while I do not choose to be relieved of the responsibility of selecting the "people" of this book, it is comforting to feel that my personal bias has not been imposed upon the reader. I really present an anthology of personalities of all types and intellectual sizes, most of them distinguished, selected by thousands of others as being worthy of attention.

Having explained the sub-title, I cannot neglect the main title of this book. "Between you and me" has four possible meanings. I reject two of them and embrace the other two. I disavow the confidential implication of the phrase. Who does not loathe the man who begins every second sentence with "confidentially"? Most often men who talk confidences, present nothing more secret than the weather forecast. They seek to confer importance on what they say by wrapping it in a mysterious package. It is a rather banal method of attracting attention and, of course, loses its magic touch with the second use.

The flattering connotation of "I would trust only you with this information" is also too obvious to be palatable, because any discerning person would realize that if the information were really inviolate the teller is breaching his trust by disclosure, even to you. Of what value then is his trust in you, if he is the kind of person who breaks his own trust? A real confidence cannot be bandied about because a confidence can no more be shared without spoiling, than virtue.

It would be particularly hypocritical of an author to pretend, for attention-attracting purposes, that he was hushing his message to the reader as a special favor. The day of private editions is done and one does not resort to the printing press to confine a message to a few eyes.

The second implication of the title which I reject is that "Between you and me" sometimes means "frankly," as though someone were willing to lift the veil of caution and speak with utter candor. The word "frankly" used as an introduction to any statement is another abomination, only slightly less annoying than "to tell you the truth." It instantly marks the user, by his own confession, a frequent dissembler or liar, who on this occasion flags you that he intends to abandon his customary habits and "come clean." The word "frankly" often brings another sin upon the head of its user—that of insufferable conceit. For men who are about to confer the most noble qualities upon themselves precede the statement with "frankly," so that it becomes, "Frankly, I have never been greedy and cannot understand why people do not give more generously to charity," or "Frankly, I am a bad liar and anyone can tell even if I were to tell a white lie, so I stick to the plain truth," or "Frankly, I am too good-natured and everyone takes advantage of me." Such persons are probably too myopic to observe it, but they are no different than the expert who testified that he was a genius unsurpassed in his field. When asked on cross-examination whether he did not recognize that his statement was rather conceited and extreme, he replied, "But I have been sworn to tell the truth and I cannot perjure myself."

The two acceptable meanings of the title *Between You and Me* are quite literal. One means exchange of thought. It is unfortunate that readers do not have the opportunity to exercise the privilege of critics and talk back to the author. Some do, of course. The responses range from garlands of approval to noxious weeds of disapproval. The one-way street of our artistic expression is being modified. Radio book forums permit Mr. Citizen a vicarious voice to speak back to authority. The growing power of theatre and motion picture critics is in the same direction, a fact little observed by those who consider reviewers tyrants rather than public representatives.

The art of conversation, so highly esteemed at one time as the mark of a cultured gentleman has come into disuse. The radio and the bridge table have displaced it. I would welcome an opportunity to exchange thoughts concerning the following pages, because the sparks which would result from the friction of discussion might cast a little light. In any event, I approve this connotation of the title even if it cannot be broadly effectuated.

The second acceptable meaning is the most literal one. Between you and me lie the intervening pages. They represent a body of impressions and thoughts of varying density. Some I hope are buoyant enough to make swimming through them an easy task. Others I fear will require hardiness and persistance. It was my intention that in any event you should emerge at the other end mentally invigorated.

So this is my jacket. From structure to title, from purpose to content, from self-revelation to expectation, from forewarning to assurance, I have told you everything—and I have told you nothing.

Because only the pages which follow can inform you whether there is a beating heart underneath the jacket.

Arizona, January 1948

LOUIS NIZER

PART II

Looking in the Window

CHAPTER 2

Exploring Inner Continents

MOST OF US think that the days of exploration and of heroic explorers are past. Every continent and island has been charted on a map. Even the opportunity of pioneering in the air to distant places has been exhausted. But there are new continents, vast continents still to be explored. They are not outside of us, they are inside of us.

There can no longer be a Christopher Columbus sailing across the ocean with three boats, none of which was larger than ninety tons. His sailors were so afraid of the unknown that they pleaded with him to return and he almost did, but finally two months and eight days after they had left Palos, they saw a hawthorn branch with berries on it floating on the ocean and they knew they must be near land. Five days later Columbus landed on Watling Island, dressed in a scarlet cloak and full armor to combat the unknown.

No, there can no longer be a Columbus but we have had a Sigmund Freud, born of Jewish parents who had fled to Austria because they were persecuted in Cologne. While studying medicine, a Dr. Joseph Breuer told him about a remarkable case of a young girl who was suffering from partial paralysis, contractures and inability to drink water. There was no physical reason for these extraordinary symptoms. Dr. Breuer questioned the young girl at length and uncovered past incidents in her life which had created certain anxieties. To his astonishment, the very revelation of these facts had a cathartic effect and the young girl was cured. This was the hawthorn branch with berries for Freud. He saw new continents and discovered many islands which others have since explored more fully. They are called repressions, inhibitions, subconscious, unconscious, psychoses, neuroses. In 1893 Freud and Breuer wrote *On the Psychic Mechanisms of Hysterical Phenomena*. It was the trail-blazing work in this field. He was the modern discoverer of these vast inner continents.

There can no longer be a Magellan who in 1519 sailed around the world with five boats laden with 20,000 bells and mirrors for trading purposes. One ship mutinied and went back to Spain. Another was wrecked. But he finally rounded the Cape of the Virgins and saw the great Pacific Ocean.

Recently, however, we have had another explorer, Dr. Manfred Sakel. He was treating narcotic patients with insulin in order to shock them and deprive them of their hunger for the drug. He observed that some of their apparitions also disappeared. Thus was discovered the insulin shock therapy for schizophrenia.

And there is the explorer Dr. Ladislaus von Meduna, who noticed that dementia praecox and epilepsy seldom were found in the same person, that one excluded the other. This gave rise to therapy by the induction of artificial convulsions and the use of metrazol for that purpose. And there are the explorers Drs. Cerletti and Bini who in 1939 discovered the use of electric shock to substitute for the more violent metrazol treatment.

No, there can be no longer a Roald Amundsen who left Oslo in 1903 in a herring boat weighing forty-seven tons and three years later reached Nome, Alaska, the first mariner to navigate the Northwest Passage. But there can be a Dr. Hans Berger who first recorded the electric currents of the brain, thus giving rise to the science of encephalography, which might be described as a cardiograph of the head instead of the heart. And there can be, as recently as 1941, a Dr. Walter Freeman, who made the first experiments in prefrontal leucotomy, surgically separating the white matter of both frontal lobes of the brain to obtain beneficial results in certain types of insanity.

The tendency is to think of post-war problems in terms of politics and sociology. We seldom think of them in terms of mental disease. It might be well for us to know that in 1923 there were 241 patients in hospitals for mental diseases for every 100,000 people. In 1939 there were 351 for every 100,000 people. In other words, in fifteen years there was a seventy per cent increase in the number of inmates of hospitals for mental diseases.

After Pearl Harbor, the army rejected 1,340,000 men for neuro-psychiatric causes. In addition, 216,000 soldiers were discharged for similar reasons. On the basis of 13,000,000 physical examinations, the army discovered that physical disturbances due to mental troubles doubled during the war. All this might seem to indicate that in a few years the situation will be hopeless. But situations are never hopeless. It is men who are hopeless about situations.

In ancient days, illness was considered an evil spirit which had entered the body. Witch doctors therefore sought to cure illness by pummeling the patient to drive out the evil spirit. This sometimes helped because the treatment was equivalent to massage which was good for many ailments. Or sometimes they would use purgatives. These were also effective in some cases though the witch doctors did not know why.

In any event, we have lost our superstitions about physical ailments. It is no longer a disgrace to have pneumonia or appendicitis. But, curiously enough, we have remained superstitious about mental diseases. We still attribute to them shameful origins. That day is passing. Man is slowly—oh, so slowly—throwing the fetters of ignorance from him and emerging free to face the unknown. Yes, there is a great era of exploration before us. It will be a daring, courageous and romantic era to discover and explore the human being.

CHAPTER 3

An Experiment on an Island

VERY OFTEN I hear people say, "We have too many laws, and they are too complicated. You lawyers make things so involved. You delight in being technical. I suppose it's good for your profession. If laymen made the laws according to common sense and without all the hocus-pocus of legal verbiage, people would know what the laws are and would be better able to obey them. As it is now, even you lawyers can't keep track of them. The judges have all sorts of difficulties deciding what they mean. One court disagrees with another. Why, even the judges of the United States Supreme Court are all confused and disagree on whether a certain thing is legal or not. The trouble is that lawyers are trained to be formalistic in language. They put so many 'whereases' and 'therefores' in the simplest proposition that it takes a squad of interpreters to unravel the situation. The legislatures are made up almost entirely of lawyers, so they try to cure everything by passing laws. The whole darn thing gets so involved, no one knows what he can or cannot do."

This is by no means all I hear about the unnecessary complexity of the laws, but I have set it forth as a typical comment. If you hold such views, I should like to conduct an experiment with you. I ask you to imagine that you are one of a group of people, let's say about two thousand, who have founded a colony on an island. There is not a lawyer among you and you don't want any; you have no laws and you start with the slate clean. The wisest and most solid citizens among you are chosen as a sort of governing council, like a board of directors of a company. You are going to make certain rules so that there will be no confusion, but as few as possible. And you are going to make them simple and easy to understand so that even a child will have no trouble knowing what it may not do to injure or inconvenience the rest of you. You are going to apply plain horse-sense to the situations. You are not interested in the English common-law or any fol-de-rol that lawyers like to invent.

All right—we're off. One day in this primitive community a horse-cart driven by Mr. Jones runs over Mr. Smith and breaks his leg. Each says it was the other's fault and your wise-men's council is called upon to decide what shall be done in a case such as this. Should Jones, if negligent, be required to pay damages to Smith? You vote yes. A dozen questions instantly assert themselves. How much damage? Only the doctor's bills? Should you add the money Smith lost while not working because his leg was in a cast? Will you allow anything for his pain and suffering? If so, how much? Well, suppose you have answered all these questions and have made an award of damages to Smith. You put the file away with a sigh of satisfaction. You have adopted in your community the simple doctrine of liability for neg-ligence.

The very next day Mr. Halloran's cart runs over Mr. Tompkins. However, not only was Mr. Halloran negligently driving on the wrong side of the street but your governing council is convinced that Mr. Tompkins was careless, too. He should not suddenly have run across the path from behind another cart. Well, now you are called upon to decide what rule you will adopt where one person negli-gently injures another and the person injured has also been careless. It doesn't matter to me what decision you make. I will suppose that (like New York and other states) you decide that if one is himself negligent he cannot recover for injuries he suffered from another's negligence. Or I am will-ing to assume that (like some states) you decide that even though both are negligent, Halloran must pay for Tompkins' injuries. In either event you have adopted a rule on "contributory negligence." You are troubled a little by your decision. While it is based on the best judgment and common sense you can bring to bear on this subject, you are not too sure in your breast that you did the right thing. More than that, you are not sure (no matter which way you decided) that the community will approve.

But all this is simple. Another week goes by—another accident in this busy little community. This time Mrs. Eldridge is driving a cart and Mr. Williams is approaching at a right angle. He is reading the local paper while holding the reins lightly. He does not even know that he is near an intersection. Clearly, he is negligent. Mrs. Eldridge has the right of way and, by God, she's not going to give it up. She sticks to her course. The carts collide and Mr. Williams' is damaged. Does the fact that Mrs. Eldridge could have avoided the accident differentiate this case from the others? You decide that it does. Even though Williams was negligent and Mrs. Eldridge was not, she saw the situation in time to avoid it. She should have. Others on the council argue for a different application of "common sense." Either way, you have adopted a rule which lawyers call the doctrine of "last clear chance."

Only a few days have gone by when the first of a hundred problems posed by the doctrine of "respondeat superior" is thrown on your doorstep. You don't call it by its Latin name as lawyers would, but you grapple with it in the same way. The most elementary question is whether the owner of a cart will be held responsible if his servant has driven it negligently. Well, you decide that since the owner of a cow or a dog is responsible for any damage it does to a neighbor's property, a similar rule should apply for the misconduct of a servant. But in the next case which comes before you, the cow-hand who was driving the cart negligently was not on a trip for his master at the time. He had taken a detour to visit a young lady whose diffidence needed the melting of his presence. Should his employer be held liable for his

negligence when he was not driving in the course of his duty?
You decide not. At once dozens of troublesome situations
spring up challenging your interpretation of "course of
duty." If the servant takes the long way home to see more
beautiful scenery, is he in the course of duty? If he is on his
way to lunch, is he in the course of duty? If he injures someone on his way to work or coming home from work, should
his master be liable? You have barely caught your breath
after a series of these decisions when a new series of problems
is presented by daily occurrences. They deal with the responsibility of the owner of a cart if he rents it to someone
else. Should your decision be different if it is an invitee who
is injured? And then someone sues the maker of a cart
because a wheel came off and injured the occupant. What
proof is necessary to prove defective construction?

By this time, someone who has lost a case has made bitter
protestation because, on a previous occasion when the facts
were similar, the council had decided differently. You answer
that the cases are distinguishable. There were one or two
facts in the prior situation which did not exist in this one
and which tipped the scales differently. Immediately you are
accused of making refined interpretations. You reply that in
any event you are not bound by the prior decision. You will
not be enslaved by precedent. Thereupon a very influential
group of citizens who previously had supported you write
a letter to the local newspaper that unless there is stability
in the decisions of the council, the citizens will never know
what the law is, what they may or may not do. You agree
with this in a general way and soon there creep into the
decisions of the council such references as "We decided in
Halloran against Tompkins (decided September 1946, see
Decision No. 42), that one guilty of contributory negligence
cannot recover for another's negligence."

So now in this simple community you are veering toward
what the lawyers call "stare decisis," the rule of precedent,
and your decisions bear reference to the exercise of your
wisdom on prior occasions, in order to establish consistency

and a definite rule upon which the community can rely in determining its conduct.

As yet, we have in this experiment touched only on one branch of law, the law of torts, that is to say, wrongs committed by one against another. You will notice that we have barely scraped the surface of one segment of that vast field of human behavior. We have not even discussed the liability of infants or their parents for negligence of infants; the rules for libel or slander and their myriad complexities; the rules for civil responsibility for striking another with fist or weapon; the rules for liability for deceiving another by fraudulent statements; and literally hundreds of other situations which sooner or later will arise in your community. You are astonished, nevertheless, at the confusion and disagreement which already exist concerning these decisions. You find that your rules are not so simple. Many are charging you with being technical.

Let us continue the experiment in a different field. In this community you must adopt rules for barter and sale. You are determined not to be technical. Once more you will avoid the lawyer's art like a plague. Simplicity and common sense will guide you. So we start at the beginning. People who give their word orally or in writing on a business transaction must live up to it. Whenever a contract is made, your council will enforce it. When will you consider that a contract has come into existence? When the bargain has been struck; when the minds of two people have met on a deal. Well and good. Soon you have a case before you. Mr. Strawbridge offered in a letter to sell two cows to Mr. Cane for $500. Before Mr. Cane could reply accepting the proposition, Strawbridge changed his mind and wrote another letter withdrawing his offer. Cane nevertheless accepted the original proposal. Should Strawbridge be required to deliver the cows and take the $500? You decide that an offer may be withdrawn before it has been accepted and thereby ripened into a contract.

You are not permitted, however, to rest upon this simple

proposition. Within a few days a more complicated situation has been presented to you. The withdrawal of the offer and the acceptance crossed in the mail. Is there a contract or isn't there? You may decide (as is the law in the United States) that the contract came into existence at the moment when the acceptance was mailed. Therefore the revocation of the offer was ineffectual. Or you may decide (as is the law in some European countries) that the contract comes into existence when the acceptance is received, not when it is mailed. Since the offer was withdrawn before the acceptance was received, there was nothing to accept and there could be no contract.

Thus far you have only been confronted with the elementary propositions of contract law which a freshman learns in his first lecture at law school. The really difficult questions which will be posed, must sooner or later arise as your community grows and its activities increase. One day a builder, Mr. Flint, sues Dr. Winkler who hired him to construct a home. He charges that the doctor refuses to pay him. Dr. Winkler argues that he ought not to be required to pay because Flint has not built the home in accordance with specifications. The roof is of gable design and entirely different from the architect's drawing. You are called upon to decide whether the builder should receive nothing unless he rebuilds the roof; whether he should receive full payment, since the roof is well constructed, though different; or whether you will apportion the contract price so as to deduct damages for the incorrect construction. You decide the latter (though you have great difficulty in deciding how much damage has been done). In other words you commit yourself to the proposition that even though a contract has been violated, you will permit the violator to recover for the major portion of the price. You have adopted the doctrine of "substantial performance."

But later a case arises in which a carpenter sues for payment of the construction of a bureau. The evidence is that the job is unfinished. Here you refuse to permit any recovery.

You decide that the bureau is valueless unless completed. This is a contract "in entirety" and in such a case it must be fully performed or the contract is breached. You will not permit recovery for partial performance.

In still another case twenty sacks of grain have been delivered although forty were contracted for. You rule that the twenty sacks must be paid for. Thus you also adopt the contrasting rule of "severable contract," the kind which may be performed only in part but nevertheless be paid for proportionately. Variations of these disputes seem to be endless. When you look back upon your decisions after a year has gone by, you find it difficult to justify them all. Some seem inconsistent and you are not so sure but that the accusation that you have been technical is not correct. For when you try to rationalize these varying rulings, you find that you are relying on some mighty fine distinctions of fact.

In the meantime the scope of the subject matter which you are called upon to decide is broadening all the time and becoming more complex. Should a bank be liable to its depositor for paying out money on a forged signature? Should a bus company be liable to a passenger who lost a business deal because its bus was late? May a farmer cut down the branches of a neighbor's tree which extend over his property and prevent the construction of a barn? Should a doctor be liable for not advising a Caesarian operation for a woman who, due to her bone construction, consequently died in labor?

Your resolve not to be technical runs into a particularly challenging case. Williams made a loan of $1,000 to Brachet. Hartley guaranteed that his friend Brachet would pay back the money. The loan was due October 1. Brachet asked Williams to extend the time to June 1. Williams did so. Hartley was not consulted. On June 1 Brachet can't pay, so Williams sues Hartley who guaranteed the payment. Hartley says, "If you had sued me on the original due date of October 1, I would have paid. At that time Brachet was solvent and I could have reimbursed myself. But without asking me, you extended Brachet's time to pay for seven months. In the meantime he has become insolvent and if I pay I cannot recover the money from him. I did all this just as a favor to Brachet. There was no money in it for me. And you can't stick me with this debt when, by your conduct in delaying the payment, you made it impossible for me to collect from Brachet."

If you agree with Hartley's argument and decide in his favor, you have adopted the rule which lawyers call "strictissimi juris"; you have held that an endorsement of a note or a guarantee of a debt, given without consideration, will be strictly enforced according to its terms. If the terms are varied, the guarantor is released. And incidentally, there will be many in the community who will say you are becoming pretty technical no matter which way you decide the case, just as you might say it about a lawyer who talked about "strictissimi juris."

All these matters seem simple by comparison to those you are called upon to decide in the domestic relations field. For the strain of living upon an island is great and there is a disproportionately large number of quarrels between married folk. What rule will you adopt for divorce? Some religious groups urge that only adultery should be an adequate ground. Others say incompatability should be a sufficient reason but they are somewhat confused as to how much incompatability there must be and of what kind, particularly where one of the parties resists the divorce. You may or may not know that there are thirty-seven legal grounds for divorce recognized in the United States. The same type of question presents itself concerning separation, that is to say, where the husband and wife remain married but live apart. Should cruelty or non-support be the only grounds for a separation? Should you permit alimony in your community, and if so, on what should it be based? Should the husband be called upon to support his wife in the manner to which she has been accustomed during marriage? Does it matter that she has some money and assets of her own? What about custody of the children and visitation rights?

Other communities have struggled with such questions. In 1700 the British Parliament passed a law providing that any woman who lures a man into matrimony "by means of scents, paints, cosmetics, washes, artificial teeth, false hair, Spanish wool, iron stays, hoops, high-heeled shoes or bolstered hips" would draw upon herself the penalty prescribed for witchcraft and her marriage would in the eyes of the law "stand null and void." In Cochin, China, persons seeking a divorce break a pair of chopsticks in the presence of witnesses and the divorce proceedings are over and done with. You reflect upon Dr. Samuel Johnson's epigram, "Nature has given women so much power that the law has wisely given them little."

You pick your way through a maze of problems, applying your common sense, but soon a body of law has grown up which is challenged by everybody. To satisfy the deep religious convictions of certain groups of your community, you compromise by permitting different standards for different sections of the community. You hope that this follows the democratic philosophy of respecting the religious and moral convictions of all. However, you find that you are excoriated for your stupidity in having different divorce laws in different parts of the island. You realize that you are struggling with your own predilections about these matters. As Benjamin Cardozo once wrote, "The great tides and currents which engulf the rest of men, do not turn aside in their course and pass judges by."

People die in your community. Though you long to avoid any of the complications of will contests, you are compelled to provide rules for the disposition of property after death. Your citizens have the familiar frailty of trying to perpetuate themselves after death by directing what shall be done with their property from one lifetime to another. They try by provisions in their wills to hold the strings on their property for generations and thus continue to exert a force long after they are gone. You decide that you must put a stop to this. So you forbid testamentary dispositions for more than two lives in being. Perhaps you adopt a different rule, but you can be sure that the contest of wills will blossom. Your determination to have simple rules, easily understood, seems to lead to a morass of interpretations as to what the deceased meant by the language he used. Aunt Tessie is sure that the clause "all the rest of the property which I possess" was not intended to include property acquired after the date of the will. One widow is reputed to have said, "I've had so much trouble over John's property that I sometimes wish he hadn't died."

In another case a wife receives nothing and she claims that the will should therefore be declared ineffective. It proves, she argues, the undue influence that "the other woman" had on him. So you must decide what is the amount and nature of the pressure which must be brought upon a man or a woman to invalidate the will he makes. You decide that the evidence must establish that the pressure constituted duress in that the testator was unable to exercise his own free will and judgment.

But you find that this is a deceptive generality behind which you are not permitted to hide. Specific situations arise demanding your application of the rule to the facts. If a daughter constantly attended her sick father and permitted no one else to come near him, is that "undue influence" as the disinherited sons claim? If a man who deserted his wife has lived with another woman and left his property to her, has she wielded "undue influence" over him? You decide this was not duress but voluntary choice and therefore the wife must lose. You may be sure your decision will not go uncriticized. Or you decide that the sexual "domination" of the mistress deprived him of his free will and you bring down upon your head the condemnation of psychologists and psychiatrists who agree that love is not a wicked force to be condemned for the compulsion it exercises.

As litigation grows in this community, the governing council is unable to cope with all disputes. It sets up subsidiary courts, parceling out jurisdiction to each. In some courts the jurisdiction is limited to matters involving no more than $3,000. Some courts are set up for criminal matters only. Sometimes the jurisdiction is determined by the nature of the subject matter, such as probate of wills or copyright or patent disputes. Before you are fully aware of it, your community has developed a complex structure of judicial forums and cases have been dismissed because they have been brought in the wrong court.

Losing litigants insist that they should have the right of at least one appeal. In the beginning you oppose this. You don't want protracted litigation with all the expense and lapse of time it involves. But when the different courts have been set up to relieve the governing council of the litigation which has inundated it, you decide that the governing council will no longer decide cases in the first instance but will act as a court of appeals. You do not realize that this apparently innocuous decision opens up the floodgates to a new series of difficult questions. Should all losing parties be permitted to appeal or only those where the lower council was divided in rendering its opinion? Should the losing party be required to post a bond so that if he loses the appeal the victor will be protected, or should an appeal be permitted without a bond lest a poor man be deprived of a remedy? Should the appellate court review the facts as well as the legal rulings, even though it has not the benefit of viewing the witnesses and forming impressions from their demeanor? Or if you permit the whole trial over again instead of deciding the case on the stenographic report, should you accept new testimony? If so, how can you decide whether the lower court erred, since it did not have the same evidence before it? There are, let me assure you, literally hundreds of similar appellate questions. You are compelled to make rules about all these matters. An enormous body of "technical law" grows up under your very nose, like weeds in your garden.

You haven't even time to despair. The situation becomes more complex every second. To take one other isolated illustration, you are required to devise rules of evidence. What does your common sense dictate concerning such questions as: Should we permit witnesses to tell us not only what they saw and heard, but also what others told them about the matter? At first, you think there should be no restrictions. "Let them talk," you say. But after some experience, the opposing argument begins to appeal to you more and more. The people who gave the information to the witness are not in court. No one can cross-examine them. It seems unfair to accept indirect testimony of this kind from one who did not hear the conversation but was told about it later. So before you know it you have adopted the "hearsay" rule which has been condemned as technical by many laymen. That is, you will permit witnesses to tell only what they know of their own knowledge, not what someone told them.

You soon discover that witnesses must be confined to the pertinent questions posed by the dispute. Otherwise they ramble on endlessly, reciting matters which have so remote a bearing that they do not aid you in coming to a decision. Before you know it, you are cutting off testimony because "it is irrelevant." Another member of your council likes to use the word "immaterial" in describing his reason for excluding certain testimony. In another case, a child is offered as a witness. She is too young to be responsible for what she says. You rule out her testimony as "incompetent." Then one day, one of the judges combines the three words and there you have that horrible concoction of the lawyer: "irrelevant, incompetent and immaterial."

You also find yourself making what seem to be strangely technical rulings, at least until they are explained. For example, Mrs. Palmer tripped on a torn carpet on the stairway of her building and sued her landlord. At the trial Mrs. Palmer showed that her landlord had replaced the carpet with a new strip one week after the accident. This evidence was objected to, but you said, "We are not lawyers and we are not technical. Common sense tells you that the fact that the landlord has replaced the carpet is some evidence that the original carpet was defective."

You felt quite content with yourself for that ruling. But three months later you agreed to reverse yourself. Why? Because owners of buildings and factories would not dare to construct safety devices or improve any condition after any accident. "It is like putting your head in a noose. Evidence of our repairs or new construction will be used to condemn us even though we were not negligent in the first place. The machine which injured my worker was not defective. He was careless when he walked by. Nevertheless, after the accident I wanted to construct a special safety fence around it to protect even careless employees. But I can't do that if my act of precaution is going to be used against me."

So you decide that because it is good public policy to encourage repairs and safety devices, you will not permit evidence of any repairs *after* an accident to prove the original defective condition. Let the injured person prove the defective condition at the time of the accident without resort to later events. So it comes about that you adopt a rule of evidence which has caused nine out of ten people who have witnessed negligence trials in the past, to fume at the "stupidity and technicalities" of the rules of evidence invented by lawyers.

You also discover that it is almost impossible to handle the many contractual disputes which are based on oral "agreements." There is not a stitch of writing to guide you. It is simply one man's word against another's. You finally grow impatient with these quarrels. "If the matter was so important why didn't you write it down so that everyone would know what you intended?" you say. "Why should we be required to guess about what was said when you don't agree on it? From now on certain kinds of contracts, such as those for the sale of real estate or transactions involving more than $100, let's say, must be in writing or we won't enforce them. If you don't take the trouble to work out your understanding on paper, don't shift your headache to us." So there you are. You have adopted what lawyers call a Statute of Frauds, requiring certain contracts to be in writing in order to prevent fraudulent claims based on oral promises from flourishing.

But even after you have made this rule (which you may be sure will be condemned as highly technical and contrary to the moral right of those who have taken their neighbor's word), your problem is not disposed of. For now every time a written contract is presented, one of the parties claims that something was said orally at the time the contract was being drawn which should be taken into consideration.

"The contract says '1,000 bales of hay' but he told me definitely that if he had 1,500 bales he would sell it to me at the same price. Now he wants to sell the extra 500 to someone else because he can get a higher price," argues one of the litigants.

You reply, "But if we permit oral conversations to change the written provisions, what happens to our rule that contracts must be in writing? You should have written down that special arrangement about the 500 bales. Now the conversation is denied. We will not allow testimony of oral arrangements which are designed to change the written agreement. We want the certainty of a writing. We can't dilute that certainty by opening up the doors to oral changes."

Well, you don't know it, but you have adopted what lawyers call the "parole evidence" rule which, I may inform you, is frequently denounced as a "technical" stratagem designed to shut off the full truth.

Incidentally, these rules lead to long contracts. The parties are determined to put everything in writing. They are forced to resolve questions which may be remote, but which, without written agreement, will leave a void in their relationship. I do not say that this is bad. It is better to "fight out" disagreements in advance, rather than have them lead to litigation later. But you soon discover that your dream about having one-page contracts is not attainable. You also find that the more the draftsman (we won't call him lawyer) anticipates and provides for, the clearer the arrangement. So as time goes on, clauses for certain types of situations become customary.

Thus, for example, employment contracts constantly grow in length. It has been found helpful to put in a "sick or disabled" clause because whenever there is none, the employer and employee find themselves in a contest. "Cancellation" and "renewal option" clauses come into use. More careful definition of the duties of the employee is resorted to, because there have arisen some nasty disputes as to whether the employer could order the employee to perform certain duties which the employee felt were beneath him. If commissions are to be paid, how should it be determined which sales or reorders belong to the employee? May he inspect the books? If so, how often and when? How should his rights be circumscribed so that he does not obtain confidential data which might be prejudicial to the employer if the employee leaves? Long clauses are devised for these situations.

Of course a similar elongating process takes place for other kinds of contracts, such as those for the purchase of literary material, the sale of real estate, the license of a patent and dozens of others. You recall, a little shamefacedly, how you used to call your lawyer (before you were on the island) and say, "Now, please, no long, involved contract. Keep it simple. Just put it into a one-page letter." Now you realize from actual experience that the more precise and foreseeing the contract is in providing for various contingencies, the less likely becomes costly litigation later. You have seen will contests which ate up half of the estate, resulting from too short and simple a will which left the heirs in the dark concerning certain situations which could have been anticipated and provided for. You no longer worship brevity as an end in itself. You find yourself recommending draftsmen who know the range of subject matter which even the parties do not envision; who therefore can anticipate questions which should be answered in the contract; who aim for clarity and who do not spare the page.

As time goes by, the rules made by your governing council and its subsidiary courts accumulate into quite a body of law. In the beginning only one copy of each of these decisions and rules was kept on file. As the community grew, more and more resort was had to these files. People wanted to know what they might or might not do. The file room became so crowded that you decided to print these decisions. At first, informal little paper booklets were issued. (Lawyers have the equivalent. They call them "advance sheets.") Later, books containing these rules were printed. They were marked by number and the practice grew of referring to a case by citing the names of the parties involved and putting after them the number of the book and its page number. So there you have your legal citation: Hartley v. Jones, 9 Community Book, P. 167.

As the rules become more numerous and complex, citizens pour into your office to ask you about them. You are on the council and are familiar with them. Before you know it, people are calling you a counselor. One morning as you contemplate your face in the shaving mirror, you see a jaw-opening image of a horrified man for it has suddenly struck you that you are acting as a lawyer!

You cannot handle all matters. Others buy the published law reports and study them. They become expert in drafting documents and advising what the rights of the citizen are. People pay them for this service. You decide that the whole matter had better be regulated so that people will not be imposed upon. Thus licenses are issued to those who possess knowledge of the rules which your council has created. Law schools are founded. Your community, which started with the resolution not to have lawyers and all their technical hocus-pocus, has reached the point of recognizing the necessity of laws, lawyers and courts, and the public service they render. To the man who said you can't live with lawyers, you say sadly, "Nor can you live without them. And you can't die without them, either."

Now I abandon the experiment which we launched on our

imaginary island. In the course of this mental excursion I have conjured up situations to demonstrate how they would tax your common sense and very likely lead you to adopt rules similar to those you might ordinarily have condemned as too complicated and technical. You realize, of course, that the hypothetical problems which we placed in our experimental laboratory were a mere speck of dust compared to the millions of acres of ground to be traversed in the field of human relationships. They were intended to represent an infinitesimal illustration of the complexities which arise in any society.

The law as it exists today is the crystallization of centuries of experience. It is imperfect because man is imperfect. It is the philosophical expression of society's moral and ethical standards. There is no absolute in philosophy. There is no certainty in it either. We struggle with close questions to determine what is right and what is wrong. Often we compromise and find that although we have achieved balance, we have sacrificed the purity of logic to stability. At best it is a groping process in which we blindly try to find our way out of the darkness of man's greed, cupidity and passion. That there is as much domestic order as we have, is no inconsiderable achievement when one views the cataclysmic explosions on the international front. It is better to try to do something and fail at it, than to do nothing and succeed at it.

The legal process is a desperate search for truth which is as elusive in courts as in life. The law weighs conflicting moral values and often finds them impossible of exact measurement. The law is not a series of edicts handed down to us like the Commandments from Mt. Sinai. It is the reflection of our customs and moral standards. If it appears distorted at times it is because our customs and moral standards are distorted. The improvement of the law depends greatly upon the improvement of man. We cannot evade this fact by condemning law or lawyers, for their defects stem from us.

They are not independent phenomena which we can make scapegoats for society's own shortcomings.

Our experiment proves nothing more. You rail at "technicalities," but if you were obliged to formulate the rules, they would necessarily be of the same nature. You demand simplicity, but the complexities of social relationships do not lend themselves to your abstract ideals. You yearn for certainty, but the varied and involved nature of men's quarrels lead you to challengeable solutions. Interpretation becomes the bridge across the chasm of inconsistency. You find yourself distinguishing one situation from another and reaching different conclusions. But frequently the fact which tipped the balance is considered weightless by others.

Having gone through this experiment, perhaps your horizon will be wider. Perhaps, through your vicarious experience as a law-maker on the island, you have had a glimpse of the struggle which has been going on for centuries to make wise laws for foolish men, a struggle which has taxed the resourcefulness of the finest minds throughout the ages.

CHAPTER 4

The Ticker

THE AVERAGE HEART is five inches long, three and one-half inches wide and two and one-half inches thick. It weighs ten ounces, and it can hold only two ounces of blood at any one time. Yet this little organ beats forty to fifty million times a year and pumps three million quarts of blood each year.

This is a mechanical miracle, isn't it? But mechanically, we can reproduce it. Oh, there is nothing we can't do mechanically in this twentieth century. Why, ten years ago Dr. Alexis Carrel built an artificial heart encased in glass and run by compressed oxygen, nitrogen and carbon dioxide. He even produced some artificial blood which he felt served his purpose better than real blood. Yet it is reputed that Dr. Carrel collaborated with the Nazis by heading a scientific institute in France, so you see there was something wrong with Dr. Carrel's heart.

Something more than a wonderful mechanism is needed to make a real heart. It is that quality which makes the heart record every shining thing and play it back through the years like a record, giving the soul a memory. It is the quality which we call courage and which makes man noble and self-sacrificing in his greatest crises. That is why man, who can be so greedy in peacetime, shows such magnanimity in times of disaster. It is easier for him to be courageous when he is in a minority than tolerant when he is in a majority. It is that quality which makes us worry about someone else's heart.

The heart is the only organ of the body which makes a noise. Its rhythmic beat is the announcement of life. Its silence is the announcement of death. It makes us all resemble clocks, ticking away life. We are wound up for a specific span and when the unknown time has elapsed, the ticking stops and time stops for us, though it runs on for others.

CHAPTER 5

The Four Little Miracles

I HAVE NEVER met anyone who believed in democracy. I have met many who prefer it to any other form of government and who are willing to die for it. I have met many who are willing to abide by majority opinion, but I have never met anyone who believed in mass judgment. That is what democracy is.

It is a great tribute to democracy that its devotees accept

it passionately as a way of life even though they do not subscribe to its essential truth. How many of us really believe that the average intelligence of the mass is high? Well, I do. The democratic process is not intended to be applied to precise scientific realms of which mathematics is the easiest illustration. It is in the fields of policy, political and economic, that public will is determinative.

I believe that two people consulting upon a decision are likely to reduce the possibility of error which one might have made. I believe that three reduce the potentiality of error even more, ten considerably more; and therefore I would rather trust to the *correctness* (not expediency) of a decision made by a million men than I would to that of one man be he the most learned in the world.

There is an instinctive quality in mass judgment which reduces error to a minimum. You may observe it in the decision of juries. They represent the average mass intelligence applied to private rather than public disputes. A juror is chosen because he does not know the litigants, witnesses, or anything about the dispute (a curious reversal of the common law doctrine which insisted that jurors be witnesses). Since opposing lawyers offset each other in seeking to obtain jurors favorably prejudiced toward their clients (the best method of excluding prejudice from the jury box), jurors as ultimately selected represent an average cross-section of the community. They are neither experts nor specialists. Yet any trial lawyer or judge will tell you that juries have an uncanny faculty of reaching correct decisions. Several judges have kept records of jury verdicts and compared them with their own reactions and with subsequent appellate decisions. They have found that juries approximate justice in an extraordinarily high percentage of cases. Statistics are available to this effect, but their load might be too heavy for the bridge over which we are passing toward the main thought. The fact is that the mass judgment of juries is sound.

Those who mock the jury process will refer to the invalid reasons upon which verdicts are often based. The real issue goes unnoticed while the jurors resent a witness' arrogance or an unsatisfactory answer to a totally irrelevant question or the conceit of the defendant, or similar seemingly collateral matters. But curiously enough, the decisions are right, although the reasons for them may be anomalous. A little thought may persuade us that this is no accident of justice. We are all likely, even in our daily affairs, to reach conclusions and search for supporting reasons later. Even if the reasons are inadequate, the original conclusion resulting from a host of stimuli remains undisturbed. Upon hearing opposing contentions we *feel* which side is right. The rationalizations follow rather than precede judgment.

A witness's manner concerning a trivial irrelevancy may rightly shake confidence in him. Credibility is the result of a myriad of impressions, each finding its roots in our own previous experience. Is this not the process of wisdom? So fundamental is this rule that appellate courts seldom reverse juries on questions of fact because the judges have not had the opportunity to observe and hear the witnesses. They do not therefore feel as qualified as the jury to form impressions of veracity. Thus we see that the "absurd reasons" for the jury's decision may often be based upon the wisdom of every man's experience.

Justice Holmes once said, "The life of the law has not been logic; it has been experience." This is what conditions our reactions to each new situation. It does not matter whether you call this, as William James did, "the total push and pressure of the cosmos," or as Cardozo unveiled it for judges, "the judicial process." It results from all those mysterious forces within, sharpened by every moment of existence. It is the instinct of knowing what is right. The lowliest citizen has it as much as the most exalted. Indeed, since the cultured man has to some extent been excluded from life by confinement to books, he may be less prepared than his uneducated brother to respond to the vigorous tests of raw experience. That is why the multiplication of individual reactions produces a better essence of wisdom than the judgment of any superior individual. That is why I trust the mass judgment. It may err, and grievously, but its chances of doing so are fewer and its resolve to correct past mistakes are stronger than may be expected from any coterie of brilliant minds.

Cynical public relations experts insist that public intelligence is low, if not moronic, and are certain that pure selfishness motivates the ordinary man's decisions. Many illustrations to contradict both of these libels can be cited from recent history. The public was far ahead of its government in desiring to be taxed for war preparation, in approving conscription which would take its sons, and in endorsing price control which hampered individual profits. The public also showed independence in its political thinking (irrespective of what one's views may be as to its wisdom) in ignoring the great majority of the newspapers which condemned the New Deal, and in repeatedly re-electing its spokesman.

But even if one were to admit that by and large the ordinary man's decision is motivated not by concern for the common good, but by personal advantage, the democratic process translates this selfishness into wisdom. For in the ordinary case, since that is best for the nation which benefits the greatest number of its individual citizens, the test of self-aggrandisement when multiplied by a great majority of choices approximates the public good. This is a little trick in transmutation which democracy performs, which fascism cannot possibly match. This is one of the miracles of democracy.

Nor would I concede that greater weight ought to be given to the vote of a well-educated person than to that of a simple, unlearned one. For the instinctive decision of ordinary man, based upon observation and the wisdom of his experience, is often superior to that of the involved intellectual processes of very cultured people. We have had many opportunities to observe the confusions which result from refined reasoning, while the naive reaction sticks to the moral core. The home-

spun philosopher is popular in every country not because
his language hovers between simplicity and slang, but because his thoughts are freed from the sophisticated involu-
tions which have led us astray so often.

The English Foreign Office, manned by the acutest brains
of the Empire, somehow manages to support England's enemies like the Mufti, the Arabs, Franco, and German "businessmen," while offending its friends. The United States,
by similar reliance on "shrewd minds," has at times been led
into equally curious support of or "neutrality" toward
Franco, Argentina and the indefensible imperialist policies
of England. The average man cannot understand the depth
of these policies, but would pursue an "obvious" course
which in its very naiveté would avoid the pitfalls of our international fiascos. There has been no proof as yet in public
affairs that higher education is a guaranty of better judgment. While the argument cannot be carried to extremes,
and we all desire literacy and minimum education as a
qualification for citizenship, neither can it be argued that
professors in universities exercise the franchise better than
their students or servants. There is always the danger that
education, like Greek wisdom, will "grow only blossoms,
but no fruit."

To those who point to the recent Bilbo, Talmadge,
Rankin and their ubiquitous successors, the answer is two-
fold. Since democracy is a human process, it is never perfect.
These demagogues are fewer than the din they make would
lead us to suspect. Narrow-minded bigots are like narrow-
necked bottles: the less they have in them the more noise
they make pouring it out. Furthermore, even if these men
express the views of a majority of their constituents it would
do little good if we were able to impose more enlightened
representatives upon them, for reform must come from
within. The very fact that the contempt of the nation spot-
lights such demagogues and makes them national symbols
of democracy's shame is a challenge to the local communities
which elected them. Vigorous opposition groups are thus

set in motion and, with a little time, a liberal, intelligent
Arnall replaces a Talmadge. Sometimes the advance is only
temporary, but the struggle is as normal and genuine as
man's own struggle for self-improvement. In the long run
the verdict is likely to be sound. The Wheelers, Nyes, Fergu-
sons, Clarks, Fishes, Shipsteads and La Follettes are rewarded
for their isolationism with political isolation to the point
of oblivion.

This, then, is another little miracle passed by democracy.
Like the human body, the body politic reacts to infectious
germs by setting up anti-bodies to meet the challenge. This
process is life-preserving. It serves no purpose to condemn
nature because infections have appeared, for it is also nature
which creates the mysterious anti-bodies to maintain the
equilibrium. Just as more nature is the cure for nature, so
more democracy is the cure for democracy.

When democracy results in grievous error, there is at least
the opportunity for correction. If a city has a corrupt political machine, the time comes when the voters rise in wrath
and turn the scoundrels out. True, great damage may have
been done in the meantime, but compare this with the practice of dictators, no matter how benevolent and well-inten-
tioned. The individual ruler, not subject to democratic
removal, is more likely to cling to his program and to disguise his failures. Pride and vanity block his confession and
reform. This is a human weakness. It applies to presidents
and senators as well as to dictators.

But here again democracy performs a little miracle. The
people do not hesitate to reverse themselves. Their pride is
lost in the millions of anonymous votes. Their vanity is dissolved by immersion in thousands of ballot boxes. The stag-
nating process of fascism is reversed. Each voter feels heroic
because the courage of the mass is projected to him. It is
always my neighbor who previously voted stupidly, but it is
always I who correct the error. This is the only way to
explain the unadulterated sense of triumph which citizens
feel when they have altered a national trend. Democracy

removes the individual inhibition to confess error and sub-
stitutes for it the elation of courageous reform.

As for the customary accusation that in an emergency
democracy is unwieldy and slow and must adopt the dicta-
torial method to survive, the answer is, first, that it isn't
true. Democracy is not inconsistent with strong, centralized
leadership. Few rulers have more power than the United
States Constitution gives to the President. Though Washington rejected the title of His High Mightiness, or His
Elective Majesty (satirizing these suggestions by referring to
Vice President Adams as His Superfluous Excellency or His
Rotundity), he welcomed the extraordinary powers conferred upon the President. When an emergency occurs, even
these great powers are greatly increased. But this is done
under constitutional authority and by special legislation.

It was never intended, as so many democrats believe, that
a democracy should not be able to protect itself by strong
federal measures under powerful individual leadership. It is
quite true that the democratic process functions best in
normal times when there is no premium on haste and centralized decision. But inherent in democracy is its capacity
to function well in emergencies too. When there is an
epidemic in a town, the health commissioner has the power
to close schools and forbid public assemblies. This is not in
violation of the right of public assembly. Such power is not
to be confused with dictatorship, for it derives from the city
charter and is part of democracy not in abrogation of it. We
must not mistake the exercise of emergency powers for dictatorship, any more than we should mistake plebiscites in dictatorships for democracy.

Furthermore, the possibility of transition from emergency
powers to normal powers is a vital distinction between democracy and dictatorship. The United States and Great
Britain demonstrated recently the feasibility of total mobili-
zation under centralized leadership, which put the vaunted
efficiency of dictatorships to shame. But when the crisis had
passed, the extraordinary constitutional powers which had

been vested in Churchill and Roosevelt lapsed. Churchill, after his great war triumphs, was actually voted out and the Congress of the United States cancelled much of the emergency legislation which had conferred unique discretionary powers upon the President. Has anyone ever heard of a dictator's powers expanding and contracting with the heat and cold of the national emergency?

Democracy may change its color for protective purposes, but not its character. Like the fish in the sea whose bellies take on the light shade of the sky to deceive their attackers underneath, so democracy may appear to have the color of dictatorship when efficiency and prompt decision are the defensive requirements of the hour. But the true character of democracy is not changed thereby. The fact that democracy can, in a war emergency, display the limited virtues of a dictatorship without adopting its vices, is another little miracle. Conversely, dictatorship cannot utilize the virtues of democracy without completely succumbing to it.

I do not merely accept democracy. I really believe in it. Why shouldn't I, in view of its four little miracles?

CHAPTER 6

Tell Me No Fortunes

THE CIRCULAR said that the professor was the greatest marvel of our day. He had astonished a group of Harvard scientists who could not explain his extraordinary feats. Other skeptics in Europe and this country had been confounded by his mind reading. They had arranged their own conditions to eliminate all possibilities of trickery but he had read their minds. Extra-sensory perception existed. The professor would demonstrate it to all unbelievers.

I went. He looked his part. He had iron-gray hair and a swarthy complexion which gave his deep blue eyes a pene-

trating quality. He was distinguished in manner and devoid
of the hocus-pocus of quacks. In a simple way he stated that
he would read the mind of any person in the audience. He
would follow the instructions conveyed by mere thinking—
no writing of the message, no moving of lips, no imparting
of the thought to anyone else, no questions by any stooge.
Then, in a matter-of-fact manner, which heightened his per-
suasiveness, he said, "I know most of you think this is impossible. I prefer not to lecture about it. A demonstration
will be more convincing. I invite the most skeptical in the
audience to come forth and determine for themselves
whether I can or cannot read their minds."

A lady responded. He told her to concentrate on any instruction she wished to convey to him and to keep instruct-
ing him in her mind only, not moving her lips or saying
anything. He then took her by the hand, walked quite
speedily through an audience of several hundred people,
entered a row, stopped in front of a man, removed his eyeglasses, and placed them on his own nose. "Is this what you
wanted me to do?" he asked. She could not speak. She
nodded her head in amazement and walked back to her seat
in another row, quite bewildered.

A friend of mine could not contain himself. "This is
bunk," he said, "I'm going up there." He did. The professor
walked him to my seat, reached into my back pocket, took
out my purse, removed a ten dollar bill from it, walked
to another part of the room where sat an acquaintance
of ours, and exchanged the ten dollar bill with one in his
purse, then returned to me and placed the money in my
folder. My friend turned white. I thought he would faint.
"That is exactly what I instructed him to do," he whispered
to me. "I thought of it at the last moment. I didn't say a
word of it to anyone. This is amazing. I can't believe it."

Before his last feat the professor reported that at Harvard
University one of the scientists had instructed him mentally
to go to the library, select a certain book out of thousands
and open to a particular page and passage, all of which he

had done. He offered to give a demonstration of this feat on
a more limited scale. An attendant placed fifty books on the
table. Various persons walked to the platform and thought
of a specific paragraph on a certain page of a particular book.
In each instance the professor correctly complied with the
instruction. It was interesting to see some of the skeptical
stagger from the platform shaking their heads incredulously
and involuntarily registering comical attitudes of bewilderment.

That night I could not sleep. I do not believe in extra-
sensory perception. I felt a trick had been perpetrated upon
us. But how! There were no stooges; I was convinced of that.
The mental instruction had not been written down, so there
was no palming and disclosure. There was no assistant who
communicated information to the professor by code in the
form of questions. He worked alone. Yet I was convinced
he had not read and could not read anyone's mind.

This was my private mystery exercise. I was determined to
get to the bottom of it. I began to reconstruct in great detail
everything that had happened. I recalled the instructions the
professor had given to each participant. "If I walk in the
wrong direction, say to yourself without moving your lips,
'You are wrong. Take five steps the other way. Five steps the
other way.' If I reach for the object and my hand is too
high, say to yourself, 'Lower your hand—lower—lower.
That's right.' In other words, break up your instructions to
me into minute detail and keep giving me orders mentally
all the time."

I also recalled that he held each participant by the hand
as he proceeded to his destination. True, he often had a
handkerchief in his hand with which he had been mopping
his brow, but there was physical contact. Is it possible that
the pulse or other reaction of the hand might indicate to
one highly sensitive to such pressures that he was on the
right track?

I decided to experiment for myself. I began with a simple
test. I asked a cousin of mine to think of an object in the

room and to give me mental instructions as I walked around the room in search of the object. Even in my first test I felt the pull of the hand as I veered in the wrong direction. Unbeknown to my cousin, his concentration upon his instructions was being revealed in the tension of his hand. I eliminated three sides of the room and was led repeatedly to one wall where the chosen object was. Soon I could select the object itself. I learned that high-strung and nervous people were most communicative. At times it was difficult to restrain my laughter at the actual physical tugging on my hand as I reached above the designated object or turned away from it. When I touched the object itself, there was a convulsive approval by the hand, registering success. Yet the subject was totally unaware of the involuntary impulses he was sending forth. Soon I could follow more complicated instructions.

Later I could perform the most startling of the professor's tricks, picking a book from many shelves of books and turning to a precise page. After the hand's "excitement" had designated the book, I would turn its pages first in general sections, until the area had been determined, and then more carefully until the grip of the hand informed me I had chosen the exact page. Then as my finger slowly passed down the page, I was halted at a particular paragraph by a tightening and sudden relaxation of the hand. The look on the subject's face, a cross between sheepishness and wonderment, sealed the verdict.

Of course the professor was not subject to the hesitancy and struggling of the amateur. He almost flew to the selected object. He had developed so sensitive a touch that he could afford to hold a handkerchief in the hand which held his subject's and still recognize the involuntary pressure signals which were conveyed. But the mystery had been solved. I seldom talk about it because inevitably I am asked to demonstrate and one feels rather foolish dragging a heavily breathing excited lady around the room groping for a designated object. Anyone can perform this feat. Usually others

in the room experiment and succeed immediately in the
simple tests. Try it yourself.

The moral, of course, is that all fortune tellers and mind
readers are tricksters or charlatans. Yet human gullibility
affords them millions of frightened, fanatical and superstitious victims ranging from those with a moronic I.Q. to
those with otherwise keen intelligence. If you wish to satisfy
yourself how easy it is to amaze people by reading their
palms, try it some day. Observe your subject's reactions while
you use standard analysis clichés, and trim your sails accord-
ingly. For example, "You are slow to make friends, but when
you form a friendship you are loyal and devoted to it even
through adversity." A self-satisfied smile on your subject's
face as if to say, "How true, how true," should encourage
you to extend this line. A stoic expression which says, "So
far I don't recognize it, but I am eager to hear more," should
cause you to change tack. The latter is unlikely because
people love to be flattered, particularly when a fault is
turned into a compliment. This affords the rich reward of
being a good sport in accepting criticism, while enjoying the
inner glow of being praised. This is the psychological key
to the highly developed monologues of tea leaf, card, palm
and other readers. Thus: "You have a love of beautiful
things which interferes with your resolution to be economical." What more delectable tribute could be paid to a spend-
thrift! Or, "You are sensitive and easily hurt, but you do
not harbor a grudge." Nobody minds being thus beaten over
the brow with a wreath.

The specific information given by readers which melts
their subject's skepticism, such as the telling of recent ill-
nesses, divorces and trips, is due to developed skills in observation and deduction. The great diagnostician, the late
Dr. Emanuel Libman, could walk through a hospital ward
and by observing the color and tone of the patients' faces
and eyes, call off with remarkable accuracy the disease from
which each was suffering. Years of observation enable us
to know the different tastes of fruits from the varying tex-

tures and color of their skin. Fortune tellers develop similar
sensitive reactions to people, which, heightened by the tell-
tale reactions of their subjects' faces (not different from the
pressure of their hands), encourage or alter the direction of
the prediction. All the rest of the awe-inspiring "accuracy"
of certain readers is either coincidence, good guessing or
indirect information.

As Mark Twain put it: "A man who goes along with a
prophecy-gun ought never to get discouraged. If he will keep
up his heart and fire at everything he sees he is bound to hit
something by and by." The only reliable fortune teller is
a credit agency. But no warning will stop the flow of millions
of dollars to pretenders of occult wisdom from insecure
people greedy for knowledge of their fate.

Some time ago one of the most famous mind readers was
booked into a leading vaudeville theatre. The demonstration which convinced audiences most was a card trick. He
fanned a deck of cards to show it was a regular bridge deck.
Then he invited anyone in the audience to take this deck,
descend the steps from the stage and, in the darkness of the
aisle, lift a corner of any card so that no one else could
see it. The mind reader would instantly write the card on
a large slate. When the patron returned to the stage and
announced his card, the "professor" held up the slate and
upon it was written the correct card. Gasps turned to applause at each demonstration.

The trick is so simple, one feels silly ever having been
deceived. The deck is of a special make. Spread one way, the
cards are all different. Turned around and spread, they are
all the same. The mind reader used a different deck for
each performance. If it is composed of sevens of hearts, no
matter where the skeptical person lifts the deck to take a
furtive look, he will see a seven of hearts.

Even more elementary is a trick which has supported a
host of mind readers for twenty years. One evening at a
leading hotel dining room which boasted a return engagement of its star performer, a mind reader, I observed the

following variation of a customary fraud. All patrons were invited to write a question on a specially printed card which was folded. On the outside of the card the patron placed his initials. A lady assistant, dressed in appropriate Turkish attire more becoming than mystifying, collected the cards in a large silver pail. After the ballroom dancing team had whirled their last number, hiding their breathlessness behind expansive smiles, the mind reader appeared. He gave a brief talk on the "established" phenomenon of mind reading and then proceeded to demonstrate. He drew a card at random, deep from the center of the silver pail, and called out the initials appearing on its cover. When the person whose initials had been called arose (while his companions at the table stirred with embarrassed glee) the mind reader proceeded to answer the question written on the inside of the card. While doing so, he not only kept the card closed, never glancing at it, but slowly tore it to small bits. In each instance he gave the correct name of the patron (which had been written on the inside of the card) and convincingly demonstrated that he knew what had been asked of him.

At times he would deliberately grope around the subject so that there was doubt as to whether he really knew the question. But finally and in triumph he would strike upon a specific answer. For example, if the question was, "Will I go to Bristol, England, this year?" he would venture the thought that the patron was interested in travel—not locally, far away—indeed, not in this country—some place in Europe —England to be exact—"Yes, you will visit *Bristol*, England, this year! Was that your question, sir?" Applause. The audience, of course, did not know that the question included the city Bristol. The form of the answer gave the impression that the mind reader supplied even this detail.

How is this done? During the five-minute interval when the ballroom dancer is ferris-wheeling his blonde partner through the air, our mind reader is selecting ten or fifteen interesting and varied questions. He memorizes the initials and the questions in couplets. Thereafter, irrespective of the card he draws from the pail, he calls the initials he has memorized and answers the associated question. It is purely a memory trick. The reason the card is torn to bits is not only to demonstrate that he does not peek at the inside, but to prevent anyone from seeing the card a little later and learning that neither the initials nor the question were on the card which the professor held in his hand.

To give this procedure an extraordinary fillip, a variation is developed to throw the skeptical observer completely off the track. For on one or two occasions the professor will call on someone who is laughing heartily and say, "Well, you seem to be skeptical but jovial about this. Did you sign a card?" If not, all the better. If she did, then, "Well, I don't know which one it is but if you will concentrate, I will try to read your mind right now without any card. First concentrate on your name. It is—I see an L— Lou—no, Louise. Right?" Startled applause from the table and nervous shifting to one foot by Louise who is quite taken back. Then, "You are wondering whether you are going to marry a young man this year. He's red-headed—why, he is with you tonight." Screams from the table. "And let me see if I can get his name. Concentrate for a minute. His name is—I see a K— no, it is an H—H-a-r-v-e-y—Harvey, that's it. Harvey. His second name begins with a B. I see Berger—man—think I see Bergerman!" It is all correct. The audience buzzes with wonder. One can see ladies leaning toward their all-wise unbelieving escorts and asking, "And how do you explain *that!*"

Well, I suspect that "that" is accomplished by waiters or even the young lady who collects the cards, who pick up information around the garrulous table. They overhear someone teasing Louise about Harvey, or perhaps the table has been arranged to celebrate their engagement. A few crumbs of information are thus relayed to the mind reader who, having spotted the victim, turns to her with a great show of spontaneity.

In vaudeville theatres, bazaars and tent shows mind readers

and fortune tellers have leaned heavily upon another simple trick. One day a performer billed as the "X-ray mind" came to my office to seek some legal advice. It is unnecessary to comment upon the the fact that if he could exercise occult powers he would not need the professional service of a lawyer torn by the uncertainties of unpredictable judges. When I got to know the "X-ray mind" better, the subject arose as to the genuineness of his performance. I did not raise it. I respected his professional secrets. But he must have sensed that I was an unbeliever and it probably pleased him to confound me. When he challenged me to state my view, I did tell him that I thought his performance was a trick. He urged me to reveal the reasons for my skepticism. I did so.

His mind-reading performance consisted of having the subject write a question, fold the paper several times and hand it to him. He would then tear the paper into many bits, put the pieces into a tray and set fire to them. While they burned he gazed meaningfully at the smoke and answered the question. He always knew what the question was. The customer, swept along by this phenomenon, was led to believe in the answer too.

I suggested that this was a palming trick; that he tore another piece of paper similarly folded, palmed the original and continued to read the question while the subject thought it was burning in the tray. The patronizing smile of the "X-ray mind" informed me I was wrong.

"Suppose," he said, "you write a question on your own piece of paper, so that I cannot have a duplicate." He went to the window and turned his back to me. I wrote a question upon a half-sheet taken from a pad on my desk, specially printed for legal memoranda, folded it and called him to the desk. He tore it to bits in my presence. He then put a match to the pieces and "answered" my question. Clearly he knew the import of the question. My solution was wrong, but I remained convinced that so were his protestations of mind reading.

It was not until much later that I learned from another source how this was done. A question is written in the center of the sheet. To make sure of this, these professors have sheets with a printed circle in which you automatically write the query. I recalled that when I took a sheet from the pad on my desk the "X-ray mind" carelessly drew a circle with a pencil and said, "All right, write down any question on your own sheet. I haven't another like it." When such a sheet is folded twice and torn in a certain way, the central piece remains untouched. Only this piece is palmed. The rest of the paper falls in many bits into the tray. It is convenient as well as impressive to burn them, for otherwise one might be tempted later to reconstruct them and find the question missing. Yet this simple device has mystified innumerable people and convoyed their credulity into the nether regions of mind-transference, spirits and Lord knows what other hocus-pocus.

Religious people are sometimes inclined to believe in fortune tellers. They have faith and often transfer it indiscriminately to those not deserving. It might be well, therefore, to remind them of the passage in the Bible, which reads: "There shall not be found among you any one . . . that useth divination . . . or a charmer, or a consulter with familiar spirits. For all that do these things are abomination unto the Lord and because of these abominations the Lord thy God doth drive them out from before thee." (Deuteronomy 18: 10-12.)

Laws have been passed to support this biblical injunction. The most eloquently outspoken of these statutes is one passed in 1825 in England, which provided: "Every person pretending or professing to tell fortunes, or using any subtle craft . . . by palmistry or otherwise to deceive and impose on any of his Majesty's subjects . . . shall be deemed a rogue and vagabond . . ." Appropriate prison sentence was attached to this offense.

There is a profusion of current statutes similarly designed to protect the public, but no one is so vulnerable as one who does not wish to be disillusioned. Ambrose Bierce put it wisely and wittily when he said: "Palmistry is the 947th method of obtaining money by false pretenses. The pretense is not altogether false however because character can really be read very accurately in this way. The wrinkles in every hand submitted plainly spell the word 'dupe.' The imposture consists in not reading it aloud."

CHAPTER 7

Economics in a Thimble

TWO SIMPLE FACTS would clarify the complicated debates about economics and the anti-trust laws which roar from our radios and splutter in our magazines. They are: First, bigness and centralized operation often increase efficiency and make for cheaper prices. This rule of economics sets up a centripetal force tending toward mergers and larger enterprises. This is a pulling-together force. Second, Americans wish to protect the small business man. He cannot compete with large organizations which enjoy the economic advantages that go with size, so the anti-trust laws come to his aid. They attack combines. This is a centrifugal or breaking-apart force. These two forces work against each other.

Despite the enforcement of the anti-trust laws by vigorous attorneys-general for the past fifty years, combinations continue to grow and prosper and the Department of Justice has had an ever busier task. The reason for this paradox is that we welcome the natural economic law that large operations give us good products at cheap prices, while we fight this same economic law by anti-trust statutes to protect the individual business man. This is a conflict in our own thinking. It is popular to praise American mass-production and enterprise. It is equally popular to defend the small entrepreneur. We choose not to notice that these are inconsistent and that the reason we have not coped successfully with either problem is that we support contending forces which offset each other. There is a continuous economic tug and pull in American life which leaves us frustrated.

There is a service rendered by the anti-trust laws with which no public-spirited citizen will quarrel. This is the prevention of monopoly and price-fixing which raise prices and exploit the public. But when, as the result of centralized operation, good products can be sold at cheaper prices, do we want to reject these advantages to protect small business? Until this decision is consciously made by the public, the economic tendency will be toward gigantic enterprise and the legal tendency will be to "break up the combine."

The battle between large business and the anti-trust laws would long ago have been won by business, were it not for an unexpected ally. The ally is not a man-made law. It is another economic law unobserved even by most business men. There is a point at which size destroys itself. It is as if one piled up a huge sand mound. At a certain point a landslide occurs and the mound is back to its original size. Since I have seen business men, time and again, expand right into bankruptcy, this simple economic proposition must be obscure. I will therefore illustrate it simply.

Suppose business A merges with business B. The overhead is reduced forty per cent because the same buyer acts for the two organizations, the rental of one office may be eliminated, the number of supervisors may be reduced, one advertising budget covers both products, etc. Duplication is avoided, efficiency is maintained. This is a sound merger.

Now suppose A-B merges with C. The overhead is reduced, let us say, by only twenty per cent because C's offices cannot be crowded in with A-B's, the buyer may need an assistant to handle the larger assignment, etc. The efficiency of the organization suffers somewhat by the spread operation. Nevertheless, there is still a gain from the combination.

This is a healthy merger, though its advantages are not as great as those from the original one.

Now suppose A-B-C expands to acquire D. The overhead saving is perhaps ten per cent. Indeed, it may become necessary at this point to organize a special home office and to hire district supervisors. There may be no saving at all in such operation. Also, there is likely to be a ten per cent decrease in efficiency, for now the organization is complex and it is difficult to "keep a finger" on each activity. This merger is of doubtful value. At best, the organization has merely held its own.

But if A-B-C-D acquires E, there is likely to be no saving in operation at all. There is a loss in efficiency of perhaps ten or fifteen per cent. This merger is definitely bad. It is the beginning of the decline.

Of course this illustration is oversimplified. Advantages from larger buying power, improved manufacturing methods, superior personnel are factors which I have ignored. On the other hand, I have not mentioned the disadvantages from depressions which many a business with large overhead cannot weather, discriminatory taxation, the competitive frictions which an expanding firm generates, not even excluding anti-trust investigations.

Though simplified, the illustration does indicate an economic truth, namely, that there is a saturation point at which growth ceases to provide additional advantages of size and tends to limit itself. Time and again I have seen shrewd business men trapped because they were blind to this principle. That is why so many successful expanding operations end in bankruptcy. I could list a dozen firms which expanded, lured by a disease common to business as well as politics—"mapitis." This is the disease of having a map on the wall and coloring in a new territory which has been conquered. On paper each new branch adds to the strength of the enterprise. But the reality is often a top-heavy struture which suffers a landslide; the lawyers call it insolvency.

I do not claim that economic laws are like laws of nature,

but there is a similarity between the way bacteria are devoured by other bacteria, and the way economic growth is
offset by economic strangulation. It is this rule of economics
which delimits the advantage of vertical or horizontal trusts.
It is this rule much more than the anti-trust laws which has
held monopoly in check.

How will the struggle between the pulling-together force
and the breaking-apart force ultimately end? I suspect that
the tendency in major industries will be toward regulated
monopolies, closely supervised as to rates and service so that
the public interest can be preserved. I am afraid that despite
our tears for little business, its future is quite restricted. The
economic advantages of size are too alluring to Americans,
trained in large-scale production, to be long withstood.
Fortunately, even this tendency toward centralization will be
limited by the offsetting economic postulate that there is a
point at which size becomes its own worst enemy.

CHAPTER 8

Splitting the Atoms or Uniting the Adams

WHEN THE LORD created Adam, He intended
him to be a symbol of all mankind. Later there were millions
of Adams. It must have been ordained that they should live
together in harmony and in peace. Soon, however, the Adams
of the world were split. They were split religiously. There
are today three hundred and fifty different religions and sects
and untold denominational subdivisions. As a result of the
splitting of the Adams of the world religiously, there were
released volcanic forces of hatred and passion which have
mushroomed up to the sky, casting angry red, purple and
yellow lights upon the night, and heavy brooding clouds
over our days. In the name of religion, these forces have
caused the destruction of millions of people. In the Crusades,

between 1096 and 1271, twenty million men were killed. The Thirty Years' War, which was, in the main, a war between Catholic and Protestant nations, destroyed seventy-five per cent of the peoples of Central Europe. These volcanic forces have emitted gamma rays which have continued down through the centuries to poison the bloodstream of mankind.

Not only have the Adams of the world been split religiously, they have also been split nationally. There are today one hundred and twenty-five nations, each sitting sulkily behind irregularly shaped boundary lines, each believing in its own superiority and nourishing its own pride and vanity. As a result of the splitting of the Adams of the world nationally, additional forces of hatred have been released, resulting in the killing of millions of people. The Napoleonic wars cost the lives of twenty million people. The first World War resulted in eight million deaths and three million additional casualties. The second World War is estimated to have destroyed thirty-five million people. The cities of Europe, so painstakingly and preciously built during the centuries and which now lie in ruins, were not destroyed by bombs, or cannon, or dynamite. They were destroyed by the hatreds released by the nationalistic splitting of the Adams.

Now we must call conventions of scientists. No, not physicists who know how to split the atoms, but moral scientists whose function it will be to unite the Adams of the world. We are all qualified to be moral scientists. All we need is a generous heart and a clear brain. We must gather the atomic fragments of different races, creeds, religions and sects and synthesize them in a cyclotron so that they will emerge a united entity of brotherhood.

We must learn to respect all religions for, after all, they have a common basic ethical foundation. A devout Hindu, Gandhi, believed that the scriptures of all great religions are equally the word of God: the Bible, Talmud, Zend-Avesta, Koran and Veda. His faith was a universal expression: "I perceive that whilst everything around is ever-changing and ever-dying, there is, underlying all that change, a living Power that is changeless, that holds all together, that creates, dissolves and recreates. That informing Power and Spirit is God. I see it as purely benevolent for I can see that, in the midst of death, life persists; in the midst of untruth, truth persists; in the midst of darkness, light persists. Hence I gather that God is life, truth and light. He is love. He is the Supreme God!"

We must support the fumbling but earnest efforts of the United Nations to bind the countries and races of the world together. For, as against the superstitions of racial and national superiorities, I would prefer the Chinese myth that the Creator made men by baking them in ovens and that the differences in the shades of skin were due to the degree of baking. Isn't it silly to hate and kill one another simply because the Creator experimented as to which of us should be done a little more than others?

There is a race going on between the physical scientists, who are learning more about splitting the atoms, and the moral scientists, who must learn more about uniting the Adams. We dare not lose this race for if there is another war it will not decide who is right, but who, if anybody, is to be left.

CHAPTER 9

The Right of Privacy

IT IS ONLY during the last half-century that the law has recognized the "right to be let alone," the right under certain circumstances to protect one's name and physiognomy from becoming public property. No mention of such a right will be found in the works of the great political philosophers and tract-writers of the seventeenth and eighteenth centuries: Hobbes, Locke, Rousseau, Montesquieu,

Paine. In discoursing on "natural rights," "the state of nature," "the social contract," and "the inalienable rights of man," they were concerned only with the power of the state to abridge the liberties of the people. Society had not yet become so complex that the individual's privacy was in danger of encroachment.

But political, social and economic changes require the creation of new legal rights. Since the common law is not the mere formal statement of an inherited traditional moral code but is newly fashioned to meet unanticipated needs, it was predestined that the privacy doctrine should be formulated. The rule was the product of its time.

The social need which became crystallized in the right of privacy did not grow insistent until the age of great industrial expansion, when miraculous advances in transportation and communication threatened to annihilate time and space, when the press was going through the growing pains of "yellow journalism," when business first became big. In an era marked by the triumph of the strong man, esoteric concepts such as the right of privacy were spectacularly flouted. In the backwash of this wave of excesses, the privacy doctrine was formulated. Its creation at that precise time was historically inevitable. Was man to have no fenced area for himself except in the recesses of his mind? One thinks of Professor Einstein's reply when, at a particularly dull academic meeting, he was asked whether he was terribly bored. "No, no," he said, "on such occasions as this I retire to the back of my mind and there I am happy." Few have so delightful a retreat and the law intends that privacy should not be so limited.

Although the doctrine of the right of privacy is of recent origin, its roots go back into the ancient principles of the common law. In earliest times the law afforded only bare protection against physical interference with life and property, but the trend has been steadily toward a fuller recognition of more intangible, incorporeal, spiritual values. The right to life includes the right to enjoy life. "Personal" rights originally included protection only against physical violence, battery. Later it was established that a real injury to human sensibilities could be inflicted when one is merely placed in imminent *danger* of battery by an *attempt* at bodily harm. At about the same time people began to value their reputations and their honor as well as their skins, and in 1356 the first known judgment for slander was recorded in the law books.

Later, applying the law of nuisances, judges granted redress for the discomfort caused by noise, odors, dust and smoke. Still later, spiritual values found protection. In 1745, for example, the cause of action for alienation of affections was recognized. The category of personal rights now includes freedom of speech, press, assembly and religion, the constitutional privilege of a person accused of crime not to be compelled to testify against himself, the right to recover damages for false arrest or malicious prosecution, habeas corpus, and the inadmissibility in evidence of confidential communications with an attorney, doctor or priest.

Similarly, the concept of property has been expanded to include not only physical, tangible things, but also the incorporeal rights surrounding those things and eventually the products and processes of the mind. Infringement upon the rights of ownership in literary and artistic creations was made actionable in 1558. Trade secrets and trademarks did not receive judicial protection until 1803. Still later, recovery for unfair competition was allowed and the courts began to grant injunctions against persons who traded on another's business reputation by the use of a name or device so similar to his as to deceive the public.

Progress in this direction indicated that in the natural course of events the common law would expand its scope to include the right of privacy. It is but a short step, for example, from an injunction against the publication of a man's private letters to an injunction against the publication of a picture of his face. A man's thoughts, emotions and sensations are as much a part of him as his arms and legs. Not all the pain, pleasure and profit of life come from physical things; man's spiritual nature, too, requires legal recognition.

Five hundred years of legal history reveal the progressive growth of the "right of inviolate personality." What were originally deemed the minimum rights of man ordained by nature itself have been expanded to include newer concepts of man's right to enjoy unmolested a fuller and richer life more consonant with the dignity of human existence.

Every lawsuit involves a choice between opposing interests. Every rule of law, being merely a generalization from a multitude of such choices, represents a compromise between opposing principles. The history of the right of privacy is a revealing chronicle of this continuous tug-of-war between two conflicting ideals. The right of privacy, in essence, is asocial. It is the right of an individual to live a life of seclusion and anonymity, free from the prying curiosity which accompanies both fame and notoriety. It presupposes a desire to withdraw from the public gaze, to be free from the insatiable interest of the great mass of men in one who has risen above, or fallen below, the mean. It is a recognition of the dignity of solitude, of the majesty of man's free will and desire to mold his own destiny, of the sacred and inviolable nature of one's innermost self.

Opposed to this ideal is the principle that the white light of publicity safeguards the public, that free disclosure of truth is the best protection against tyranny. Liberty is not the right of one but of many. The advance of civilization depends upon the dissemination of knowledge and society has an absolute right to be informed on matters bearing upon its protection and education. Frequently the public has an interest in an individual which transcends his right to be let alone. Since the whole is greater than its component parts, private rights must often yield to public interest.

Each of these ideals bears within it the germ of excess. If the pendulum swings too far in one direction, society is reduced to anarchy, with each individual retaining all of the rights which he would have exercised in a state of nature;

at the other end of the trajectory lies totalitarianism, where the individual is a slave to the state. In any single case these two opposing forces press in upon the judge. On the one hand, he is urged to uphold the right of free speech, the right of society to know the truth, the right to make full use of the wonders of modern civilization which spread intelligence instantaneously to the farthest ends of the earth. On the other hand, he is urged to protect the sensibilities of the individual from the brash and vulgar attentions of the mob, to fence off a small corner of human existence against the predatory advances of selfish commercial interests. Thus every lawsuit based upon an alleged infringement of the right of privacy poses a dilemma in which the court is called upon to find a point at which the rights of the individual and the rights of society are in equilibrium; a succession of such points constitutes the line along which the privacy doctrine has progressed.

"Names make news" is a primary tenet of the journalistic craft. It would be manifestly impossible, however, to publish a newspaper if it were necessary, before going to press, to obtain written consents from the hundreds of individuals whose names appear in each issue. Since the safeguarding of a free press is of paramount public importance, all courts agree that the right of privacy does not prohibit the publication of news and pictures in connection with items of legitimate public interest.

The determination of what is or is not a subject of public concern frequently requires a delicate appreciation of intangible psychological factors. The criterion is not, as the earliest cases intimated, the prominence or distinction of the person whose name or photograph is used; the differentiation between "public" and "private" characters which was advanced during the formative stages of the privacy doctrine has not been accepted. The courts have recognized that public curiosity is a mysterious thing and frequently concentrates most heavily on those least deserving of attention. Thus not only persons outstanding in the arts and sciences, in statecraft, industry and finance, but also criminals, prize fighters, fan dancers and people who try to set endurance records, are natural targets of public interest and their names and photographs may be used with impunity in reporting their exploits.

One frequently becomes an object of attention through no affirmative act of his own, but simply because he has been an unwilling participant in an event of general interest. For example, a wife was walking along the street with her husband when he was mysteriously assaulted and stabbed to death. A newspaper described the event and printed the wife's picture. She sued the newspaper claiming that her right of privacy had been violated. The court stated that although everyone has a right to live his life in seclusion there are times when one becomes an actor, sometimes involuntarily, in a newsworthy occurrence. When this happens, he emerges from his seclusion and the publication of his name and picture is not a violation of his right of privacy.

What is an obvious truism with respect to a sensational headline story on page one may, however, become a close question when the less world-shaking items on the inside pages of the newspaper are concerned. How keen must the public's desire for information be in order to permit a person's name or picture to be used in a "human interest" story, rotogravure section, serialized biography or sports commentator's column?

American newspapers customarily publish a wide variety of material which, strictly speaking, is neither news nor fiction. Such articles include travel stories and descriptions of distant places, tales of historic personages and events, reviews of past news stories and surveys of social conditions. Although these stories do not necessarily chronicle events of very recent occurrence, they are based on fact and are semi-educational in character. In general the courts have been quite liberal in interpreting almost any article which has appeared in a newspaper as "news," irrespective of whether it has been printed in the news columns, feature pages or magazine section, on the ground that the individual's right of privacy is outweighed by the public policy requiring unhampered circulation of information.

The same test is applied to the publication of a person's name or photograph in a magazine. If the use is in connection with a factual report of important or interesting happenings, the privacy doctrine will not be invoked. If, however, the informational factor is secondary, relief may be granted.

Books, although less timely than newspapers or magazines, frequently contain material of such immediate public concern that the right of privacy is inapplicable. However, the unauthorized use of one's name in a book of fiction may be actionable.

The growth of the motion picture industry has created new and difficult problems. Potentially the camera is mightier than the pen, at least as an instrument for the invasion of privacy. For one thing, it is possible to write a news account of a parade, a riot, or the reactions of a crowd at a football or baseball game without mentioning the name of any individual. A newsreel picturization of the same scenes, however, would necessarily reveal thousands of faces whose owners might all claim that their privacy had been invaded. The impossibility of securing written consents before publishing a newspaper is multiplied many times over in the case of newsreels.

Furthermore, a photographic record of any occurrence requires the physical presence of the cameraman, whereas a written description may be fabricated after the event by a "rewrite man" who may have received his information at second or third hand. Assuming that a particular person has no right to prevent the use of his name in a newspaper story describing a particular event, does that same rule require him to tolerate the presence of a camera man on the premises to record the event while it is going on? An Alaska case has held that an explorer and his equipment were legitimate objects of public concern and that photographic news of his expedition might be gathered and distributed despite the fact that he had sold "exclusive" rights to a rival company.

A debatable question is presented by the use of photographs of medical or surgical subjects. Here it is frequently very difficult to choose between public interest and individual privacy. Where the pictures are used in a salacious context and do not have primarily an educational appeal, there would be little dissent from the view that the subject's right of privacy has been violated. In an advisory opinion the attorney-general of New York held that photographs of cancer patients may not be exhibited publicly by the Department of Health without the consent of the patients, despite the "distinct social value for the general instruction and information of the public."

In every state which recognizes the right of privacy, the name or photograph of a living person may not be used without his permission for purposes of advertising or trade. Thus one could hardly take exception to the frequently recurring case which grants relief where privacy has been violated by a spurious endorsement of merchandise, or the decisions which have condemned the unauthorized use of a lady's photograph in a fashion magazine. Nor could one question the correctness of a ruling that an artist's name may not be used without his permission in connection with the sale of pillows adorned with a reproduction of one of his paintings, or a decision that a university president's name may not be used on a set of books with which he has had no connection.

The right of privacy doctrine, in the brief span of its existence, has mirrored the contemporary struggle between the rights of the individual and the rights of society. Every new offensive weapon is met by a corresponding improvement in defensive armament; so the right of privacy doctrine is the protective bulwark built up against the threatened annihilation of man's personal life by unprecedented advances in communication and transportation. The privacy doctrine is the law's answer to the abuses made possible by unrestrained and irresponsible operation of newspapers with their far-flung agencies for gathering information, high-speed printing presses, and huge circulation; by motion pictures, which bring vivid impressions of the vast panorama of life to many whose mental world would otherwise be bounded by the confines of their own narrow existence; by nation-wide net-works of radio stations; sending words instantaneously into millions of homes; and by supporting forces of telephone, telegraph, teletype, cable, facsimile printing, microfilm, television and other mechanical devices by which it may soon be possible to know everything about everybody everywhere.

Once the right of privacy has been recognized in its true light, its development will be foreseeable. It gives expression to an ideal which conceives of the individual as a unit not to be obliterated by society. Everyone has a right to live his own life in quiet and solitude. Modesty and reticence need not be sacrificed entirely to public clamor. No one owes an obligation to permit others to profit by his mistakes or his success. One's home is one's castle, and one's private life is a precious possession which cannot be wrested from him.

Carried to its ultimate extreme, this reasoning would lead to the destruction of social obligation. It is prevented from doing so by an opposing ideal which is as firmly established in the law—that man is a social animal and that, in order to exist peaceably, he must give up a portion of himself in return for the mutual advantages which flow from communal existence. To guarantee liberty we are called upon to surrender some freedom of action. Consideration for others requires reciprocal concessions. There are times when the public interest demands disclosure of one's activities and achievements. So society, as an entity, also has rights which are frequently paramount to the rights of the individual.

The right of privacy is the child of these two opposite ideals. Like every new rule of law, it sprang from the spark struck off by clashing principles. With gradual adjustment

of the weight to be given to these forces, a balance of values
will be achieved and the right of privacy will reach its full
stature as a mature expression of one phase of man's relationship to his fellow men.

CHAPTER 10

Word Cartooning

GREAT CARTOONISTS will struggle for hours
to eliminate a line. They seek to create a likeness with as
little drawing as possible. It is as if they were striving for the
unattainable, a blank page which would immediately suggest
a certain face. What a humiliation it would be for the subject if some cartoonist finally achieved perfection!

Obviously it is not a miser's instinct which causes cartoonists to economize on lines. They know that although millions
of faces are composed of similar features, the miracle of their
being distinguishable lies in some individual difference un-
observable to the untrained eye. Nature having contrived so
many billions of separate identities out of a pair of eyes,
a nose, a mouth and a chin, it remains for the artist to discover the secret combination which unlocks the mystery of
identity. For this purpose most features are surplusage. They
are not sufficiently different from others to contribute much
to individual recognition. Finally the shrewd observation of
the cartoonist finds *the* line. It may be only an angle, as in
the face of Gershwin, whose forehead and nose formed a
straight perpendicular line at the bottom of which jutted
a cigar at a forty degree angle, thus revealing the contour
of the mouth; or it may be only a heavy curve, like Roosevelt's jaw, with the mouth forming an uptilted loop a little
wider on the right side; or it may be a rectangle, like Hoover's head, with a pair of inverse parentheses to represent the

heavy cheeks; or it may be the barest outline of hair, like the forelock and mustache of Hitler.

The cartoonist, having placed his pencil on *the* unique feature of the particular face, proceeds to emphasize his discovery as if he were presenting a magnifying glass to those with ordinary vision. He can by such dissection also reveal character. For this reason cartoons can be devastating, not by making people funny-looking, but by informing us how they really look. In 1880, Carle de Perieres, an illustrator, was challenged to a duel as a result of his caricature of Sarah Bernhardt. He lost and immediately sent a message to the actress to say he was at her feet and did not wish to live unless she would pardon him. She combined forgiveness with an unrelenting note. "I forgive you," she wrote, "if you will get away from my feet."

Oscar Wilde, however, who was frequently lampooned, turned insult into compliment in characteristic manner. "Caricature," he said, "is the tribute that mediocrity pays to genius."

I often wonder (beauticians undoubtedly have studied the subject more closely) what it is about a face that conveys the age of a person. As you walk by people on the street you can usually tell within two or three years how old they are. The total impression of age is clear, but the disassembling of that impression into its component parts is a baffling task. Is it the jowls? Well, often you will see fifty-year-old persons whose jawlines are tight and round. Is is the bags under the eyes? Often teen-age children have puffed eyes, but they look young nevertheless. Is it the texture of the skin? You have seen older people with peachy, smooth complexions and young ones with lines on their faces. Is it obesity? Well, look at a slim middle-aged woman and a fat twenty-year-old girl of the same height. You will tell the difference in age immediately, even if the young girl happens to have gray hair and the older woman natural jet-black hair. Is it the lines from the nose to the mouth? Children's faces surprisingly often have such heavy lines, while older people reveal their ages even when there are no furrows surrounding the mouth. Masseurs will tell you that they can judge age best by muscles, particularly those of the legs and hips. But these we are not customarily privileged to see and the muscles of the face are by no means as tell-tale.

The cartoonist's art includes depicting the age of his subject with the same economy of line with which he makes the face recognizable. This is an even greater achievement and more mysterious, since age is not designated by exaggerations as are features.

Photographers have attempted to portray character by the method of analogy, showing human beings and animals side by side in poses which show remarkable similarity. Non-descriptive comments which act as clues to identity constitute the photographic analogy translated into words. For example, I would associate the following personalities with these comments:

Dwight Eisenhower: Tact is the ability to inject a needle without pain.

Thomas E. Dewey: Politics is like a horse race; a good jockey knows how to fall with the least damage.

George C. Marshall: Bold in what he stands for, but careful in what he falls for.

Katherine Cornell: The saying that beauty is but skin deep is a skin-deep saying. There is inner beauty in artists.

Fritz Kreisler: The best of all trades is to make songs, and the second best is to play them. He follows both trades.

J. Edgar Hoover: God help him who helps himself.

George Jean Nathan: He has spent the best jeers of his life in the theatre.

Grover Whalen: He has applause in his buttonhole.

Bennett Meyers: Most of the stumbling blocks people complain about are under their hats.

Charles Kettering: Ideas are funny little things. They don't work unless you do.

Robert A. Taft: Inflation is a period when two can live as steep as one.

Gypsy Rose Lee: Burlesque is not an original show. It's just a take-off.

Lee Shubert: A stage production budget is a plan for worrying before you spend, instead of afterward.

Bert Lytell: Better a small role than a long loaf.

Anne O'Hare McCormick: Women usually know less than men and always understand more.

Leonard Lyons: He has know-who as well as know-how.

Joseph Stalin: He is the kind of man with whom one should eat, drink and be wary.

Bernard Baruch: We call loudly for a man of vision and when we get one we call him a visionary.

Kate Smith: Woman's fondest wish is to be weighed and found wanting.

Harry Hershfield: He serves the greatest cause of all, the cause of making us happy.

Russell Birdwell: Many a live wire would be a dead one except for his connection.

Andrei Vishinsky: It takes you to make a quarrel.

Theatre critics: Pan-Americans.

Harold Stassen: A moderate of the most violent extraction.

Tom Clark: Some people think the only honest law suit is that worn by a policeman.

Robert R. Young: A financier is one who makes capital out of his mistakes.

Tommy Manville: Love is the feeling that makes a man think almost as much of a girl as he thinks of himself.

Henry Wallace: A third party is as unpopular in politics as in love.

Cartoonists are neither literal nor symbolic, but catch the image by a partial revelation. Some day a writer will seek to reveal by an economy of words rather than by lavish use of them. Such an effect was attained by a tenant who received a notice to vacate his premises. Confident of his rights under the federal rent law, he replied: "Dear Sir, I remain, Yours truly."

Benjamin Franklin, who could be magnificently rhetorical, also knew the art of succinctness. One remembers his famous note to one who opposed American independence:

"Dear Sir:
          You are my enemy, and I am
                    Yours,
                         Benjamin Franklin"

Even more economical was Victor Hugo's inquiry concerning the success of his new book. He sent a postcard to his publisher upon which was nothing but a question mark. The publisher replied: "!"

CHAPTER 11

The Second Knock on the Door

DEMOCRACY HAS many branch offices. One is entitled Democracy in Politics; another Democracy in Economics; and perhaps we should add another, Democracy for Youth. It is the young people whose lives are most affected by war and it is they who ought to have a very definite say concerning the kind of world they want to live in. Are they too inexperienced to make a wise choice? Well, for one thing, their elders have not done happily by them thus far and the risk is therefore at a minimum. For another, we are living in an age chiefly fit for youth, for it requires limitless imagination and courage. Every castle on earth was once a castle in the air.

Even in other eras young men have excelled. Benjamin Franklin wrote *Poor Richard's Almanac* when he was in his twenties. It was he who said, "Experience keeps a dear school, but fools will learn in no other." William Pitt was

Prime Minister of England at the age of twenty-five. He did not quail before tyranny. He said, "Necessity is the argument of tyrants; it is the creed of slaves." John Keats wrote *On First Looking into Chapman's Homer* when he was twenty, and his friend Percy Shelley wrote *Queen Mab* when he was twenty-one. They put wings on words and made them soar. It was Shelley who said, "It is not a merit to be tolerant, but rather a crime to be intolerant." Johann Goethe began writing *The Sorrows of Young Werther* at the age of twenty-two. Concerning youth, he said, "The destiny of any nation depends on the opinions of its young men."

So it is for the young men and women of the world to develop a higher form of patriotism, not one which sets up sovereignty as a pagan image before which we must shed our blood every twenty years, but patriotism which recognizes that sovereignty is preserved by sharing it with other nations which are willing to do likewise. Certainly young people should not despair because new crises arise. What else can be expected after the cataclysms we have passed through? The greater the conflict of interest, the greater the necessity for international collaboration. Sulky withdrawal is no solution. Isolationism is not only politically wrong; it is cowardice. We can't solve our problems by turning our heads away. So we pray for the democracy of youth. For these are moments when no matter what the attitude of the body, the soul is on its knees.

But suppose youth fails? Are we doomed? Why, no, life offers many opportunites. An old young man is usually a young old man. The young must continue to try until they are old. There is inspiration for them here, too. Talleyrand was French Ambassador to Britain at eighty. Tennyson wrote *Crossing the Bar* at eighty. Voltaire finished his tragedy *Irene* at eighty-four. Gladstone was Prime Minister of Britain at eighty-five. Verdi composed his opera *Falstaff* at eighty-five. Michelangelo designed the great dome of St. Peter's in Rome at eighty-seven.

Persistence is the first requisite for the solution of any problem. When Thomas Edison was looking for a filament for his incandescent lamp, a friend commiserated with him upon his failure after two thousand experiments. Edison replied, "Why we have made real progress. These are two thousand things we do not need to try again." So if youth has little else to look forward to, it can at least look forward to old age.

CHAPTER 12

Gin Rummy—the Great American Illusion

JUST AS METEOROLOGISTS can foretell storms which will suddenly strike certain sections of the country, so there ought to be "cardologists" who can predict when certain card games will sweep the country. Then we could have been forewarned many years ago that a great blizzard called bridge was about to descend upon us. It chilled thousands of friendships and provoked domestic quarrels on a scale never before known. "Another word out of you and I'm a widow," announced one wife, thus giving expression to the thoughts of thousands of spouses. The post mortem for every hand was not a quiet and respectful commentary such as befits a hand which has passed away. Recriminations and corrective lectures took place between partners. Pride and conceit resisted learning. The furore was great, the excitement was of a rather bitter variety.

Still, bridge is mainly a game of skill. Players, no matter how grudgingly, recognize the superiority of other players, just as golfers cannot deny the mathematical test of the score. Consequently, bridge did not become a gambling game for the masses. The average player would not risk large stakes against better players. Also there was sufficient skill involved to make a small game interesting.

But then followed another storm. Its name was gin. It has swept the nation and its grip is undiminished. The great secret of its attraction is its simplicity. Everyone can play it. It is the great equalizer. The lowly are wise because everyone is an expert. Since there are no strata as in bridge, the temptation is great to match skill at higher stakes. Consequently, gin has become the greatest gambling game for the masses. The rates are constantly increasing and all America is in a fever. A new kind of card widow has been created. She does not quarrel with her husband because he failed to finesse. She simply doesn't see him.

Gin nights have become the great American habit. They last into the early hours of the morning. This is not due solely to the fascination of the game. High stakes make for high losses and losers are more eager to recoup losses than to sleep. So a great strain on family relationships has again developed. "Aren't there other things we can do once in a while than play gin—gin—gin?" is the scornful question in thousands of homes.

Whether the rate is one half cent a point or two dollars a point, many players are playing for higher stakes than they can afford. In Hollywood one executive lost four-hundred-thousand dollars in one evening. In New York a man of only comfortable wealth lost two-hundred-thousand dollars in a few sessions. The two-hundred dollar and three-hundred dollar losses, and even the fifty dollar and sixty dollar losses, are proportionately disastrous in thousands of instances. There is no sign of flagging interest. The lure of gin seems to have a lasting quality. It is the great national indoor sport. So let us examine this new American phenomenon.

The gin craze is based on an illusion. The illusion is that a great amount of skill can be applied to the luck of the cards. This belief is as convenient as it is pat. Thus, if a player loses, why he simply can't overcome bad cards. If he wins, he is slyly radiant at the maneuvers which brought about his triumph. What could be more nourishing to the ego, and Lord, how hungry most egos are! This theory is a thing of beauty because it achieves the impossible, relieving the player of responsibility when he loses and giving him full credit when he wins.

The reason this fatuous conviction is held by the great majority of players is that they ascribe greater skill to the game than it possesses. True, a learner is at a disadvantage against an experienced player. He may be unaware of such elementary points as how to arrange combinations of cards so as to have the greatest opportunity of filling runs; or he may be totally oblivious to the cards his opponent has lifted, and therefore innocently "feed" him; or he may be unaware of the advisability in playing "Hollywood" (three games across), of knocking as soon as possible to "get on" score and insure himself against "schneids"; or in playing partnership, he may not take into consideration his partner's winning score and therefore may not eschew ginning to protect it, or his partner's losing score which may necessitate his going for gin; or similar considerations which everyone learns after a while. One who plays against such a rank amateur will have an advantage. But when these elementary propositions have been learned, as they are by almost all players (since it requires no great intellect to absorb them), the skill of players is approximately equalized. Any real advantage disappears and the luck of the cards is the overwhelming determinative factor. That is why, as so frequently happens in this game, one side will "schneid" the other three straight games and then immediately thereafter be "schneided" back.

In games where skill is a large factor, there is seldom such a disparity of result in so short a period. In bridge even bad cards played by superior players will often set the opponent or reduce his winnings. In pinochle, skillful bidding and playing can offset better cards to a great extent. Even in backgammon there is greater leeway for tactics to reduce the advantage of good dice. But in gin the factor of skill is so small after it is balanced by basic knowledge of the game by almost all players, that it plays practically no part. Of course thousands of players will resent this conclusion either with howls of protest or with a silent and smug shrug of the shoulders as if to say, "I know better, why argue? I wish I had that fellow on a slow boat to China."

But let us examine this conclusion a bit farther. How often in a game do you hear the surprised and somewhat anguished cry, "Why that was the safest card in the deck!" Gin players can quickly diagnose the cause of the pain from such an outcry. A player has decided in the course of "scientific defense" to play the card which, according to all the averages, will least benefit his opponent. So, for example, if he has two queens, and a ten of clubs has been played, the queen of clubs should be a reasonably safe card. But, no sooner has he removed his finger from the card than his opponent seizes it and, with ill-disguised elation, cries, "Gin! Boy, you filled it right in the middle." He had the jack and king of clubs.

This is not a freakish or unfair illustration. Players know that when cards are "against" you, the safest cards—that is to say, those which according to the averages should be safest —turn out repeatedly to be the most dangerous. "Well," says the scientific player, "that only illustrates that defense in gin is a wrong tactic. You must play an offensive game or you are lost." The trouble with this theory is that it is likewise entirely subject to the whim of chance. It will not stand up scientifically. Often you decide to throw caution to the wind and play "strange" cards which you do not need. When luck is against you, such cards will be seized and you will be trapped with pairs of kings and queens, thus accelerating the "schneid." On the other hand, when the cards are running in your favor, the most dangerous cards thrown by you seem to have no attraction for your opponent. Similarly the player who likes to throw aces rather than kings will, when in a "bad run," find himself annihilated because the ace makes it possible for his opponent to knock with ten and catch him at the beginning of the game with a high score. Once more, these experiences are not isolated. They are, indeed the regular run of the game, occurring quite frequently, often shifting from one side to another in the course of the same evening. So, offensive play is not a scientific theory as players know who derive an inner glow of false superiority from the fact that they frustrated an opponent by safe playing. Then, of course, they think of defensive tactics as skill.

Another illustration of the fact that science in gin is an illusion, is the practice of many players to ignore an opponent's "pick" and "feed" him rather than hold a card as a possible throw-off. Such players, for example, knowing that their opponent has picked a nine will nevertheless throw another nine, announcing jauntily as they do so, lest the play be considered an error, "Here's another one. Go ahead and have a good time." While occasionally such a play will not injure, either because the opponent has a sequence and doesn't need the nine, or because, having three nines and a sequence of four, he foregoes the card in order not to spoil his gin possibilities just as often the fed card results in the hilarious announcement of "Gin!" Surprisingly enough, most players so tricked by their own "scientific" theory of not cluttering up the hand with dead cards, do not feel humiliated. Nor do they admit error. They simply accept their fate philosophically with the self-comforting comment that "in the long run" their method (a disguise for the word science, for few players have the temerity to utter the word seriously) will triumph over dumb luck. Thus even disaster fails to disprove their theory. There is no greater obstinacy than that of the self-satisfied gin scientist.

Incidentally, what becomes of the theory or skill when it is possible to justify the abandonment of the first principle of the game: to remember what your opponent took so as not to play into his hand? On this theory of "feeding" an opponent, the learner, who doesn't even notice what his opponent took, turns out to be the scientific player. There ought to be some persuasion in the fact that the rankest amateur and the most advanced theorist meet at the same point, one playing by oversight, the other with deliberation, but both doing the same thing.

Those who argue that skill is a vital factor in gin rest on

two final propositions. The first is an admission designed to be disarming. They concede that luck is a major factor, perhaps as high as sixty per cent, others will say seventy or even eighty per cent. Then follows the second proposition: "However," they say, "there is a large percentage of skill left and no matter how little the difference in skill between two players, in the long run the more skillful one is sure to win. The averages even out the luck between them and skill finally becomes the decisive factor."

The chief fallacy in this argument lies in the words "in the long run." How long, mister? One hour? Three? An evening? A week? A month? Will you guarantee that luck will average out evenly in a year? You shy away from a definite period. Will you even bet that it will equalize itself in three years or ten? Assuming that two players are exactly equal in skill, are you willing to predict over what period of time they will be approximately even? If experiments were conducted and two such players did come out even after a certain period of time, could you honestly say that this was not a coincidence and that two unequal players might not have reached the same result? Or to put it conversely, if the same two equally skilled players tried it again, would you be confident that they would come out approximately even over the same period of time?

Not only do I not concede that substantial skill is involved in the game, but I challenge the importance of the law of averages which is set forth. I challenge it not as a mathematical formula but as a practical guide, because in no one game does the average hold true, nor in any specific number of games. In the first place, as Ely Culbertson has pointed out, every new deal is an independent event offering exactly even chances. "What happened in the past has no bearing upon the probability of the next event." So when a coin is flipped ten times and head comes up ten times in succession, the odds on a head in the eleventh throw are even. The sergeant was wrong who said, "I have had so many close calls I feel like a fugitive from the law of averages." It is of little comfort to the player to know, even if it were so, that if he continued to play indefinitely he would come out all right. He is playing one evening and that particular evening the averages almost never work out. For example, he has three deuces. The chances of buying the fourth and last deuce out of the thirty-one cards left is very small. Yet in this particular hand, as so often happens when one is "running strong," the fourth deuce is the second or third card, or perhaps even on top. On the other hand, when he is in bad luck, the card he needs and for which he has waited patiently turns out to be one of the last two cards and therefore unobtainable. Such deviations from the average frequently occur all evening.

Indeed it is common to experience winning streaks for weeks or months. The same of course is true of losing streaks. On such occasions, players who simply will not accept the truth about the complete domination of chance begin to doubt themselves. "Perhaps," they think, "I am really playing badly. After all, I am taking beating after beating now for four months. It can't all be just a typographical error." They change their style of play. They play more cautiously, then very recklessly. They try to knock quickly and not aspire for gin. Then they shift and go for gin all the time. Nothing avails them. They continue to lose. The averages are no more guide to them than a defective compass.

Then without warning a winning streak hits them. They can do no wrong. They carelessly fail to pick cards which fill runs, but they gin nevertheless. They undercall when the opponent knocks, often throwing off cards which they had no reason to think could so be used or they beat their opponents to gin. Suddenly it dawns on them that they are good players. While as a matter of courtesy and good sportsmanship they may comment on an opponent's "bad luck," in their inner thoughts they have a little compassion for him. "Poor fellow, he doesn't really know how to get the best out of his cards. I'm playing rings around him. He's really confused."

You can't depend on averages any more than the professor who came to the city for the first time and was advised to have his bags carried from the train to the hotel. He inquired of the porter what the customary charge was. "Well," said the porter, "different people pay different amounts, but the average is five dollars." With a grimace, the professor complied and gave him five dollars. In an unexpected burst of appreciation the porter cried, "Thank you, sir. Thank you. You are the first gentleman who ever came up to the average."

Although some skill is required in gin, the simplicity of the game makes it possible for all experienced players to acquire approximately the same degree of skill. It is therefore cancelled out as a decisive factor in winning or losing. The luck of the cards takes complete control. You cannot depend on luck averaging out over any given period of time, particularly a limited period, such as one evening's play. Therefore it is not true that luck will equalize itself and superiority in skill, no matter how infinitesimal, will determine the winner. On the contrary, in gin a run of good cards so overwhelms any possible refinements of scientific play that the latter is not worth calculating as a factor.

Of course this does not mean that you can play recklessly, ignoring the few simple rules of skill, for we have proceeded on the theory that all players abide by these minimum standards. That is why, despite everything said above, certain players are preferable as partners. One who concentrates upon the simple rules and adheres to them can have an advantage over the reckless or unorthodox player who disregards them. But this is a far cry from the mistaken notion held by most players that there is such a wide area for ingenuity that a master's touch is necessary to derive the most out of the game.

A dramatic illustration of this point occurred recently. Several players who were arguing that the science of the game cannot be underestimated held forth, as Exhibit A, a brilliant bridge player whom they also considered the

greatest gin player they knew. They claimed that his superiority was so great that they would be willing to give odds
on him against any ordinary experienced player. He won far
too often, they urged, to attribute his success to mere luck.
Although they possessed excellent "card sense" themselves,
they spoke of his feats in awed tones. On one occasion he had
three queens. He suspected that his opponent had the fourth
queen and would use it as a throw-off to undercall. As the
game neared the end, to the astonishment of the on-lookers,
Mr. Genius broke up his three queens and threw one. Instantly his opponent released the blank queen he was holding, whereupon Mr. Genius picked it up and knocked. His
opponent, having deprived himself of the throw-off by this
deceptive maneuver, was unable to undercall.

On another occasion Mr. Genius had picked a king of
hearts to fill a run of three kings. His opponent, however,
was not certain whether it was a heart sequence or a run.
Finally he guessed that it was kings. He therefore threw a
ten of hearts which was of no use to him. Without a moment's hesitation, Mr. Genius picked it up, though he did
not need it. His opponent then was certain that he had made
a wrong guess and that Mr. Genius had a heart sequence up
to the king. He was compelled to this conclusion because
several tens were out and therefore the ten of hearts could
only be used for the jack, queen, king of hearts. Therefore
he threw a king of clubs which he now considered safe. This
gave Mr. Genius four kings. He threw back the ten of hearts
which was just a decoy and announced "gin."

I was impressed, even though I could imagine Mr. Genius
in the first illustration breaking up his queens only to find,
first, that his opponent was not holding the fourth queen as
a throw-off and that it was in the deck or secondly, that the
queen he threw happened to fill a sequence for his opponent
which otherwise was completely blocked. I could also imagine
Mr. Genius in the second illustration picking the ten of
hearts, which he did not need, and being obliged to throw
a card from his hand which ordinarily he would not have

thrown, this card making gin for his opponent who threw away the king of clubs as the eleventh card supinely unaware that he had been deceived.

The dénouement of this true story is this: Several months later I heard that a certain player who had accumulated large winnings had lost them all and suffered an additional loss of $150,000 in a period of several months. He was unable to pay his losses and had been given time to make payments in installments. He was now playing for smaller stakes, trying to get back on his feet. Furthermore, his large business enterprise was now in jeopardy. When I inquired about the name of this victim—yes, you guessed it, his name was Mr. Genius.

When his admirers were faced with this fact, they explained that he had only one weakness: he played aggressively and would not pull in his horns with a "little safe play" no matter how bad his luck was. It did no good to point out to them that his aggressiveness was one of the qualities they had particularly praised a few months earlier. "He has the heart of a lion," they had said then, using a heroic phrase much more suitable, I thought, to more dangerous pursuits. "He does not change his game because he happens to be on a 'schneid.' He plays as if he were ahead, even though the stakes are high. That kind of aggressive player is hard to beat." So Mr. Genius applied his superior skill aggressively and, to use the ungainly phrase which has become part of gin vocabulary, "got his brains beaten out." But my friends who thought he was a prohibitive favorite against any ordinary player are not convinced. They still hold to the great American illusion that skill is the decisive factor in gin.

Like most card games, gin develops a series of types who become familiar wherever the game is played. There is the "belly-acher" who bemoans his fate after each lost hand as though he were the victim of the most outrageous ill-fortune which ever befell man. "Isn't that extraordinary!" he cries. "I had two runs right from the beginning and couldn't improve the hand." Or if his hand is entirely bad, he terms the situation "Unbelievable, I haven't a run in my hand." Or if he has all sorts of possibilities but hasn't filled them, he thinks the situation is "Fantastic. Here I am sitting with all this and never filled a run." Of course he fails to observe that in each hand played there must be a loser and that one of the possibilities he has referred to must occur. He just whimpers on. When he wins, the "belly-acher" is oblivious to his good fortune. He accepts his success as natural and rather enjoys his opponent's discomfiture.

Then there is that strange phenomenon, the "sore winner." He is outraged when you get off a "schneid." He slams his cards on the table in disgust and yells, "Imagine that, ninety-two on a schneid and you're off." Anyone entering the room and hearing the outcries would imagine that the score was reversed and that the loser was exercising his privilege of cursing his bad luck. The "sore winner" considers every crumb which falls to his adversary an outrageous diminution of his own bread supply. He is dissatisfied with close games because he won little. He is equally unhappy with one-sided games because they fall short of being "schneids." He even grumbles about "schneids" because there are too few boxes. He never enjoys his triumphs because he constantly recalls the occasion when he lost and he doesn't think the situation is sufficiently reciprocal. He is the kind of man who, when he sees the sun, thinks only that it casts shadows.

Then there is the "replayer" who after each hand, win or lose, insists on telling you precisely what he started with, how his cards developed, what choices he made and why. He goes about his task with such avidity that you would think he was under contractual obligation to render a report. He projects his own excitement over his cards to everyone else around the table and is sure you are hanging on every syllable as he traces the course of his cards. It does not help to deal the cards quickly to him. He will put them down until he has explained the history of his prior adventure. Your stiletto stare will go unobserved. You might express

your boredom delicately, like the lady who, being pinned
down by her friend's endless recitation about herself, pointed
to a man yawning at the other end of the room and said,
"My dear, I think we've been overheard."

Sometimes it will help to say with mock innocence, "That's
fascinating! How did the hand come out?" But you may be
sure your rebuke will have only temporary effect. A replayer
is a replayer.

Then there is the superstitious player. He, of course, is
common to all card games, but a particularly annoying breed
grows in gin. He does not confine his petty beliefs to changing seats, walking around them, or keeping other people's
legs off the rung of his chair. He insists that no one touch his
score pad or pencil; that the cards he has shuffled be not re-
shuffled but only cut, or sometimes the converse, that it is
his right to shuffle the cards after his opponent has "made"
them; or occasionally he insists that his opponent prepare
and deal the cards for him. There is no limit to his eccen-
tricities. He will touch his tie or take off his coat to change
his luck. He somehow believes that the mysterious gods of
luck have nothing more important to do than hover over
him and watch whether he complies with some inane ritual
before they confer their favor upon him.

I have not listed as superstition the changing of decks
or the more extensive shuffling and cutting of cards. These
practices come under a different heading and are not superstitions. There is a rhythm in the game which cards frequently fall into, not because of any mysterious force but
because the hands as finally put down are arranged in definite patterns. They are seldom shuffled very thoroughly for
any card manipulator can tell you that the customary "rif-
fling" of the cards, one into the other, does very little to
change their position. Often successive "riffles" place them
right back into their original positions. Only the overhand
kind of shuffling which repeatedly shifts small groups of
cards, substantially changes their position one to the other.
Even such shuffling preserves large groups of cards approxi-

mately in their original positions. The final cut by an opponent affects only two cards. Consequently, when the cards are dealt alternately, the relationship of the previous runs and sequences is maintained to a great extent in the players' hands or in the deck and the players' hands. This often accounts for the remarkable runs of luck to one player. Everything he needs seems instantly to be offered to him by his opponent or by the deck. Conversely, if one is out of rhythm with this maintained relationship of the cards, the card he needs seems always to elude him by one or two draws. So, for example, having a jack and a king of diamonds, he discards the king and the next card in the deck is a queen of diamonds.

Some light is cast upon the persistence of lucky runs when one considers the arranged position of the cards at the end of each hand and the ineffective shuffle. Lucky runs are not entirely the whims of chance. Curiously enough, it is difficult to break this lucky rhythm once it is established. Extra shuffling and cutting frequently fail to affect it. That is why it is fairer for losers rather than winners to deal. At least they can attempt by more thorough shuffling to break up the arrangement of the cards resulting from the prior hand. This is also why it is not a superstition to change the decks. It provides an additional opportunity to alter the rhythm. The winner's barbs ought not deter the loser from changing cards any more than the dowager was discouraged when she instructed her new maid always to serve from the left and take the plate from the right. "What's the matter," inquired the maid condescendingly, "are you superstitious?"

Gin has created its own idioms and its own slang. These are not confined to any type of player. Noel Coward once wrote a devastating sketch of a bridge game in which the players, apparently bored with the traditional terms, changed them so that they sounded like a lover cooing to his new bride. The first player bid "a cloob"; the second, "one little deeamond"; the third, "a heartie"; and the last "a spadie-wadie." Similar tendencies can be observed in gin. There is the player who will never use the word "gin," as if to do so were an insult to his sense of originality. He will announce "name of the game," or "Timoshenko," or "Tschaikowsky," or any other irrelevant expression. Similarly he will not announce "I undercall." He will shake his head as if in a sad gesture and hold out a three. He silently awaits the anxious questions of his opponent as to whether this means that this is all he has to meld, and will finally break down and confess the situation. He enjoys having his victory dragged out of him.

Then there is the player who expresses his protest at an early knock by yelling with feigned anger (which is so real that one marvels at the simulation), "What's your hurry? Why don't you play the game? Where do you think you're rushing to? Sit back and take it easy, will you? I never saw such a man!"

Another affectation is that of the player who throws a very low card, announcing modestly, "Fearless, they call me," or "I am a courageous fellow," or "When in doubt, throw an ace." The frequent retort is, "Say, you must be pretty prosperous."

The jargon of gin includes, "That's 'schneid' insurance," referring to the first score on the game; "So you sent out a salesman," referring to the playing of a card in order to attract the same card in a different color; another comment for the same situation is, "Dirty playing if I ever saw it"; "Go ahead, have a good time," when an unshown card is thrown; "Don't you ever throw a card a fellow needs?" a grievance against a long drought of filling cards; "Come on, throw it, so you'll be killed," an encouragement to a hesitating player to take a risk; "You have to throw a card sometimes," or "You're the slowest player I have ever seen," to harry a deliberate player; "Lucky fool, he's already thrown off twenty-two points," a protest against an opponent's reduction of his hand after a knock; "Nobody ever won with ninety-nine," referring to the superstition that one who comes so close to a winning score of one hundred and falls short is doomed to lose; "I like to start like that," expressing another superstition that losing the first hand is a lucky omen; "Just for investment," to indicate that the card does not fill a run but is picked for future possibilities; "That's a nice haul," a comment upon a large count after a knock; and "They got us by the boxes" referring to a one-sided score due to a large accumulation of boxes.

More annoying than gin clichés and gin types are the tricky devices resorted to by some players to deceive their opponents. While acting, gestures and misleading comments are not barred by the rules, they are generally considered bad sportsmanship. Some players will look at a card long-ingly and hesitate before picking it to give the impression that they do not need it when they actually do. Such simula-tion practiced consistently only results in delaying the game, for the opponent sooner or later learns that the pause before the pick is of no significance. Another gesture is that of the player who takes the precaution of placing each card picked from the deck in his hand before discarding it, so as to avoid informing his opponent that his hand has not been im-proved. A more tricky gesture is that of a player who, having only two or three points in his hand, is waiting for an under-call, but shakes his head in despair each time his opponent picks a card as though he were facing disaster from a quick knock. Even worse is the stratagem of throwing a card of which one has a pair, but with a comment upon how dan-gerous it is, in order to lure an opponent into throwing the same card in another color. Another offensive habit, though often innocently indulged in, is the loser's adding up his hand after his opponent's knock, announcing his score and throwing the cards into the deck. The opponent is thus compelled to accept the loser's count or give the impression of distrusting him. No leeway is given for his desire to check the count so as to avoid an unintentional error. It is only fair that each losing hand should be placed on the table for an open count.

Despite these and other irritations, gin has prospered as

few games have in pleasure-loving America. It is about as difficult to quit as it was for the country boy who visited an automat for the first time and bought thirty pieces of apple pie. "Why don't you stop?" inquired a stranger. "You can't eat all that!" "What, stop now," he screamed, "when I am in the middle of a winning streak?" Yes, gin is a fast, active and thrilling card game. Above all, it has done more for the inferiority complex of millions of Americans than any other sport or game. It has made self-satisfied, self-admiring experts of incompetent men and women as well as of talented ones. Millions believe that they display exceptional skill at the game. This is the great American illusion. Long may it wave.

CHAPTER 13

Illegitimate Parents

THE PROBLEM of juvenile delinquency is a frightening one. We may as well be frank about it. We have failed to solve this problem. Seventy-two per cent of all ju-venine delinquents who are sent to jail continue in their careers of crime. Imprisonment does not act as a deterrent. In 1945 children under the age of twenty-one committed fifteen per cent of all murders in the United States, sixty-two per cent of all automobile thefts, fifty-one per cent of all bur-glaries, twenty-six per cent of all arsons, thirty per cent of all rapes, and twenty-one per cent of all crime. The arrest of girls under the age of eighteen increased by one-hundred-ninety-eight per cent from 1939 to 1945. These are the stark facts.

The Chinese say, "Always strike your child once a day; if you don't know why, he will." This is more than a witticism, for the Chinese accept parental responsibility for juvenile delinquency. It is interesting to observe that there is prac-tically no juvenile delinquency in China despite its poverty.

It is obvious that children, even when they are bad actors, don't need critics. They need models. The parents must be the models, but in the United States adolescents often rear their parents.

We have tried the Chinese theory in the state of Colorado. There, under state statute, the parents may be punished for the offenses of their children. Judge Philip S. Gilliam in 1945 convicted forty out of forty-five parents brought before him for neglect of children who had committed offenses. In addition one hundred and thirty-two parents were fined or jailed on the theory that they were responsible for their children's depredations. This may sound startling but if you have a domestic pet and it bites another, or trespasses on another's property and causes injury, you may be sued and held responsible for its conduct, provided you have had notice of its dangerous tendencies. Shall we apply a lower standard for parents of children than we do for owners of animals?

In New York we no longer permit certificates of birth to record the illegitimacy of a child. The philosophy behind this law is that it is the parents who are illegitimate, not the child. Are the parents less responsible for the derelictions of their children after birth? Ought they not demonstrate that they have done their duty and have not contributed to the delinquency of their children? They cannot shift responsibility like the mother who sighed about her son, "I'll be glad when he's old enough to go to the reformatory."

But even all this is an over-simplification. There are hundreds of thousands of orphans. There were two million mothers in the United States in 1944 whose children were under ten years of age and who had to work because their husbands were earning less than two thousand dollars a year. Society often prepares the crime. The criminal merely commits it.

Therefore it becomes a governmental function to substitute for the parents in taking care of children and leading them on the right path. In New York City there are only eight child guidance units in the school system. There should be hundreds. There is only one psychologist in the school systems for every forty-six thousand children. There ought to be dozens. Children who need such attention have to wait months for an interview. There is only one institution, the Rockland State Hospital, which treats mentally defective children under the age of twelve free of charge.

If we would spend the cost of one battleship for these purposes we could direct hundreds of children toward useful lives instead of permitting them to drift into lives of crime. The only thing more expensive than education is ignorance. There ought to be a youth bureau in each state under the guidance of state authority, supervising through its psychiatrists, welfare workers, nursery homes and child guidance departments a veritable war against juvenile delinquency.

President Lincoln used to take walks behind the White House for relaxation. One day he saw a child struggling up a hill with another child on his back. "Son, isn't that too heavy a burden for you?" he asked. The child replied, "Sir, that is no burden; it is my brother."

These juvenile delinquents are not somebody else's burden. They are our children. We must all accept the responsibility for them.

CHAPTER 14

The Art of the Jury Trial

IN WRITING this I reach the peak of my audacity, for this chapter may imply a degree of knowledge and expertness which I, of course, disavow. In a certain sense there is no right or wrong way to try a case, any more than there is a right or wrong way to paint a painting or to write a poem. The right way to try a case is that in which one expresses one's personality and talents to the full, because the art of persuasion—and that is what a jury trial is—is such a complex combination of psychology, insight, learning, facility in thinking quickly, felicity of expression, and the myriad forms of personality, that there is no precise, scientific yardstick for it.

We all know of the successful trial lawyer whose method is to boil with righteous indignation, to attack witnesses boldly and loudly, to permit his sarcasm to spill over his adversary, and even to cross swords with the presiding justice himself. We know that that kind of lawyer will often set the atmosphere around him aflame and that those flames will sometimes leap across the barriers of the jury box and set fire to the convictions of the jurors.

We also know the extreme opposite type of trial lawyer: the man who is suave and quiet, kindly, almost timid; who approaches even a hostile witness with great friendship and who, even when he inserts the knife in cross-examination, does so bloodlessly; who is deferential to his adversary and obeisant to the presiding judge and who, nevertheless, persuades the jury of the justice of his case by the calm, reasoned effort he is making for his client.

Between these two methods there is a variety of compromises, as many as there are personalities of men. So, obviously, if a lawyer is the kind of person who becomes righteously indignant about a cause, he should not pattern his style after the suave lawyer. The jury is very likely to resent his imitation of another as well as the ineffectualness of his pretended calm. If, on the other hand, a lawyer is quiet and unassuming, he should not pattern his style after the lionesque type of lawyer because the jury is likely to resent his hypocrisy as well as his bad acting. That is the best method which best represents the individual. We hate affectation in court rooms as well as in drawing rooms. One can best express his talents in his own way.

There is only one thing that I shall be didactic about; more than didactic, I shall be arbitrary about it. I shall brook no disagreement on this subject. I shall be defiant if you differ and I shall be supported in that obstinacy by all of the trial lawyers who have ever tried cases and, indeed, by the unanimity of expression of all the literature on the subject, and that is that the most important qualifications for an able trial lawyer are *thorough preparation, hard work* and *industry*. I don't think that should disappoint any lawyer. There is all the opportunity that he may wish for flashes of insight, for ebullient improvisation, for balancing like a gyroscope in a difficult storm, but all of these qualities and many more are satellites of the great sun around which they swing. The sun is hard work, preparation and industry.

From the moment that a lawyer begins to ferret out the facts from his client and witnesses, from the moment that his client's papers are brought to him, his industry begins. Even the irrelevant, musty papers should be dusted off and carefully listed, because most likely during the course of a trial some witness will state a fact which no one expected him to state and there will swim into the lawyer's recollection that musty, old, irrelevant document. He will have the case in his hand.

When the trial begins, the lawyer's industry begins all over again. After the court has adjourned, he must work till two, three, four, five in the morning, see the sun come up, wash his face and go to court. In order to prepare for the next day, he will dispatch messengers who will find new witnesses to testify concerning matters not previously anticipated. He will prepare a trial memorandum of law for the court overnight with respect to the admissibility or inadmissibility of an imminent bit of evidence. And this must continue day after day, night after night—sleeplessness, hard work, industry, preparation, until the case is over.

I should say no trial lawyer is worth his salt if he does not lose at least six pounds during the course of a trial. The physician, Sir William Osler, once put it this way: "There is an old folk lore legend that there is some mystic word which will open barred gates. There is, in fact, such a mystic word. It is the open sesame of every portal. The great equalizer in the world, the true philosopher's stone, which transmutes all the baser metal of humanity into gold. The stupid man it will make bright, the bright brilliant and the brilliant steady. With the mystic word all things are possible. And the mystic word is 'work.' "

Suppose a novice says, "I am persuaded. I am ready to work as hard as you require of me because I want to be a good trial lawyer." But suppose he also says, "How am I going to apply all this industry so as to attain my objective?" That would be a very fair question.

Well, let us start the trial with the selection of the jury. Some lawyers who have experience may say, "Certainly you don't need any preparation for that." May I respectfully differ? A lawyer must consider very carefully in advance what kind of juror he wants in that particular case. Does he want more women jurors than men jurors? If it is a case in which he hopes to obtain a large verdict in terms of money, he does not want women jurors. The attendants in the court rooms will tell you that women jurors usually give smaller verdicts. They are not, as a rule, people of large business affairs, and they do not often grant large verdicts. If the lawyer is for the defense, obviously he wants more women jurors. Does he want young jurors or old jurors? There are many considerations which will determine his decision in that field. I shall not stop, in such a brief article as this, to list them all. Does he want men of experience in certain fields of endeavor, specialists or industrialists, or does he want the ordinary man on the jury?

A few hints with respect to the selection of the jury would not be amiss. There are two schools of thought on choosing jurors, as there are on most subjects except that of thorough preparation. One is that although we all pride ourselves on knowing human nature and reading faces, none of us really has the gift. We are always taking a chance. And so, some say, it is best, once a lawyer has satisfied himself that the jury does not know counsel or litigants and has no apparent prejudice in the case, to waive further examination and, with a grand gesture, say, "Jury satisfactory." Many good lawyers do that. They hope to profit from the fact that the jury will say, "He has great confidence in his case because he did not question us much."

And there is the other school which says, "It is not given to you in other fields to pick your judges. But the law gives you an opportunity to pick the judges of the facts. It is a precious opportunity and it should be used with all the resourcefulness at your command." I cast my vote for the second school on this.

It is important to select a jury very carefully and, since we do not read faces as well as we read voices and mannerisms, it becomes important to induce prospective jurors to talk. That is a very difficult art, because a lawyer is not permitted to engage them in conversation. He must do so in the form of questions which are rather limited. Very often a juror's hard, severe and cold face lights up in a kindly manner when he speaks. Also, very often (and this is the only part of a case in which I really depend on my intuition), I sense a bond of sympathy or receptivity between the juror and myself. Such a juror is a good juror even if other qualifications are lacking.

In addition to that, a lawyer is permitted to ask specific questions to elicit whether the juror is prejudiced and I find that many good lawyers ask this type of question, although I have never, myself, been able to discern any good reason for it. Let us suppose it is a case in which a young lady sues a large corporation. The lawyer says to the juror, "Have you any prejudice against a corporation or any prejudice in favor of a young lady who is suing a large corporation?" Invariably the answer is, "No, I will decide this case on the facts and on the law." What could he expect the juror to say? Does he expect him, sitting there in the presence of strangers, to make a confession that he is prejudiced?

But now suppose, instead of that wasted question, the lawyer made it palatable for the juror to admit his prejudice in this manner: "In the first place, I want to apologize for asking you some of these questions and prying into your mind. You understand it is not curiosity. The law places upon me the heavy responsibility of selecting a jury which is unbiased, so that we start from scratch on both sides. You understand that, sir. Now, we all have some prejudice or leanings. (I like the word leaning. It is much softer.) We all have leanings. I have them. Sometimes, subconsciously, you have them. Now, if I were in your place and if you were to ask me, I would feel I had a duty to be candid with you. So, in that spirit, I shall take your answer at face value and rely on it. Sometimes, subconsciously, we lean in favor of an individual who is suing a large corporation. You may have such a feeling in this case. If you have, I should appreciate it very much if you would be frank with me."

After such an approach the lawyer might get the answer: "I think I might be a little more in favor of the plaintiff under such circumstances." I do not say that he will, but he might obtain the admission of prejudice. I do not think he will ever obtain it the other way. A juror's candor must be wooed like a woman's love. It cannot be earned by a formal question. It is rare to find a juror such as a prosecutor in a murder case questioned. "Do you believe in capital punishment?" he asked bluntly. The juror replied, "Generally, no, but in this case, yes!"

After the jury has been selected and sworn in, counsel make their opening statements. Here again there are the customary two schools of thought. One school says: "Make your opening as brief as possible. Simply state your facts, those that you hope to prove. Do it succinctly and be conservative. Don't promise too much. Let the witnesses tell it from the witness stand. The jury will be more impressed when they hear it from the witnesses for the first time."

The other school says, "No. The opportunity of an opening statement, if taken advantage of skillfully, gives you a leaping start over your adversary. It should be exploited to the full." Once more I should like to cast my vote for the second school of thought.

I think it is extremely important that counsel, by thorough preparation, so design his opening statement that, although he is merely listing what he hopes to prove and does so conservatively, the juxtaposition of his thoughts and the analysis of his promises, the points at which he drags in his adversary's claims and then states what he is going to prove with respect to these claims, the manner in which he does it, the sincerity with which he conveys the feeling at the very outset that his client is right, that the facts point to the justice of his cause—all these offer an invaluable opportunity through counsel's mouth to condition the jury favorably toward his client.

I know the adversary may arise, "Your Honor, I object. This is a summation, not an opening." That is a risk an attorney must take. But I think that there is such a fine line, such a thin line, between a carefully selected statement of what he intends to prove and a persuasive statement of what that proof means if he adduces it, that his skill and thorough preparation can transform one into the other without violating in the slightest the rules applicable to opening statements.

As for dulling the effect of the testimony by its predigestion, any persuader can deliver a long preachment on the necessity of repetition. I would rather say that a jury might enjoy recognizable testimony and assimilate it more quickly, just as most of us enjoy a familiar tune more than a strange one. Of course, surprise elements should be hoarded. An opponent should not be educated as to matters concerning which he is still in the dark. Obviously the traps should not be uncovered. Indeed, a lawyer may cast a few more leaves over them so that his adversary will step more boldly on the hollow ground believing it is solid. All this requires that the opening statement be most carefully prepared for its omission as well as its contents. I can only confess for myself that I have sometimes labored five or six hours to organize in my mind a statement which was delivered in twenty minutes. In this way one can avoid the error of the young attorney who was permitted by senior counsel to open the case because he did not consider that the opening statement was very important. The junior, being suddenly cast into the limelight, made a magnificent, eloquent opening. When he was through, the client approached him and enthusiastically congratulated him on his fiery opening statement. The senior attorney dolefully said, "Yes, it was a very, very eloquent opening. He opened the case so wide I don't know how the devil I shall ever be able to close it."

I do not think a lawyer should ever launch into his opening statement without some explanation. He must not assume that the jury knows why the lawyer is going to make a speech. Jurors sometimes resent the lawyer's intrusion. Some such introductory statement as this I think is useful: "Ladies and gentlemen of the jury: As this case progresses there will be witnesses on the stand who will give testimony for the plaintiff and other witnesses for the defendant. Sometimes it is difficult for a jury to see the relationship between each bit of testimony given piecemeal and the entire case. The law recognizes this and therefore gives me and my distinguished adversary the opportunity of making an opening statement to you, in which each of us will tell you what he hopes to prove. Thereby, knowing in advance the nature of our case, you will be better able to follow each bit of testimony and recognize its bearing on the entire case. I avail myself of that opportunity and I shall now make an opening statement to you of what my client intends to prove." I think some such introduction sets the proper state of receptivity for the opening remarks.

I hope you are never represented by the kind of lawyer who puts a witness on the stand relying upon the preparation of his assistant who hands him a note as to what this witness will testify. I hope you are never represented by the kind of lawyer who puts the witness on the stand after he has himself only perfunctorily examined him to determine the nature of his testimony, for such a lawyer is overlooking some of the elementary facts of life.

Put yourself in the position of the witness. He has never faced an audience before in his life. Suddenly he is placed on a platform and to his right sits a judge in a black robe, which in itself is sufficient to put him in awe and terror. To his left there are twelve jurors looking at him very skeptically and critically, examining every motion he makes as well as every word he utters. In front of him is a sea of faces and by this time he sees, out of the corner of his eye, already dimmed, the leering faces of the defendant and his witnesses looking up at him. In front of these hostile faces he sees opposing counsel sitting anxiously on the edge of their seats. He imagines by this time that the cross-examiner is slowly sharpening a knife, waiting to spring at him and cut him to pieces. And while all these confusing surrounding circumstances are pressing in upon him and his blood is pounding in his head, you stand there presenting questions to him. It is surprising that he can even answer the first questions put to him by the court attendant: "What is your name and where do you live?" If one expected him, in the light of these circumstances, to be descriptive, to be articulate, to be finely sensitive to a point that his lawyer wishes him to develop, well, one simply expects too much from human nature. It is useless for the attorney to go to the restaurant during recess hour and complain about his fool witness; how he made incredible answers against his own interest and in violation of the truth. The fault is the lawyer's. If he puts the witness on the stand without greater preparation and takes that risk, the blame is not upon the witness.

The law permits an attorney—it does more than permit him, it makes it his duty—to examine his witness carefully in advance to refresh his recollection as to dates and details by exhibiting documents to him which establish these matters; to acquaint him with the sequence of questions so that the truth may be established in orderly fashion and without confusion which may throw doubt upon it. It is the only way, in fact, in which he can present the truth. For the truth never walks into a court room. It never flies in through the window. It must be dragged in through evidence, so that the jury is subjected to the stimuli of the facts which the attorney possesses. Incidentally, if the lawyer examines his witness carefully in advance, he will find out what kind of person he is. If he is timid, he must encourage him and lead him. If he is impulsive and talkative, he must restrain him. Also, he learns whether or not he is an impressive witness. This has nothing to do with his intelligence or culture. Very often a lowly, humble witness talks with such sincerity that one knows he is making a good impression.

The lawyer must learn these characteristics in advance from personal contact with the witness, not at the time he reaches the jury box. Such knowledge enables him to determine the sequence of witnesses, a very important consideration. Ideally speaking, it is good to have a very strong witness to open the case, a very strong witness to close the case, and the weaker witnesses in between; but this, of course, must be adapted to the necessities of developing the facts in certain sequence. But if the attorney foregoes these considerations and simply puts a witness upon the stand, he is taking a risk. Usually he loses the gamble and he has disserved justice, because such a witness often, in his confusion, will make slips and, as frequently as not, will distort the truth against himself.

I shall not even comment upon the obvious distinction between legitimate review of the facts to be elicited and the illegitimate suggestions grafted upon the witness' memory. The lawyer so unmindful of his oath, of the nobility of his profession and of its ethics as to ignore this distinction is a rarity, although the public is not as aware as it should be of how rare a specimen he is. Suffice it to say that, even apart from this reflection on the high character which is the customary equipment of every competent trial lawyer, unethical practices are simply bad trial tactics and bear their own punishment. For when the truth is tampered with, a thousand unknown facts spring to life to bedevil the culprit.

When I am faced with a dishonest witness I am most confident of winning. If I am properly prepared, such a witness cannot survive and, when he falls, the jury's contempt for him makes his fall fatal. A jury will often overlook a mistake, but never a deliberate lie.

Now suppose that the lawyer has carefully reviewed his direct testimony with the witness. What else is necessary? Why, he must prepare him for cross-examination. That is a field which I am afraid a good many lawyers completely overlook or at least underestimate. Once more, remember the panicky position of the witness placed suddenly on the witness stand and asked to fence on cross-examination with a trained, carefully prepared adversary. I believe every witness should be subjected in advance to a drill in cross-examination. One can anticipate what the other attorney is likely to ask. The lawyer knows of some documents in the case which will be used against him. He knows that perhaps the last paragraph of a certain letter refutes the point the cross-examiner will wish to make. But will his witness be confused? Will he utilize the last paragraph? The lawyer must train him in his office. I would say: "From now on I am your enemy. I am preparing you for cross-examination." Lead him into traps and show him how he has been lured into the traps unjustly. That is proper preparation. It is essential preparation.

Incidentally, most witnesses do not understand the rules of evidence. How often does one see a witness confused when he testifies, "Then the man got very angry and walked out," and the lawyer says, "Objection. He has stated a conclusion." The judge says, "Sustained. Strike out that statement." The witness does not know what the trouble is. If the witness makes this statement in the course of preparation, the lawyer can explain to him that the law does not permit him to say that "he got angry." That is a conclusion. He must state the facts from which he deduced the anger. Why does he think the man was angry? "Well," he says, "he banged his fist on the table and said, 'I don't have to stand for that,' and

walked out." "Won't you please say that instead of 'angry'?"
the lawyer cautions him. He is then a better witness. He tells
the facts more vividly and he is no longer going to be bad-
gered by a lawyer or a judge.

Similarly, a witness may not understand the nature of an
objection. He testifies that the parties "agreed." It is objected
to as a conclusion. He does not understand why it is that
you cannot say "agreed." It must be made clear to him that
only what the parties said or did may be related in order
to demonstrate agreement. His mere conclusion that they
agreed is insufficient. If the witness is prepared in advance
he will not think the court room is caving in upon him
because objections to such testimony have been sustained.

Assuming the lawyer has not opened the case too wide,
that his star witnesses have gone off the stand unscathed,
and that the defendant's witnesses are now upon the stand,
I approach the subject of cross-examination which, of course,
is a subject upon which volumes can be and have been
written. Most lawyers who will tell you of a brilliant flash
of insight which broke the witness or other feats of cross-
examination will not confess this, but the plain truth of the
matter is that ninety-nine per cent of effective cross-examination is once more our old friend, thorough preparation.
Perhaps through this the lawyer has obtained a written document with which to contradict the witness. Thus armed, he
mistakes his weapons for his own great skill. However, there
is an art in introducing the written document contradicting
a witness' testimony. The novice will rush in. He will obtain
the false statement and then quickly hurl the document in
the face of the witness. The witness, confronted with it,
very likely will seek to retrace his steps and sometimes will
do so skillfully, and the effect is lost.

The mature trial counsel will utilize the document for
all it is worth. Having obtained the denial which he wishes,
he will, perhaps, pretend that he is disappointed. He will ask
that same question a few moments later, and again and again
get a denial. He will then phrase—and this requires prep-

aration—a whole series of questions not directed at that particular point, but in which is incorporated the very assertion which he is ready to contradict, each time getting closer and closer to the language in the written document which he possesses, until he has induced the witness to assert not once but many times the very proposition from which ordinarily he might withdraw by saying it was a slip of the tongue. Each time the lawyer draws closer to the precise language which will contradict the witness without making the witness aware of it, until finally, when the document is sprung, the effect as compared with the other method is that, let us say, of an atomic bomb against a firecracker.

Is there opportunity for preparation in cross-examination? Endless opportunity. In the first place, there is a field of cross-examination which is undramatic, uninspiring, certainly insignificant in its effectiveness upon the jury and the judge, who will sometimes think the lawyer is wasting time. But he must stick to his guns. If he has carefully prepared this kind of cross-examination, it is of great value. It is the kind of cross-examination by which he does not contradict anything, but by which he selects certain facts and dates which the witness may admit, as, for example, that there was correspondence or conversation between the parties in a certain month, nothing more, which the witness does not deny. In fact, the witness does not see the purpose of denial and at times, considering it unimportant, he is led to concede the point readily. Such an answer, utilized later in summation and fortified by information other witnesses have given, may become an admission so strong that it undermines his other testimony.

This kind of cross-examination, which is really not "cross" at all, is the result of the lawyer's studying his witnesses' testimony, knowing what his adversary is likely to testify to, and saying to himself, "How many of the facts which I wish to establish can I get him to concede without his being aware of their import; such 'innocuous' facts as that he met the plaintiff many times during a certain year; that he corresponded with him at certain times; that there was a certain directors' meeting at which four or five directors were present," and so forth. His admissions may appear harmless but, when joined with later testimony, may be more influential upon the jury than all the dramatic cross-examination which the lawyer may conduct.

There are other fertile areas for preparation of cross-examination. The plan of attack often determines the form of the question. Sometimes it is vital to obtain the admission of the witness in the first instance. The lawyer doesn't want the witness to contradict falsely. He wants any admission he can obtain, rather than the advantage of contradiction. In such a situation the questions must be framed so as to induce the concession. Since leading questions are permitted on cross-examination, the form of the question, as well as the tone in which it is put, may push the witness toward admission.

Sometimes it is desirable to induce denial. The lawyer can destroy a witness' credibility by leading him into a denial of a fact and by then proving it. These various objectives, which must be carefully thought out, require different approaches.

The subject on which the lawyer examines the witness first and last is important. Often the very sequence determines the nature of cross-examination. There is a negative rule about cross-examination upon which almost all trial lawyers agree. One should not cross-examine aimlessly. The lawyer should not simply take the witness over his direct testimony in the hope of finding a crevice. His repetition, without any substantial contradiction, will only italicize the impression he may already have made. It is far better in such an instance to waive cross-examination and to endeavor to minimize the effect of the testimony in summation. Fishing expeditions on cross-examination are almost always disastrous. A fisherman being pulled into the water by his catch is an ungainly sight.

But if the attorney has foreseen the testimony which will be given against him and has prepared one or two points on which the witness must yield, or which at least align probability against the witness, and if the attorney limits himself to these, waiving the witness aside after he has made his limited inquiry, he may find that the cloud over one or two of the witness' statements may also cast a shadow over the rest of his testimony.

It is difficult to formulate rules for spontaneous cross-examination. The different factors—the witness' mannerisms, his temper, his evasion or undue assertiveness, his confusion, the jury's reaction to him (do they enjoy or sympathize with his plight?)—all affect the persistence and method of the cross-examiner. Trigger judgment must be used. Sometimes one additional question gives a witness a chance to retreat. Sometimes relentlessness brings a great and final reward. The psychological factors are numerous and intriguing.

I pass on to the subject of summation. I should like to suggest that the lawyer obtain the minutes of the trial overnight, particularly in an important case and, during those early hours of the morning when his adversary is sleeping, cull out admissions, inadvertent statements, and categorize them. In a long case he will generally have at least one evening to collate this material for final use. Then in his summation he can advise the jury: "In order to persuade you that there is no real controversy in this case, that the defendant concedes the justice of our position, I shall quote only from his testimony and from the testimony of his witnesses. I have the minutes of the trial here, ladies and gentlemen, the official minutes. I shall not quote my client. I shall quote only the words of the defendant and his witnesses." Then, if he has his points carefully categorized, he says concerning each point, "Let us see what the defendant said," and turns quickly to that particular admission and reads in *haec verba*. He is by cumulative effect creating an impressive case much more irresistible, I am sure, than the greatest eloquence applied to generalities. The day is past when a lawyer could make mere emotional appeals. Emotion is futile when it is not based on sound fact and reason.

One final thought with respect to summation: It is wise to tie all the arguments together upon one strong point, so that they are not scattered. One can often gather them on the string of a single illustration. Suppose the attorney claims the defendant has not answered a single real issue and has simply attempted to escape by using all sorts of artifices. Well, it might be a good idea for the attorney to put his pearls together on the following string: "There is a curious fact about an octopus. When an octopus is attacked he emits a cloudy fluid and escapes in the confusion. The defendant in this case has used this method. Whenever he was in danger he emitted a cloudy fluid." Thereafter, every time the attorney points out evasive evidence, he says, "Some more of that inky fluid by the octopus," and the jury is able to correlate his different arguments by the image which he has implanted in their minds.

After summation, the lawyer must be ready to submit "requests to charge" to the presiding judge. These are instructions which the judge is requested to give the jury. There is the story about the lawyer who said, "Your Honor, I am perfectly willing to waive summation." His adversary said, "Your Honor, I am willing to waive summation, and the charge, too." That privilege is not afforded lawyers. It is therefore necessary to prepare the requests to charge. This must be done at the very last moment or they will not be effective. They must be prepared in the light of the testimony which has developed in the course of the trial. That again means hard work and late hours.

The jury system is a magnificent system for determining the truth, but only if one assumes that the lawyers have brought into the court room all the necessary evidence from which to derive the truth. When a jury occasionally goes wrong it is often not the jury's fault. The reason is that the attorney who has the wrong side of the case has presented so much evidence and the other side has defaulted with respect to so much of it, that the jury, subjected to that uneven ratio of evidence, has made a wrong decision. But it is the right decision on the evidence adduced. Therefore, the responsibility imposed upon lawyers to aid the jury is a very heavy one.

I conclude with this anecdote about Rufus Choate, who was a charming and brilliant trial lawyer. On one occasion a leading citizen of the community happened to be on a jury before whom Rufus Choate represented a plaintiff. The juror knew of Choate's great reputation and reported to a friend the experience he went through as a juror. He said, "I knew about Mr. Choate's skill and the way he charmed juries and could make them believe black was white. So I set myself against him and made up my mind not to permit him to play his tricks on me. And I did more than that. I advised all my associates on the jury to be on guard against Mr. Choate's devices. As a result, no matter what Mr. Choate did during the trial, although he tried every possible trick, the tricks did not work." The friend said, "Well, were you unanimous against Mr. Choate's client?" "Oh, no," he answered, "we decided *for* Mr. Choate's client, but that was only because all the facts and the law happened to be on his side."

The goal of an attorney is to submerge his talents in the interests of his cause. He is never jealous of his adversary's personal triumphs so long as they do not sweep the verdict along with them. When a skillful trial lawyer faces a jury, it may think that his opponent is more scintillating but, curiously enough, the facts and the law happen to be on the side of the less able lawyer.

CHAPTER 15

An Editorial Lost in a News Item

I ALMOST SKIPPED this item. I do not read reports of personal tragedies which are printed in newspapers. They may attract the curious, but in a world tottering toward another war, of what importance is a lover's death or a child's disappearance? But a subheading held my eye: "Posse Holds Hands." I began to read.

It appeared that a young child had been lost in a thicket. The parents frantically summoned friends to aid them in their search for the child. Twenty hours had passed and the child might die from exposure. The police joined the search. Neighbors gathered and looked. Every bush was carefully examined, but the child was not to be found. Precious hours passed. The parents and their army of searchers grew more desperate.

Suddenly one old lady called out, "Why don't we all hold hands in one huge circle. Then we'll be sure we have covered every inch of ground." The suggestion was adopted. The neighbors, friends and police joined hands and moved forward cautiously.

In less than an hour, the crumpled body of the child was discovered. It was dead. The father cried out in anguish, "O God, why didn't we join hands sooner!"

I was stunned by the story. Here was the perfect aphorism for our troubled international scene. This story belongs on the editorial page, I thought to myself. And so I have written it here, as though the stricken father had uttered a cry on behalf of all the peoples of the world. For it is not yet too late to save the next generation of children.

To this lesson in cooperation I would like to add one on tolerance. There is an Aesop fable of a woodsman who came into a forest to ask the trees to give him a handle for his axe. It seemed so modest a request that the principal trees at once agreed on it. They decided that a plain, homely ash, the least important among them, should be sacrificed. No sooner had the woodsman fitted the staff into his axe than he began laying about him on all sides felling the noblest trees in the wood. The oak, now understanding the whole matter too late, whispered to the cedar, "The first concession has lost all; if we had not sacrificed our humblest neighbor, we might have stood for ages ourselves."

CHAPTER 16

Paternity and Fraternity

I CONSIDER this evening largely devoted to my father and, therefore, I remember the words of Diogenes: "If the son speaks foul, slap the father's face. If the son be noble, heap praise upon the father."

For this reason, I shall not disavow the compliments you have bestowed upon me this evening, for I consider myself merely a conduit through which they pass directly to my father. Indeed, my only regret is that you have not seen fit to be a little more flattering, so that you could give him more pleasure and honor.

When you requested me to present the Thirty-Fifth Anniversay Jewel to my father, you gave me two opportunities. One, to evaluate him and, two, the opportunity for great embarrassment. For, ordinarily, I would not discuss the intimate relationship of father and son at a public dinner. There are some occasions when wisdom has two precepts. First, to have something to say and, second, not to say it. This is such an occasion. For, to discuss one's own father is to court the danger either of maudlin sentiment, or of such restraint as would do him and this occasion an injustice.

But I hope that you will be indulgent and tolerant with me, because this evening is not only the thirty-fifth anniversary of his association with this fraternity, but if you turn the numbers 35 around, it is also the 53rd anniversary of the marriage of my mother and father, both of whom are on this dais this evening. Therefore, I hope that you will permit some personal recital. After all, it is you, who, despite my refusal, insisted that I perform this task, and, in the law, we have a doctrine called "the assumption of risk." You have assumed the risk.

Every man has in his mind certain memories. Indeed we often live twice; once, when the events occur and, the second time, in the reflection of the memories which those events have produced. If those memories are vivid enough and colorful enough, they become paintings, precious paintings, as if they were done by the great masters. Tonight, I invite you to visit the gallery of some of the paintings in my mind.

My mother and father married in London at the ages of 17 and 18. Those were such tender ages that they did not permit of any exercise of wisdom or judgment. Everything was excluded, except love, and here you have an object lesson of what a solid foundation love is for a long and successful marriage.

A year or so later, I was born in London, but for the next year and a half, my father rarely saw me awake. Those were the days of rugged individualism, when no one interfered with the right of a man to work 18 to 20 hours a day. My father always left too early to see me awake, and returned so late that I was asleep. When he came home, he would look at the infant sprawled in careless innocence on his stomach. This is the first painting in my mind. It is done in the style of Rembrandt, with heavy black light occupying most of the canvas, gradually turning into warm glows of dark brown. From the door slightly ajar, there is a golden trickle of light which shines on the face of my father as he looks down into the crib. The light reveals his tenderness and exhaustion. Behind him, enveloped in the shadows, with only sufficient outline to reveal her intensity and happiness, is my mother.

My father decided to come to the United States and adopt it as his country. Those who are fortunate enough to be born in the United States seldom can understand the compliment of choice which immigration involves. My father's passionate patriotism and devotion to our beloved country has been something moving and sincere throughout my life. To this very day, at his home in New Hampshire, he unfurls a huge flag every morning in front of our porch and then, at twilight, brings the ladder again and removes the flag, reverently. Even, when a year or so ago, the doctors told him that he must not climb any ladders and lift objects, the one exception he would not yield to, was his personal attendance to the display and removal of the American flag. This scene of my father removing the flag is another painting in my mind, done in the Rockwell Kent style of fervor and simplicity.

My father did not have enough money to bring my mother and his son with him to the United States; so, he proceeded alone to this country—a pioneer determined to build a steamship ticket. A year and a half later he sent for us, and we arrived on a foggy day, the front of the ship parting the fog as if it were seeking the journey's end and the buildings of New York rising like spectres in the mist. We saw my father with derby hat, bow-tie and flower in his button-hole eagerly scanning the ship for us. And, as we came off the gangplank—I, dressed in blue velvet pantaloons with a pink silk cord and a whistle at the end of it and a Napoleonic type of hat with a pompom in the center, and my mother in the tightly corseted skirt and waist style of that era, and we dashed into his arms to be smothered by indiscriminate kisses—another painting formed in my mind, done in the style of Turner, who knew how to capture mist and atmosphere, as if they were solid objects.

Then, my father proceeded to build his future in this country. From shop to candy store in Ellery Street in Brooklyn, to a cleaning and dyeing establishment in Sumner Avenue of the Williamsburgh section, to the acquisition of the building in which the store was located, to the acquisition of other properties. With his bare ten fingers, he built security for himself and his family. In the early years, we went through all the hardships of that struggle, living in flats in which icicles dropped on the inside, as well as on the outside of the windows; but which rooms were made warm by the sentiment and love of the family. A happy family, says the Bible, is an early heaven.

My father was a man of indomitable will in the most
literal sense of the word. One can change a vice into a virtue
by simply using a different word for the same quality. If
I were to say that he was stubborn, that would be a vice.
If I were to say that he was persistent, that would be a
virtue. Well, depending upon the degree of irritability
throughout the years, I would say that my father was stubborn and persistent. Once he set his mind upon a certain
course, that course would have to be consummated, even
if, while doing so, he knew that there might be a better
road. I suppose this strange characteristic was based on the
theory of complete integrity—a promise made to yourself
must not be broken, any more than a promise made to anyone else, no matter what the consequences. I cannot possibly
imagine my father changing a horse in mid-stream. Indeed,
if my father were ever on a horse in mid-stream and it fell
dead in the middle of the stream, I know that his procedure
would be to get off and drag it the next ten miles to his
destination.

One of his stubborn resolves was that I was to have every
opportunity for education which had been denied to him.
I have never confused education and wisdom. Mark Twain
put it most brilliantly when he once wrote: "When I was
14 years of age, I found my father so ignorant, that I did
not want my friends to meet the old man. But when I became 20 years old, I was amazed to find how much he had
learned in the last six years." I was never amazed to find that
my father was a wise man, despite the lack of formal education. His determination that I should have the best education pointed to Columbia College and Columbia University
Law School. He chose well, and I went to those institutions.
A father is a banker provided by nature, and I drew heavily
upon the drafts of his generosity during those years.

I shall not ask you to stop in front of the paintings of my
graduation from Columbia College or Columbia University
Law School, but, rather, I choose another painting for your
momentary pause and inspection. It was while I was in col-

lege that I entered and won first prize in the Curtis Oratorical Contest at Columbia. At the height of this "triumph," when I was receiving congratulations from the contestants, students, professors and other distinguished visitors, my father approached me and, with an accusing finger, said: "You were not entitled to better than third prize. There were two other boys who, I thought, were better than you were." I can still remember the look of pain on my mother's face at this terrible judgment, but I think it was part of my father's calculated scheme, in those days, to goad me on—never to make me feel that I had achieved anything which I might consider adequate. I must confess to you that, since then, his skepticism and critical faculties have dissolved. He now is a loyal adherent, and I am sometimes worried that he feels that I have reached the maximum of my potential achievement. I must also confess to you that I felt more comfortable when he was a severe critic, than an idolatrous father. But that scene of my father's criticism drawn in the style of Degas when he was at his ironic best, is a painting in my mind. It held a lesson for me that when one thinks he is at the top of the world, it is good to remember that the world turns upside down every twenty-four hours; as well as another lesson which he taught me—that even a clock, which has stopped, is right twice a day every twenty-four hours. Between one extreme of humility and the other of tolerance, is a good path to traverse.

It had always been my father's ambition to have me enter your fraternity and your lodge as soon as I was of age. No sooner had I reached the admissible age, then I was rushed into the lodge to take the degrees and become a member with my father. You recall how generous you were to me, elevating me, in short time, to the highest position in the lodge—that of Noble Grand, although that was achieved not without some opposition from some of you who, I am happy to see here and who, by this time, I hope, have acknowledged the error of your ways.

Then, a number of lodges elevated me to the position of

District Deputy Grand Master at a time when I was one of the youngest to have held that post in the history of the Order. I am grateful, not for these titles and promotions, but for the fact that I was drawn into the symbolism of the Order and the study of fraternity and brotherhood. The Odd Fellows are one million five hundred thousand strong, but if we had been several hundred million strong, there might not have been the two holocausts through which we have lived.

I may not reveal the secret degrees, but perhaps I can symbolize the noble principles of the Odd Fellows Order in this parable:

There was a man in hell who was suffering the torments of the burning fires, and he prayed for deliverance. Finally, a silk thread of gossamer tenderness descended to him. He seized upon it knowing that it would break but, mysteriously, it was strong enough to lift him upwards. Then, others seeing him ascend, seized desperately upon his body ar.d two; three, five and ten others held on, and the silk thread lifted them all. The man feared that the silk thread would not stand the strain and, violently, kicked the others off from his body, one by one, until once again he hung alone on it. Only then did the thread break and throw him back into the pit. Then, a voice from above said: "This thread was strong enough to lift you and your brothers; it is not strong enough to lift you alone."

This has been the symbol of our fraternity. We have been the moral scientists who have preceded the atomic age. The atomic scientists have worked to split the atom, while we have labored to unite the Adams of the world; to throw all races, creeds and colors into a cyclotron and derive therefrom a synthesis of brotherhood and unity and peace. And one of the paintings in my mind, done in the El Greco style of elongation and beautiful purple and red tints, is the scene when I was elevated to the position of District Deputy Grand Master dressed in all the regalia of splendor and my father alongside of me, beaming as if this were the ascendancy to princehood. But perhaps you will accept a perverse thought that one of the lessons I learned from all the pomp and regalia that we wore, was that you cannot judge men by their appearance.

I have not told you, yet, of the outstanding characteristic of my father, and the one that is symbolized by the most beautiful painting of all. It is gaiety, his irrepressible exuberance, his joyousness, his constant laughing and dancing and singing. Whether it be in New Hampshire during the summer, or in Florida during the winter—whenever he walks on the streets there are the loud, joyous calls of recognition, as if in anticipation that only laughter and heartiness is a proper greeting. From earliest childhood, I cannot remember talking to my father as often as I can remember singing with him. That has been our most frequent form of communication—for song wipes away the dust of everyday life from the soul, and ours has been a communication of joy and happiness.

A man who spreads as much sunshine to others as my father does, cannot help but have it shine on himself. He is a philanthropist in the benefactions of good will and joy, which he extends to others. This is best symbolized in the religious ceremonies that I was reared to enjoy in my home, and the painting that I have in mind is typical of this spirit of gaiety on the first Passover Night. My father, dressed in a white satin skull cap and white robe; the table filled with gleaming silver and wine filled glasses which shine like huge rubies; the candles flickering with golden little flames that bend back and forth as the rush of song beats against them; the sacramental bread covered by gold brocaded satin; my father holding the silver chalice of wine and singing exuberantly, so that the wine flows over his hand and upon the spotless white tablecloth and, with the other hand, he is violently leading all the others as a choir to give harmony to his song. The verses are many and the music lasts long into the night. This is the unforgettable scene, painted in the style of Peter Brueghel who knew how to depict wild scenes, such as the Wedding Feast, in splashing whites, yellows, and vibrant reds representing explosions of color. And, in the background of all these paintings, deliberately choosing to be in the background, is my mother—always conferring sweetness and goodness for the hard-driving willed personality of my father. She is like tender ivy, which clings to the wall and covers every crevice or crack, to give it beauty.

There is one other painting that is going to be added to my gallery. It is being painted this evening. It is about to be finished. It is you and this scene. You, seated here with expectancy, indulgence and kindliness on your faces; my father and mother on the dais next to beautiful Mildred, surrounded by friends and neighbors, by the distinguished humorist, Harry Hershfield, who has given us so much joy over the years, by leaders of your fraternity and by many of you who have known my father for forty odd years. And, in this scene, I am presenting a jewel to my father—I call him to the dais as I do now. I refer to the aphorism of the king who wished to present a jewel to the noblest in the land. His Prime Minister selected the foremost painters, writers, scientists and philanthropists. On the appointed evening, the Prime Minister, from the galaxy of famous men, led to the center of the room a simple little man whose face and achievements were unknown. The king inquired on what theory this man had been chosen over all the others in the realm, to receive the jewel, and the Prime Minister replied: "He is the greatest of all, your majesty. He is your teacher."

A father is a thousand schoolmasters, and I present to my teacher, on your behalf, this jewel with your affection and my love.

PART III

Looking at the Neighbors

CHAPTER 17

Irving Berlin

BEFORE THE ADVENT of newspapers and radio, people used to learn the news through songs. Minstrels were the reporters of their day. Homer recorded his period in epic songs. The adventures of Beowolf were sung by Anglo-Saxon bards called "scops." Perhaps it is from this word that the newspaper term "scoop" is derived.

If a historian of the next generation desired to analyze the events of our day by studying the songs of our period, there is no doubt but that he would have to review the works of Irving Berlin for these have been sung by tens of millions of people throughout the world.

Such a historian would discover the high-spirited era of the beginning of the century by listening to *Alexander's Ragtime Band* and *My Wife's Gone To The Country*. He would learn about the grim wartime spirit by listening to the songs *We're On Our Way To France* and *For Your Country And My Country*. He would learn about peactime conversion from Berlin's song *I've Got My Captain Working For Me Now*. He could trace the romanticism of the 1920s by listening to the beautiful ballads *All Alone, Always,* and *Remember*. Music is love in search of a word. Berlin supplied the word and married it to his music. He could then discover the rising tide of optimism in his *Blue Skies* and *Putting On The Ritz*. He would become aware of the crash and disillusionment of the 1929 from the simple song *Say It Isn't So*. He would learn about American resurgence and recuperative power from the songs *Easter Parade* and *Top Hat, White Tie and Tails*. He would understand the desperate fight which our beloved country made for its own liberty and for that of the world by hearing the songs *This Is the Army, Angels of Mercy* and *God Bless America*. He would learn of our dedication to liberty in a divided post-war world from the strains of *Freedom Train*.

It is very likely that Irving Berlin never realized when he was painting his musical canvasses that they would reflect the history of our times. I suspect that Berlin was simply *Doing What Comes Naturally*. Few men are geniuses but even fewer geniuses are great men. Berlin has grown to the stature of both. He carries his music with him and his brief-case is his heart.

When I think of the streams of melody which have flowed from him and which will continue to flow into the hearts of the generations to come, I venture to say that it is not too lavish a prediction to make that he will be one of the hand-ful of immortals of this generation. For he is the Homer of our present era.

CHAPTER 18

Eddie Rickenbacker

ON JULY 4, 1914, at the Sioux City two-mile dirt racetrack, Barney Oldfield and the other great automobile racers of the day had gathered. The prize was $25,000. As the race neared its climax, one car driven with particular daring and skill was out in front. Suddenly its tire exploded. It seemed as if the car would take several somersaults and its driver would be killed. However, the driver held on to the wheel with herculean strength, righted the car, refused to slow down, and managed to win the race. Then out of the car, holding a kitten which was his mascot, stepped a young man, his face black with dirt but with a white flashing grin. It was Eddie Rickenbacker.

Three years later our country went to war. This same

young man organized the dare-devil racetrack drivers and sought to enlist the whole group as an air squadron. The army, however, rejected the idea and this young man wound up an army chauffeur. Well, not just a chauffeur, the chauffeur for the commanding general, General John Pershing. Then using his influence with his commander, he manipulated his way into the air force.

From that moment on, history was written in the air. He shot down one German plane—two German planes—three —four—five—six. His name became legendary in the German air ranks. They sent their best fliers against him but each time, flying recklessly but with extraordinary skill, he downed his enemy. Seven—eight—nine—ten—eleven— twelve opposing planes shot down in flames. One day he tried a new experiment. He was going to capture a plane and bring it in. He crippled his German foe in a dog fight and then directed him to fly in. He got the plane back to the American air field but as it was about to land, the German became so confused that he crashed and his plane exploded. Rickenbacker continued to make history in the air. Thirteen —fourteen—fifteen—sixteen planes. When the war ended, he had shot down twenty-two German planes and four balloons to become the foremost war ace of our flying forces.

He had become the commanding officer of the 94th Air (Hat-in-the-Ring) Squadron. This was the only air squadron accompanying the occupying forces when they went into Germany.

In 1925 he fought courageously for Billy Mitchell, his friend. When he returned to civil life, he became president and general manager of Eastern Air Lines. Then he applied his daring and skill to executive functions behind a desk instead of behind a stick.

In 1941, the plane in which he was riding crashed. Eight were killed. He was fatally wounded or so the doctors thought. For months he hovered between life and death. He was swathed in bandages but he smiled his way out of them. A nerve in his leg had been cut, never to heal again, and he was told he must never fly again. So he immediately went up in a plane and did a couple of loop-the-loops. When the plane landed, he limped out with that same flashing white smile and announced to the doctors that he was complying fully with their instructions.

In 1941 our country went to war again. This young man was no longer so young. Secretary of War Stimson asked him to perform official missions for the government. He visited thirty-two fighting fronts. On one occasion, while flying to a small Pacific island, there was a strong tail wind. The plane overshot its mark, was unable to find the island, and made a crash landing in the sea. Then eight men clung to a raft for eighteen days, sharing four oranges, two raw fish and a sea gull which, seemingly in answer to a prayer, landed on Rickenbacker's shoulder. One of the young men on the raft, unable to withstand the blistering sun, the starvation and the thirst, died. Rickenbacker, with greater reserve than any of the others, prevented their minds from cracking and their bodies from withering until their rescue. After this group had been miraculously saved, Rickenbacker, wan and worn, but still flashing that white smile, continued with his mission and finished it. This incident has become a religious and spiritual inspiration to the people of America.

So there he stands, dare-devil auto racer, chauffeur, war ace, executive, religionist. All together they spell simply— an American.

CHAPTER 19

Paul Muni

A GREAT ACTOR will sometimes perform a role so realistically that he becomes identified with the character he is playing while his own personality appears to be imaginary. It is on this theory that I think Paul Muni is not Paul

Muni at all. He is Zola, Emile Zola who left the comfortable citadel of literature to fight injustice, to afflict the comfortable and comfort the afflicted.

He is not Paul Muni. He is Louis Pasteur, the scientist who achieved distinction not by killing millions but by waging war against disease and giving life to millions; who learned that the greatest friend of truth is time; its greatest enemy, prejudice; its constant companion, humility.

He is not Paul Muni. He is Juarez, the fearless fighter for Mexican independence, who knew that liberty has restraints but never frontiers.

He is not Paul Muni. He is Wang Lung of *The Good Earth* who symbolized the resistance of the Chinese to oppression. "Come unto me with few and I will overwhelm you; come unto me with many and you will overwhelm yourselves."

Yes, he is all of these: Zola, Pasteur, Juarez, Wang Lung. He is also known by the alias of Paul Muni.

CHAPTER 20

William O'Dwyer

THERE ARE all sorts of careers. Businessmen follow careers of efficiency; professional men follow careers of proficiency. Some men follow careers of character. That is the career of Mayor O'Dwyer. Then there are others who follow careers of crime. Even in such a career one must pour torrents of energy and spend a lifetime of effort. That is why careers of crime start early, with juvenile delinquency. I would like to contrast a career of character and a career of crime.

On June 11, 1890, another son was born to the O'Dwyer family in County Mayo. He was one of eleven children. They called him William. Seven years later in New York

City, there was born to the Buchalter family another son. By a strange coincidence he too was one of eleven children. He was named Louis.

William, whose parents were school teachers, went to the Mayo schools, then to Salamanca University in Spain for two years before emigrating to the United States. He arrived in New York City in 1910, friendless and with $25.35 in his pockets. He began his career of character immediately. He worked as a coal passer on a steamer to South America and then as a stoker on the Hudson River Day Line.

Then he joined the Hod Carriers' Union. When the tallest building in the world up to that time was being constructed on lower Broadway, if you had looked up at the myriad criss-crossing of scaffolding which corrugated that building, you would have seen that one of the men who was aiding in the construction was William O'Dwyer.

Louis was not engaged in construction. He had begun his career of crime and was engaged in destruction, for that very same year he was charged with setting fire to a loft.

After becoming a United States citizen in 1916, William decided to join the Police Department, the lowest and most important stratum of law enforcement. Louis joined a local gang, the lowest and most important stratum of crime.

William decided to study law at night at Fordham University while he was pounding the streets during the daytime. Louis also decided to become educated. This was the time when rackets were evolving into their full glory and he studied the complicated techniques of extorting money.

In 1932 William was appointed magistrate. He was now a judge of the lowest criminal court of this city. Louis by this time was also appearing in the Magistrate's Court, but on the other side of the bar, charged with stealing money from pushcart peddlers.

While magistrate, William decided that criminals between the ages of sixteen and nineteen ought not to be considered in the same category as mature criminals. He organized the Adolescent Court. He was one of the first to turn to psychiatrists, welfare workers and clergymen to aid him in solving the problems of adolescents.

Louis was also interested in adolescents. He was organizing them systematically into local gangs. He had an organization which preyed upon storekeepers, an organization which later blossomed forth in its full terror against the fur, leather and garment industries.

By this time William was affectionately known by his friends as Bill, and Louis by his friends as Lepke.

In 1938 Governor Lehman appointed Bill to the County Court, one of the higher criminal courts of New York City. Lepke had also progressed. He was no longer appearing in Special Sessions; he had been promoted to General Sessions. There he was charged with grand larceny and dealing in narcotics, for each of which crimes he served two years in Sing Sing. He was beginning to learn that money can be lost in more ways than won.

In 1939 Bill was elected district attorney of Kings County to give battle to the iniquitous forces which had entrenched themselves against the public welfare. He prosecuted "Murder, Incorporated." Then for the first time the man who followed the career of character met face to face with the man who followed the career of crime. Bill and Lepke met, one heading the forces of law and order, the other the forces of disorder. Lepke, together with many others, was found guilty of murder.

Then Bill left the district attorney's office to join other forces of law and order, the United States Army, to give battle to an international "Murder, Incorporated," while Lepke, although in perfect health, stayed at home to face dangers from lawful authorities.

On the bleak day of March 8, 1944, Lepke's career of crime came to an end. That morning at six o'clock prison attendants entered his death cell to shave his head and slit his trousers so that electrodes could be strapped upon him. Then he was helped through a long and dank corridor while words of religion were intoned in his ear, words which should have been spoken to him many years before. The other inmates of the death cells, in accordance with tradition, screamed epithets at the jailers, shuffled their feet and banged their tin cups against the iron bars to create a frightening din. This was the last applause for Lepke.

He had hoped to end his career in a blaze of glory. He was to end it in a blaze of electricity. They swung open a large iron door revealing a brilliantly lit room in the center of which stood an ugly chair which looked like a throne, a throne for princes of crime. Lepke was strapped into the chair and then, at a signal from the warden, 20,000 volts of electricity hurled his body straining against the straps. He turned blue. The current was released and Lepke slumped in the chair, the room filled with the sickening odor of burnt flesh. He was placed upon a stretcher and carried out. This was the ignominious end of a career of crime.

Bill continued his career of character, being promoted from major to brigadier general. In 1944 President Roosevelt designated him head of the Allied Control Commission for Italy with rank of minister and, thereafter, American representative on the War Refugee Board.

Finally, in 1945, Bill, who thirty-five years before had stood, a friendless boy, shivering in Battery Park in New York City, was elected chief magistrate of that city, a post second only to the presidency of the United States in its administrative complexity and importance. It is not difficult to predict that, after his brilliant service as Mayor of the City of New York, higher posts await him, for he is a man of tactical efficiency and efficient tact.

I wish these true stories of a career of crime and a career of character could be told to all juvenile delinquents. Perhaps their dramatic impact would pierce their minds, a thing which mere moral preachments have failed to do. We must concentrate on preparing youth for the path at least as much as on preparing the path for youth.

CHAPTER 21

Walter Winchell

(A Column For Him While He Vacations)

I AM AFRAID to write this column because a columnist must have so many talents.

1. He must be a humorist whose column wears a pun-striped suit. For example:

Alimony is the high cost of leaving.

Sales resistance is the triumph of mind over patter.

Sex magazines are the filth column of America.

Today we have many sulfa-conscious young doctors.

True pals stick together 'til debt do them part.

He adored her and the feeling was nuptial.

Politicians, like the earth, are flattened at the polls.

Time wounds all heels.

What some patients need is a good five-cent scar.

2. A columnist must be a movie and theatrical critic who can unload atomic devastation with a phrase. For example:

It took the Curies 30 years to find radium; it took Sir William Ramsay 16 years to discover helium; it took this play only 2 hours to produce tedium.

The sets were beautiful but some dreadful people strutted in front of them, interfering with the audience's view.

Anticipating the Thanksgiving season, New York was treated last night to a fine new turkey.

3. A columnist must be a lexicographer who can invent new words which tickle the brain and surprise the eye. For example:

Bilboorish, Rankinjustice, Teutonic Plague, guesstimate, sindicated column, kilocyclopedia, Bacall of the Wild, infantuation, Bulldogmatic.

4. He must be a philosopher who disguises his wisdom in simplicity so that he does not appear pretentious. For example:

It's better to give than to lend and it costs about the same.

Suggested sign for a museum:
"Touch as much as you like with your eyes, but don't see with your fingers."

I am afraid of senators who have a difficulty for every solution.

Love at first sight often ends with divorce at first slight.

Man argues that woman can't be trusted too far. Woman argues that man can't be trusted too near.

The reason a dog is a good friend: his tail wags, not his tongue.

Philosophy is the ability to explain why you are happy although you are poor.

The President has the power to appoint and disappoint the members of his cabinet.

5. He must be a religionist who realizes that religion is caught, not taught. For example:

An atheist is a man who has no invisible means of support.

The best reply to an atheist is to give him a good dinner and ask him if he believes there is a cook.

6. He must be an ironist who does not hesitate to master the art of insult. For example:

She dresses like a bad photograph, underdeveloped and over-exposed.

An editor is one who separates the wheat from the chaff and then sees to it that the chaff is printed.

His mind is like his farm, naturally barren and made worse by mistaken cultivation.

She looked as if she were poured into her dress and forgot to say "when."

He is addressing his speech to posterity, but his audience will be there before he finishes.

A woman's tongue is her sword and she sees to it that it never becomes rusty.

7. He must be an economist who knows what two and two are for. For example:

Those who complain about shortages ought to remember that there was no sugar until the 13th century, no coal until the 15th century, no potatoes until the 16th century, no coffee until the 17th century, no matches until the 18th century and no gasoline until the 19th century.

Socialism: If you have two cows, you give one to your neighbor.

Communism: If you have two cows, you give them to the Government and the Government then gives you some milk.

Fascism: If you have two cows, you keep the cows and give the milk to the Government; then the Government sells you some milk.

Nazism: If you have two cows, the Government shoots you and keeps the cows.

Capitalism: If you have two cows, you sell one and buy a bull.

8. He must be an internationalist who keeps the conscience of the people boiling. For example:

A good motto for war criminal trials is: "The prisoners, not the sentences, should be suspended."

Don't relax. Germany has more intelligence per square head than any other nation.

An apostle of conciliation asked George Clemenceau whether his hatred of Germans was based on a study of the people. "Have you ever been to Germany?" he inquired.
"No, Monsieur," replied the Tiger, "I have not been to Germany. But twice in my life-time the Germans have been to France."

Under fascism, the only virtue is strength; under democracy, the only strength is virtue.

9. He must be a historian with a human interest touch. For example:

The spelling backward craze goes back a long way. In 1808 there was a political fight over Jefferson's embargo. His political opponents ridiculed him in cartoons as "O Grab Me."

Artists get inspirations from strange things. Schiller loved the smell of rotton apples when he composed. Beethoven dipped his hands in cold water. Goethe could only work if his room was tightly closed without fresh air. Conrad would write in his bathtub through a haze of cigarette smoke. Mark Twain always wrote in bed. Rubens had someone read to him while he painted. Caruso always smoked before he sang.

10. He must be a reporter who can reveal information kept secret even from many government officials. For example:

Our Army found in a German chemical laboratory a new secret gas so powerful that a drop no larger than a pinhead would kill a human being. Hundreds of tons of this gas, never used, were captured. The Nazi laboratory chief revealed that Hitler lost his nerve. He was afraid to use this weapon because he had been informed that the Chemical Warfare Division of the United States Army had even more fearful gases and in much larger quantities!

Yes, to be a columnist, one must be a humorist, a critic, a lexicographer, a philosopher, a religionist, an ironist, an economist, an internationalist, a historian and a reporter— all rolled into one. That's why I can't write this column.

CHAPTER 22

Nelson Aldrich Rockefeller

NELSON ALDRICH ROCKEFELLER struggled during his youth. His handicap was not, according to the Alger formula, his poverty. It was his wealth. He desired to demonstrate his capacity generated by his own motive power. He was determined not to be a snob nor to talk as if he had begotten his own ancestors.

At Dartmouth, he was elected to Phi Beta Kappa. He played on the soccer team and became editor of the school magazine, *The Five Lively Arts.* These were the early signs of his simple rearing which had left his natural talents unfettered.

He has been president of the Museum of Modern Art and is president of Rockefeller Center. His artistic and financial bent soon flowered into government service. He became, under President Roosevelt, Coordinator of Inter-American Affairs, and did yeoman's work in establishing hemispheric solidarity in fact as well as in theory. Ever since 1941 he has taken vigorous steps to counteract Nazi influence in South America. As chairman of the Inter-American Development Commission, he stimulated the development of a long-range commercial program which would develop the industry of South America and foster better trade relationships in the whole hemisphere.

At first his committee was termed the "army of amateurs" but he proved that energy intelligently applied can achieve success in the diplomatic sphere. In the old days of diplomacy an ambassador was a man of virtue who was sent to another country to lie on behalf of his own country. In those days he had to concern himself with formalities and ignore moralities. In those days we honored him for what he said but judged him by what he did. The two were never the same. But in recent years of more open diplomacy, ambassadors have talked with candor and sincerity and have fulfilled the mission of statesmanship rather than intrigue. Nelson Rockefeller thawed out the State Department's distaste for the amateur. In a year and a half he did more to obtain the good will of the South American countries than Goebbels achieved for Germany in a decade of propaganda.

His grandfather made gifts of $650,000,000 to be spent for philanthropic purposes in eighty-eight different countries. Nelson Rockefeller carries on the great tradition of his family and, what is more significant, the great tradition of America. He does so by contributing a keen mind and a good heart.

We hear so much about the character development of underprivileged boys who achieve wealth and fame by dint of hard work and determination. As great a saga of achievement is that of the boy born to riches who abjures the easy life almost thrust upon him and ventures to build reputation by his own solid achievements.

Character is like a word square. No matter how you read it, horizontally or vertically, it spells the same. No matter how you look at Nelson Rockefeller's life and activities, they read the same—character.

CHAPTER 23

John Golden

SOONER OR LATER the color, excitement and achievements of John Golden's life will be projected into a motion picture. I should like to envision that motion picture. It will probably have a lurid title, such as *The Golden Heart,* and the first scene takes place on a boat. It is a boat coming from Manchester, England, to the United States, and upon it are Joel Golden and his wife. In this scene, Joel entertains his friends by playing three or four instruments, a talent which will later be inherited by his son.

The Goldens settle in Ohio, but later come to New York City where, in 1874, nine years after the end of the Civil War, a son is born to them. They call him John. This scene reveals that upon his birth John cries endlessly until the father, mother and doctor clap their hands. Then he smiles contentedly. A producer has been born.

When this scene shutters out, the next reveals John at the age of eight, being taken by his mother to a performance of *The Mikado.* He laughs, cries and quivers with an inner excitement all afternoon. His mother is so alarmed that she tells his father that they must never take John to the theatre again. What they do not know is that he has already contracted an incurable malady, one that will keep him at fever pitch the rest of his life, one that will lend excitement to his life. It is the malady of being in love with the theatre. John proceeds to learn all the Gilbert and Sullivan operettas, and can recite and sing them to this day.

At the age of fourteen, John joins the architectural firm of Horgan & Slattery. He is advised to start at the bottom. So he becomes a bricklayer and helps to construct a building which still stands on Thirty-fifth Street in New York City. He is in ecstasy as he pats each brick into place because he is building a theatre. Little does that boy know that twenty years later there will appear in that theatre a show called *Turn to the Right,* of which he himself will be the producer. Nor does he know that twenty-five years later another theatre will be built which will bear the name of that little boy, the John Golden Theatre.

In the next scene our hero takes up chemistry. He experiments with chewing gum in his home. He has an idea that if he can get clove flavor into chewing gum he will have not only a pleasant but a useful product. He finally devises a formula and calls the product "Cafe Cloves." To this day errant husbands can return home breath-less because of young John Golden's ingenuity.

Then he begins to write songs, hundreds of them. All sorts of songs, from comedy songs such as *He Swallowed a Thermometer and Died by Degrees* to *Poor Butterfly,* which he composed in a cell of the Hippodrome from which an elephant had been vacated to make room for him. In the course of his composing efforts he gathers a host of collaborators. One of them is called Jerry; second name, Kern. Another is called Victor; second name, Herbert. Another is called Oscar; second name, Hammerstein.

Another has burning black eyes and a pale, intense face. Together they compose a song called *The Zoological Girls.* At two in the morning the song is completed, but the young man with the burning black eyes says, "Let's try it again from another angle." So they work until four-thirty in the morning. Golden is ready to quit, but the young man with the blazing eyes says, "Let's try it again from a different angle." At six in the morning the intense young man is satisfied. Golden wearily says, "Goodnight, Irving," and Berlin runs down the stairs.

The motion picture will undoubtedly present many production numbers based not only on the songs but on the complete shows which John Golden has written. Perhaps it will include scenes from Marie Dressler's first starring show, called *Miss Print,* or any one of the Hippodrome shows which he wrote. This will depend upon the mood at the story conference at the motion picture studio. I cannot anticipate this story conference and therefore skip over this portion of the picture.

I am sure, however, that there will be the scene in which Lillian Russell invites Golden to one of her birthday parties. He feels greatly honored but also greatly frightened. How can he compete with the many young men who will bring diamond tiaras and other expensive gifts to bribe a smile from Miss Russell? So he composes a one-act musical called *The Village Beauty,* puts a pretty blue ribbon around it, and with a great flourish presents it to Miss Russell. At the same time he says slyly, "Too bad this will never be produced." She replies, "Why not? We have DeWolf Hopper and all the stars here this evening. Let's do it tonight." Everyone is commandeered by Miss Russell to go into rehearsal immediately. John Golden cannot find, amongst the guests, anyone adequate to the part of the hero, so he therefore reluctantly assigns the rôle to himself. Late that evening *The Village Beauty* is produced, Miss Russell resting in the hero's arms during most of the performance, which is produced with fidelity to the script.

I imagine the director of this motion picture will be unable to resist the temptation of scanning the camera away from *The Village Beauty,* to a corner of the room where lie in lonely estate the precious gifts presented by the young men who are now merely in the supporting cast of John Golden, while Miss Russell beams her favor upon him admiringly.

As the next scene opens, John Golden is writing songs for a new musical comedy. A girl called May is going to sing most of them. Golden discovers, each time he looks at May, that she is a menace to normal breathing. He composes a song called *Goodbye, Girls, I'm Through,* and then lives up to the lyrics and marries May.

I am also sure that the motion picture will depict scenes between John Golden and various Presidents of the United States. For example, there will be the scene between Golden and Woodrow Wilson. Golden has read one of the President's speeches in which he found the phrase, "Every man must be awake, and watchful for his country's sake." "My!" says Golden, "the President writes in couplets." He thereupon culls other sentences from the President's speeches and composes a lyric which he sets to music. This brings about a meeting with Wilson. "I can get a thousand dollars advance royalty for this song, Mr. President." "Let's take it," says Wilson, "and give all royalties to the Red Cross." So it is agreed and the song sheets bear the words: "Written by Woodrow Wilson and John Golden."

Then there will be a scene between Golden and President Coolidge. The *Lightnin'* company has come to Washington to perform and it is arranged that the President should greet Frank Bacon and the supporting cast at the White House. Secretary of War Weeks introduces John Golden, the producer of *Lightnin'* to the President in flattering terms and Golden, to relieve the embarrassment, says, "He's my press agent and I take him wherever I go." Weeks laughs thunderously. Golden laughs feebly. Coolidge does not laugh. He says with great simplicity, "Yes." After a silence that seems to last several hours, it is time for the actors to be ushered in. What Golden doesn't know, however, is that they have exploited the opportunity and have invited all their relatives to come along so that they may shake hands with the President. The procession seems endless. There are six-month-old infants in mothers' arms and eighty-five-year-old grandfathers hobbling in to shake the President's hand. When the number of actors has exceeded two hundred, and they are still filing in, the President says, "You have a big cast, Mr. Golden." John replies, "You see, we have understudies, Mr. President."

Then there will be a scene between Golden and President Roosevelt. It will have to be selected from many meetings between them. Perhaps this will be the humorous one in which John Golden is seated at the bedside of President Roosevelt while he is having breakfast. Jimmy Byrnes is waiting outside. The President's unquenchable spirit and gaiety bubble out of him, despite his worn and anxious face. "Have you heard anything amusing, John?" he asks. "Well," says Golden, "I don't know whether it's amusing, but on the train down to Washington, I saw a horse playing gin rummy with a man. Someone approached the man and said, 'Smart horse you have there.' 'Not so smart,' said the man, 'I just schneided him twice.'" This President is not silent. His bell-like laughter peals through the room and through all the surrounding corridors.

There will be other touching scenes in the picture which will visually mold the character of John Golden for the viewers, perhaps the scene in which John Golden hears that Stephen Foster's home is about to be sold. He buys it and presents it to the state of Kentucky to be preserved as a shrine to American music. As Golden presents the house to the Governor of Kentucky, you can be sure that in the background the strains of My Old Kentucky Home will be heard.

The final reel of the motion picture will undoubtedly be devoted to the achievements of John Golden. In the first World War he organized entertainment for the soldiers on a huge scale, comparable to the morale factor involved. In the second World War the organizations which he inspired gave twelve million tickets to soldiers. He conducted a playwriting contest among soldiers. Hundreds of one-act plays were written by them. Five were produced under the title of The Army Play by Play. Two hundred and fifty thousand dollars were raised for Army and Navy relief purposes from this venture. He has become a spokesman, not only of the theatre, but for the theatre.

He has produced or directed three hundred plays, of which seven have run more than five hundred performances, a record never equalled by any other producer. He has been conscious of the theatre as a cultural force. He has not only taken from the theatre; he has given to it. He has organized and financed the Equity Library Theatre so that people might be able to go into the library and see a play as easily as they take a book.

He has, in the course of an active life, made hundreds of friends and been of aid to that wonderful community composed of theatre folks. He has become distinguished for his clean entertainment and has demonstrated the falsity of "Nothing risqué, nothing gained." He has shown that one can find gold in the theatre without digging through dirt.

And now I see the final scene of the motion picture. Distinguished men and women of all the arts and of government have gathered at a great dinner to honor him. The camera, starting at the ceiling so that it can take in the great panorama, pans slowly towards the dais until it has focused upon the toastmaster and John Golden, who sits beside him. As music written by John Golden wells in the background, the toastmaster is heard to say: "Ladies and gentlemen, all the arts are related. When God conceived the world, that was poetry. When He molded its austere mountains and its gracious valleys, that was sculpture. When He colored the earth with lustrous flowers, green trees and faint blue skies, that was painting. And when He put human beings upon the earth, that was the divine drama. John Golden has lived the divine drama in himself and in his work."

CHAPTER 24

Joe Louis (And Other Champions)

CHAMPIONS usually have their own methods. They do not merely imitate their predecessors. This is apparently a rule of evolution because proficiency in athletic events is constantly increasing. It is not merely superior equipment which accounts for new records.

Tilden, the greatest champion in the history of tennis, developed the full blasting swing on every stroke from serve to backhand and overhead volley. True, his virtuosity required him to become master of chops and slices too, but the distinguishing feature of his game was its ferocity. In a sense he hurt American tennis, because all his admirers adopted his method, the kill on each stroke. Naturally control is diminished as the swing is lengthened and produced with full speed. Only Tilden's genius enabled him to combine a high degree of control with blinding speed. Others aiming for unstoppable speed, fell into frequent error. The Frenchmen La Coste and Cochet decided to capitalize on the high percentage of "outs" and "nets" which Americans imposed on themselves. La Coste trained with a machine on the other side of the net. It shot balls at him at arranged speed and angles for hours at a time. He merely returned them, until he had become almost as steady and dependable as the machine. Cochet, on the other hand, used a different method to develop "errorlessness." He practiced the half-volley, a sort of pick-up as the ball bounded toward him. This was his method of preventing Tilden's speed from acquiring full momentum after the bounce. By playing control against speed the French won the Davis Cup. Even Tilden, then beyond his peak, could not maintain speed plus control. His successors were never able to do so over any long period. Budge and Vines held the spotlight for only limited periods. Tilden's individual style of play could not be successfully copied.

In golf, Byron Nelson reversed this process. He became the greatest golfer of all time, not even excluding Bobby Jones, by developing a modified type of golf swing which gave him superior control. He doesn't swing in the complete classic arc. His swing resembles a "punch" at the ball more than that of any other top golfer. But it gives him added control and has made his golf scores in competition the most

phenomenal ever recorded in that ancient game. Even
though he has recently receded somewhat from an excellence
which left him unchallenged, his athletic achievements are
probably the greatest of any champion in any sport. For no
other game requires such precision combined with power.
Nelson's average score of 68 for twenty-two tournaments is
therefore a unique standard of athletic efficiency. His individual method has not yet fully impressed itself upon golf,
but already foremost professional golfers are studying his
more upright and controlled swing with firm grip to determine whether his style may not have been as responsible
for his prowess as his reflexes.

So too in football, the ascendency of the forward pass has
been due to newer and higher standards which players like
Sid Luckman and Sammy Baugh have created. Luckman's
long passes are so accurate in allowing for the speed and
shift of the receiver that few but experts realize the importance of his stance and balance while avoiding tacklers to
gain time. He contributed a new kind of dodge to football,
escaping tacklers by side-stepping or moving forward only at
the last second and for merely a step or two, while keeping
his eyes and his arm ready for the receiver. This new method
by a champion forward passer has resulted in a host of new
records, such as eight touchdown forward passes in one game.
Baugh, on the other hand, has developed so sure and speedy
a short pass that opponents have given up trying to stop him.
They merely concentrate on stopping the runner promptly
after the pass has been thrown right at his stomach.

In basketball, champions like Hank Luissetti have demonstrated the possibility of shooting for the basket from any
position and with either hand. The set shot is scorned by
them. The classic defense is of no avail against a player who
can regularly, with his back to the basket, pivot and throw
in a shot; or who can shoot underhand with either hand
around a defensive player.

Baseball was virtually revolutionized by Babe Ruth. His
batting stance, hands held at the very end of the bat, his feet

together until he stepped into the ball, all gave full sweep to a booming swing designed for power hitting. His sixty home runs in one baseball season not only still stands as a record, but also put into the shadow during his reign all the tactical phases of the game, such as base-stealing, sacrificing and bunting. Power overcame all such refinements.

Prize-fighting is the most exciting of all sports because it represents the most primitive method of besting an adversary, something which all sports gratify in us. John L. Sullivan was as unscientific and powerful as a bull. Jim Corbett was a dazzling boxer, depending on feet and hands alike. He once said that the most important thing a man must do to become a champion is "Fight one more round." Jim Jeffries was as sturdy and heavy as a freight train. Bob Fitzsimmons had a paralyzing punch launched from a frail body with spindly legs. Jack Johnson combined an extraordinary defense with an uppercut as his chief offensive weapon. Willard was huge and lumbering. Then came the ferocious Dempsey. He fitted the traditional conception of a great fighter. He was a frenzy in action, speedy, snarling, punching continuously with both hands. Gene Tunney showed how a mechanical defense could stop a slowed-down tiger.

Now a great champion has contributed something new to an ancient art. Joe Lewis is the first shuffling type of champion we have had. He moves forward slowly, almost imperceptibly. He is therefore always in balance for heavy punching. He does not rush forward like Dempsey and other aggressive fighters who find themselves tied up in clinches after the first blows have been struck or avoided. He is not off balance from fancy footwork, or unable to unlimber his mightiest blows because he is on his toes. His speed is reserved for his arms which punch with incredible piston-like movements.

The rest of his demeanor in the ring is likewise unorthodox. Lacking are the usual facial expressions: snarls, cruelty, gritty determination, courageous contempt, or fear mixed with vengeance. Instead there is an impassive mask. Emotion, that fiery flag flown by most fighters, seems completely lacking. If it were not for a sense of complete concentration, his face would represent boredom. There is something terrifying about such a blank face. An opponent is likely to feel that he is faced with destiny, passionless, unchangeable and inevitable. Even the ferocious scowls of a Sullivan or Dempsey seemed reassuring by comparison for they gave notice that their possessors were human and might err. But what hope is there against an unemotional machine which strikes with lethal effect

The knowledge that a blow with either hand will dull an opponent to the verge of unconsciousness makes Louis patient and unhurried. He doesn't waste a move. He doesn't strike ten blows in the hope of landing one. He doesn't depend on a ceaseless torrent of punches which made Henry Armstrong a champion at three weights only to fade out quickly when his energies lagged and permitted only a normal pace.

Opponents of Louis also know that his lack of motion is no comfort, but that it is the ominous prelude to one swift blow which will render them senseless. So even when they are unharmed, there is a growing fear which paralyzes them. No other fighter in ring history has terrorized so many opponents and prepared them for complete helplessness before he had even landed a glove. It would be appropriate for the manager of more than one Louis opponent to say to his charge after the first round, "I have an idea for you. The next time he hits you why don't you hit him back?"

This attitude that a predestined fate awaits his opponents is carried out by Louis even after the knockout. No fighter before him could avoid the release of joy upon final triumph. From handsprings and tears of elation to a conqueror's scowl, winning gladiators have registered their emotions when their hands have been held high by the referee as a signal of victory. But observe Louis during such a moment. His face is still a mask, non-revealing and unconcerned. The bedlam and hysteria around him do not seem to touch him. He is still the machine which has done its work with inevitable finality, and machines do not express elation.

This monotone of impassivity does not however connote lack of wiliness. Despite his simple, uneducated rearing, his weapons as a warrior are constantly sharpened by observation. Not only was he an apt pupil of his manager, Roxborough (who got into legal difficulties and then died), but he learned from each bout. Notice his improvement whenever he fought the same opponent twice. Schmeling knocked him out in their first meeting, but was annihilated in their second encounter. The German clung to the ropes after the opening two minutes of the fight, screaming with pain like a woman. No better fate awaits Joe Walcott. All his other opponents in return matches were dispatched to dreamland many rounds earlier than in their first battle.

Above all, Louis has exhibited in his quiet way a sense of dignity befitting a much higher art than boxing. As a humble soldier and in his many public appearances, he has not posed, bragged or been affectedly modest. His simplicity is so genuine that at times it takes on various colors, such as wisdom or humor.

I recall a great U.S.O. mass meeting at Madison Square Garden during the war. Many celebrities appeared. While the audience hummed with recognition, dazzling motion picture actresses walked to the microphone and said trite things, such as "How glad I am to be here for this great cause." Then Joe Louis was introduced. I had expected that he would show himself, thank the audience, and walk off. Instead he stood fumbling for a moment in front of the microphone, and then spoke eleven words which became one of the most famous statements of the war. He said, "I know we will win, because we are on God's side."

I am not sure to this day whether or not this was an inspired mistake and whether he had intended to say, "God is on our side." In any event the distinction was so profound that it sounded the keynote of that evening which leading political figures, famous writers and speakers had failed to provide.

This incisive simplicity was once evidenced by another great Negro fighter. He was Sam Langford. Although he was never a champion, many experts consider him the peer of any fighter who ever lived. There are thrilling stories of his exploits: the time he hit Fireman Flynn so hard on the top of the head (as he was covering up his face) that he broke his ankle; or the time he chased a frightened opponent and hit him in the seat knocking him clear out of the ring. On one occasion when Langford was in San Francisco he was taken by Harry Hershfield to a restaurant on the evening preceding the fight. The owner, embarrassed by Langford's presence but awed by his prowess, decided to hide him and his white guest in the very last seat at the rear of the restaurant. Langford pretended not to notice. But when the bill was being paid, he kept searching among the toothpicks. The owner finally said, "Is there anything you want, Mr. Langford?" "I was just lookin' to see if you had a black toothpick," said the Negro quietly, and walked out.

The facility for expressive though simple phrasing gives Louis most unexpectedly a sense of humor. On one occasion he was invited to see the first motion picture showing of one of his fights. He declined saying, "I was there."

Prior to his second fight with Billy Conn a great discussion raged in the newspapers as to whether Conn's speed and cleverness would triumph over Louis' hitting. In their first fight Conn had been winning for thirteen rounds when Louis had finally crashed through an opening and knocked him out. Now sports column after sports column was filled with speculation as to whether Conn could evade Louis the full fifteen rounds and score enough points to take his title. Finally, a sports writer asked Louis his opinion of this matter. His reply in eight words has been added to ring lore as a classic comment. He said, "He can run away, but he can't hide."

This prediction turned out to be a perfect description of

the fight. Conn fled, but there were bright lights blazing over the squared arena. He couldn't hide. Louis found him in the eighth round and dispatched him to unconsciousness.

Unlike Jack Johnson, who had front gold teeth inserted to express affluence and whose wild life was a constant irritation to his people, Joe Louis has felt keenly the responsibility which a world's championship has placed upon his shoulders. Despite his profession, he is very sensitive, and the final measure of the man is his moving statement: "If I ever do anything to disgrace my people, I hope I die."

CHAPTER 25

George Jessel

YOU CAN'T EXPLAIN the talents of Jessel, who has been a composer of songs, a writer of plays, an actor on the legitimate stage, a singer, a comedian, and a toastmaster, simply by telling about his life. You can't, for example, explain Irving Berlin by telling how he began his career on the Bowery as a singing waiter. There are two thousand years of melody pouring out of Berlin even though he may not know the source. And you can't explain a George Gershwin, who had not even taken a music lesson at the time when he was writing undying melodies, by explaining his life in New York City. There are several thousand years of the cantor's art of singing which preceded Gershwin and which poured forth from him; and when he combined this melody with Negro rhythm, a new musical form was created. So you can only explain the versatility of talents of a Jessel by beginning his biography several thousand years ago.

You will notice, for example, that most Jewish comedians are also singers. There is a great tradition which explains that. To the Jews, music is the magic unity. It washes away from the soul the dust of everyday life. That is why Jessel is a singer. But you will also notice that he is not a comic singer as one might expect of a comedian. He sings sentimental and romantic songs. The trademark of his personality is a song called *My Mother's Eyes*. Here, too, there is a great tradition, the reverence for mother.

Sarah Bernhardt in her autobiography relates that in 1872 when she appeared for the first time in the Comédie Française in a play called *Mademoiselle de Belle Isle*, her mother as always was in the audience. Because of an impending heart attack her mother left a few minutes after the performance began and Sarah Bernhardt was so distraught that for four acts she performed miserably. Then when she was told that her mother was well she gave an ecstatic performance in the last, the fifth act. The next day the critics wrote that for four acts she was disappointing, but when she realized that her audience was bored she rose to magnificent heights in the last act. Little did they know that it was love for her mother which was responsible for the uneven performance.

When Jessel is through with his song he uses an imaginary telephone to talk to his mother whom he has just sentimentalized and in conversation with her throws barbs of satire and wit at the audience. This extraordinary gift of shifting instantly from tragedy to humor is also in a great tradition.

When Heine was on his death bed he gave instructions that his wife Mathilda should remarry as soon as possible. When his tearful companions asked why, Heine had to have his joke even though he was to die the next day. He said, "I want Mathilda to marry because then I will be sure that there will be at least one man who will regret my death."

Jessel is also a toastmaster of extraordinary felicity of expression and nimble-mindedness. There is historic precedent for this too, going back to the *badchen,* or the itinerant poet and singer, who was prevalent in the thirteenth century. The *badchen* was usually an erudite man who preached at weddings, but who also amused the audience by making extem-

poraneous rhymes and engaging in delightfully witty repartee
with guests. This gift of extemporizing, of original humor
which has come down through the centuries, is the source
of Jessel's skill.

Jessel is also an actor of great skill. John Golden said that
Jessel was the greatest natural actor he had ever seen, and
if you have seen him perform in the *War Song* and *The
Jazz Singer* you will recognize that he lives up to the precept
that the perfection of art is its concealment.

Thus we have all of these gifts combined pouring forth
richly from the sources of great tradition:

He is a comedian too witty to require preparation.

He is a singer too rhythmic to require a great voice.

He is an actor too natural to require technique.

He is a toastmaster too nimble-minded to require the inspiration of a dais.

He is a sentimentalist too steeped in tradition to require improvisation.

CHAPTER 26

Albert D. Lasker

HERE IS an extraordinary, true short story.

The hero was president of Lord & Thomas, one of the
largest and most successful advertising agencies in the world.
Years ago, he went to see a play. It was called *You Can't
Take It With You.* A year passed. One day he left his office
to go to lunch. On his desk were memoranda of telephone
calls to make and of important letters to write upon his
return from lunch. However, when he left the dining room,
a seed which had been sown in his mind when he saw *You
Can't Take It With You*, suddenly sprouted.

"Why am I doing all this?" he asked himself. "Why am I not devoting my time and energies to more important things?" He found himself walking away from the office and to his home. When he arrived there he said to his wife, "Mary, I'm never going back to that office!" When she recovered from the shock, she said wisely, "If you feel the same way a week from today, I'm for it."

He did feel that way a week later, and he never returned to his desk. Instead, he called his attorneys and accountants to his home and directed that the business be dissolved and its assets distributed among his associates. Even the name of Lord & Thomas was wiped out.

He had learned that just as there is no sound without someone to hear it, so a man's wealth is zero without someone to receive the benefit of it. He must spend it, give it away, express it in some way in order to have it. "Money," said Francis Bacon, "is like manure, of very little use except it be spread." It takes at least two to make a millionaire.

You can retire a man, but not his influence or his impress upon the times. By retiring from his labors, Albert Lasker has increased his influence, for one can preach a better sermon with his life than with his lips.

CHAPTER 27

Eleanor Roosevelt

IF BEING the first lady of the land meant submerging her opinions and her powerful personality to be celebrated solely for the prestige of the presidency, then Eleanor Roosevelt was not the first lady of the land.

If being the first lady of the land meant being calloused to the suffering of people and believing that injustice, bigotry and prejudice should be the concern of others, then she was not the first lady of the land.

If being the first lady of the land meant surrendering her right as a citizen to speak and write the truth as she saw it, then she was not the first lady of the land.

If being the first lady of the land meant being timid and having enough energy only to preside at cellophaned social functions, then she was not the first lady of the land.

But, if being the first lady of the land meant having the fortitude of Martha Washington, who spent eight winters with George Washington and his troops in the campaigns from 1776 to 1783; if it meant having the industry of Abigail Adams, who ran her own farm for ten years and climbed Penn's Hill to watch the Battle of Bunker Hill; if being the first lady of the land meant having the energy of Louisa Adams who, in the winter of 1814, crossed from Russia to France in a sled with her six-year-old son; if being the first lady of the land meant having the courage of Dolly Madison, the last woman to leave Washington when the White House was burned by hostile troops in 1814; if being the first lady of the land meant having the passion for justice which impelled Elizabeth Monroe personally to help Madame Lafayette escape from the terror of the French Revolution in 1795; in short, if being the first lady of the land means having the nobility of simplicity and the royalty of kindliness, then Eleanor Roosevelt was for twelve years the first lady of the United States.

There is something in great personalities which is challenging and when the challenge is directed to traditional beliefs and customs, not to speak of prejudices, it arouses violent reaction. How else is one to explain the way in which Lincoln was maligned? The attacks upon him were so vulgar that they would be censored even today for their abusiveness. Yet many of these vicious words appeared in important newspapers of his day.

Mrs. Roosevelt, who is gentleness personified, nevertheless has provoked similar animosity against herself. She has courageously championed the rights of the Negro. She has pleaded the cause of the underprivileged and nothing is more irritating to those with guilty consciences. They demand to know why she doesn't "mind her own damn business."

It happens to be a fact that she had made this her business thirty years before her husband became internationally famous. Mrs. Roosevelt's devotion to settlement work, correction of juvenile delinquency, economic betterment of poorly paid workers, and improvement of the miserable lot of Negroes, was no Albany mansion or White House-conscious activity. She had been immersed in this work since the early 1900's when no other motivation but idealism spurred her on. Can there be a better test of sincerity than the consistency of a lifetime of service? Even then she realized that unemployment is a terrible scourge not because the unemployed man is hungry but because he is nothing. His distress comes from the realization of his own unimportance. To wake up in the morning having nothing to do because there is nothing to do leads him to desperation. It corrodes his self-respect and gnaws at his ego. This is a process of demoralization far more dangerous even than hunger.

Yet time and again I have heard her charged with hypocrisy, meddling, tactlessness and, indeed, stirring up racial and labor troubles. Men who are temperate about vital matters which touch them go into uncontrollable paroxysms of hate at the mere mention of her name.

But no woman is more loved by the American people as a whole and no woman is more respected by the peoples of the world. She has grown in stature with the years. Her feeling for people seems to grow more intense and her vitality never fails to keep pace with the demands which she and others make upon herself. Her graciousness is not, as in the case of many famous people, a condescension to be humble despite high position. It is genuine kindliness and regard for others, no matter how lowly their estate.

One does not have to agree with all her views in order to appreciate her. Her noble spirit and sincere direction have evoked the admiration of millions of people throughout the world who need a friend in high place and who find that friendship in her. Water that flows from a spring does not congeal in winter. Sentiments which flow from the heart cannot be frozen by criticism.

As the American delegate to the United Nations Assembly in London and New York she has distinguished herself and carried on the tradition of moral leadership linked with the Roosevelt name. Her refusal to consider political office (the senatorship or governorship of New York State was a distinct possibility) demonstrated her determination not to capitalize on her husband's fame or turn her own into political preferment, despite the snide assertions of her enemies that this has been her main objective.

Like a finely bred mind which naturally makes sound decisions, or like a sensitive heart which instinctively reacts to evil (observe Toscanini's rejection of Mussolini and fascism when it was popular to recognize the "great man"), Mrs. Roosevelt's mind and heart have responded faithfully and truly to most great issues of our day. This has given her dignity in the finest sense of the word. It is an effortless and unconscious dignity. It is the dignity of highmindedness and devotion to principle. She is no longer the first lady of the land. She has become the first lady of the world.

CHAPTER 28

Frank Case

FRANK CASE was the owner of the Algonquin Hotel for forty-four years. He became as much a landmark in New York City as his hotel. His distinction as the author of several books was equal to that of his reputation as a hotel man.

I was not surprised to learn that he was an author. Many of the talents required for a good hotel man and author overlap. An author must have a sense of drama, a sense of suspense. So must a hotel man. All you have to do is read the menu at the Algonquin. You order Cuts Bordelais d'Esterhazy and sit back in suspense until you receive ham and eggs. Or you order Pomeranian Snow de la Terre and while you are licking your chops in expectation of an extraordinary, exotic dish you are served rice pudding.

There is also the talent for vivid description which is common to hotel men and authors. Fried chicken is never just fried chicken. It is golden brown, sun-toasted, crisp, delicious, saliva-prompting, juicy chicken, southern style, probably with marvelous sauce. They feed you adjectives and you pay according to the high rate per word of a distinguished author.

But above all, an author and a hotel man must have the ability to create an atmosphere. Whenever I ate at the Algonquin, I had the feeling that Frank Case, walking up and down the aisle, was the king of his domain and that I, amongst a few others, was his personal guest. He stopped at tables and bowed in a courtly and gracious manner. You would have to see a Frank Case bow to appreciate it. It was never so low that you forgot that he was the king. It was always low enough to give him just a touch of obsequiousness. In any event, encouraged by this atmosphere, you ordered lavishly and in accordance with your rights as a guest at a princely feast. But there came a time at the end of the dinner when the illusion was broken. One of the king's lackeys in a small white jacket began writing on a piece of cardboard. Then you looked up, hoping to catch the eye of your host who, up to this time, was ubiquitously present. You were sure that if you saw him he would tear the cardboard from the lackey's hands with indignation that one of his guests should be disturbed by such a triviality. But by a curious sense of timing, which was inexplicable to me, no living human being ever caught the eye of or saw Frank Case at such a critical moment. He vanished into thin air and there you were, left to your own resources. So you see, the qualities of dramatic suspense, vivid description and atmosphere make any good hotel man an author.

Frank Case had all the qualities of a gentleman in the most old-fashioned sense of the word. He was a friend of distinguished artists. His sincerity, wit and courtesy made him an equally distinguished figure in his own right. Despite his 70 years, he was handsomely erect, slim and young. His gaiety was harnessed to a benign natural dignity. One knew how he felt toward his wife, Bertha, when he repeated her witticisms with the appreciative laughter of a lover, not a raconteur. He was the kind of a husband who lays down the law to his wife and then accepts all her amendments.

But then his wife took desperately ill. He struggled to hide his grief, but one could measure her daily retrogression by the cloud of concern on his face. I stopped inquiring about her health because his answer was made with his tear-filled eyes. One day he seemed really cheerful. I knew Bertha was better. I dared to inquire about her health. "It is a miracle," he said, "but you would not believe me if I told you how it happened."

"Christian Science," I said promptly.

"Yes," he replied, somewhat relieved that I had not dragged the answer from him. But a week later, the medical bulletin on his face caused me to withhold the question. One month later she was dead.

It was as if a Siamese twin had died and the link with the other body doomed the survivor. Instantly his youthful appearance disappeared. His face acquired that peculiar gray-ivory colorlessness which is the announcement of death. He would not leave the hotel, for "Here I am not as lonely. I see all my friends."

He was stricken with a heart attack and lay motionless for weeks. When he returned his eyes had a curious, far-away look, as if they would say in H. G. Wells' recent awesome phrase: "Don't disturb me. Can't you see I am busy dying?" Two months later he was dead. One of the last courtly figures of our generation had passed to join his beloved.

CHAPTER 29

John Fulton Sheen

EXTRAORDINARY MEN often spring from ordinary parents. In a democracy distinguished leaders can seldom pattern their activities upon the achievements of their forebears. But I believe most men select spiritual ancestors from whom they derive inspiration. Thus writers and painters are usually influenced by some outstanding predecessor whom they hero worship. This is likewise true in the political realm. For example, I think that Winston Churchill followed in the great pathway of another Prime Minister of Great Britain, William Pitt. Pitt was also faced with a tyrant, Napoleon, who had conquered Europe and who stood poised to cross the English Channel to strike England down. England then, too, showed doggedness and high courage which confounded the military experts. It was William Pitt who said, "England has saved herself by her energy, now she must save Europe by her example."

Franklin Delano Roosevelt had a spiritual ancestor. He was Thomas Jefferson. If you were to sum up the pronouncements from Cairo, Teheran and Yalta, you could do so in the few simple words of Thomas Jefferson: "We mutually pledge to each other our lives, our property and our sacred honor."

Monseigneur Fulton Sheen also has a spiritual ancestor, literally as well as symbolically. He is St. Thomas Aquinas. St. Thomas was a writer, a lecturer, and the greatest scholastic philosopher his church ever produced. John Fulton Sheen is also a writer. He has written more than thirty books. He is a lecturer and, through the modern instrumentality of radio, he addresses millions of people each week on the Sunday Catholic Hour. Two million copies of his speeches have been distributed. He is the foremost religious and scholastic philosopher of his day and has for many years been professor of philosophy at Catholic University in Washington, D. C.

I find a curious fact in his background. His uncle was a lawyer and a partner of the famous atheist, Robert G. Ingersoll. I do not know whether it was his uncle who made the famous retort to Ingersoll on atheism but I should like to attribute it to him. It is said that Ingersoll was in a museum one day with his friend and admired a painting of a sky studded with stars and in which a bright moon lit up a turbulent sea. Ingersoll was fascinated: "What a magnificent painting this is," he said. "Who did it?" The gentleman next to him, who I hope was Monseigneur Sheen's uncle, replied, "Why, Bob, no one did it, it just happened." This was the classical reply to atheism.

The final incident in the life of the poet Shelley is full of appropriate meaning. He was living on the coast of Italy. One day he got into a boat with his friend Ned Williams to obtain some supplies from a nearby store. A squall came up and carried them out to sea. Two days later their bodies were washed up on the shore. Both were dead. At the age of twenty-nine the life of the great Shelley had been snuffed out. His distinguished friends, Byron and the writer Trelawney, rushed to Leghorn to take charge and decided to cremate his body. Trelawney wrote in his biography of Shelley that as his body was going up in flames, one part of it refused to burn. It seemed to be indestructible. It was Shelley's heart. Trelawney reached into the flames and snatched the heart from the burning pyre to save it for posterity.

What a magnificent symbol! For the past few years the body of civilization has been set aflame in the burning pyre of Europe. Just when it seemed that civilization was about to be destroyed, men of goodwill and religion snatched the indestructible heart from the flames to preserve it for the future of mankind. Fulton Sheen is one of the men who reached into the flames to preserve the future for us.

CHAPTER 30

Fiorello H. LaGuardia

LaGUARDIA PLAYED many roles. He appeared in many productions. Indeed, the critics said that his artistry was equalled only by his versatility. Perhaps you recall his first production after he became the star of New York City, Inc. The title of it was *Crime Doesn't Pay*. He played a James Cagney tough man role. In this production he smashed the food and other rackets. He reduced murders from fifty-four to six a year. He increased radio patrol cars by one hundred per cent. I recall a scene in that production in which our star addressed the Police Department and said: "I want you to put so much fear into the heart of every crook that when he meets a policeman he will tip his hat." The critics rightly hailed this performance as irresistible and vigorous.

Then in sharp contrast with this role he played a sort of Father Flanagan role in the production called *Boys' Town*. In this production he increased park playgrounds by fifty-seven per cent and recreational facilities by two hundred and seventy-three per cent. He wiped out slum districts and thus reduced juvenile delinquency by fifty per cent. He reduced fatal accidents to children by fifty per cent. Our star demonstrated that children are not inherently wicked; they are the victims of circumstance. The critics rightly hailed this performance as full of understanding and compassion.

Then do you remember *I Want Wings* played at LaGuardia Airport? This production began with a comic scene. Our star was riding in a plane from Chicago to New York. The plane landed in Newark. All the passengers got out as they should, but our star remained seated. In his best bland, comic manner and in a high-pitched voice (something like, let's say, Costello's, of Abbott and Costello) he said: "My ticket says 'New York' and I want to be taken to New York." Do you recall how the aviation officials registered resentment, then bewilderment, and finally surrendered? This lone passenger was flown to New York. The impetus of that drive did not stop until our star had constructed, at the cost of forty million dollars, the largest airport in the world, from which two hundred and sixty planes, carrying three thousand passengers, leave daily. You will recall the sentimental ending of that picture. The airport was named in honor of our star as a tribute to his foresight and zeal.

Then do you recall his role in that great scientific picture, *Pasteur?* In this production he reduced infant mortality rates to the lowest in the history of this city. He instituted a twenty-four-hour anti-pneumonia service which reduced pneumonia deaths by fifty per cent. He provided for a mass X-ray drive in which 325,000 X-ray photographs were taken, which reduced tuberculosis by twenty-five per cent. He built fourteen new health centers. He purified the milk. He constructed a new water system from the Delaware River, the largest engineering feat of its kind. In this production he demonstrated that our very lives are dependent upon good government.

Then *Goodbye, Mr. Chips.* In this production our star built sixty-seven new schools and two hundred and sixty-two playgrounds costing millions of dollars. He built vocational guidance schools and special schools for music and art, a novelty in education. Like Benjamin Franklin, he knew that if you pour your purse into your head no one can take it away from you. He knew that boys will be boys and more important, that boys will be men.

Yes, and he appeared in the first anti-Nazi picture. You recall the dramatic scene in which he suggested that a chamber of horrors should be constructed at the World's Fair to represent Hitler and his Brown Shirts properly. There was

an apology by the State Department for that statement. As
the plot ironically developed later, the State Department
looked into our star's ample vocabulary in order to express
more adequately its own condemnation and resentment of
the very "statesman" to whom it had previously apologized.
Later we had *Mr. Smith Goes To Washington.* When the
United States Corporation decided to produce the greatest
epic of all time, called *Civilian Defense,* and it sought a star
of sufficient magnitude to carry such a vehicle, we had to
lend LaGuardia to it. There were some minority stockhold-
ers who expressed a grievance about this, overlooking the
fact that our star received not one cent of compensation
for his extra service and that he rendered it to a holding
corporation in which we all had equal shares.

I could, of course, tell you of some of the short subjects
our star made. For example, there is the travelogue in which
he took you through the city, showing you the many aque-
ducts, bridges and roads which have been constructed. You
know how these end: "And as the sun sets we reluctantly
take leave of the Holland Tunnel." Or there was the serial
he made in which each episode left you breathlessly suspended as our hero rushed to a fire.

While we are in this candid mood I may confess to you
that our star, like most stars, had a great deal of tempera-
ment. We had our trouble with him. He tore up the script;
he left the lot once or twice. Was it not Burke who said that
"a vigorous mind is as sure to be accompanied by passion
as fire is by heat"? But these minor difficulties we had with
him shrink to proper insignificance when you realize that
before he joined our company it was on the verge of bankruptcy. We had assigned all our assets to the banks and our
bonds were selling far below par. Today our corporation has
prospered. We have paid off the banks and made new loans
at low rates of interest. Above all, he gave distinction, dignity
and prestige to our company, New York City, Inc.

His versatility not only made him a radio commentator
and UNRRA chief but also was the key to all his talents.

He was a showman. We should appraise his flair for show-manship more highly than we do.

When the historians of the future analyze the great international tragedy through which we have passed they are likely to find that the profession of public relations has deep roots. Dictators have used the art of dramatization to create a public acceptance of evil. Intellectuals and men of executive capacity permitted them to have a monopoly of this art because they considered it beneath their own dignity. But I think we have realized that the art of drama-tization belongs peculiarly to a democracy because democracy functions best when public opinion is aroused and active. In other words, showmanship should be used to support decency instead of evil. Several democratic leaders have realized this. President Roosevelt practiced it. Prime Min-ister Churchill understood and used it. One of the pioneers in this field was LaGuardia.

Thus when he was a Congressman and fought the Volstead Act single-handedly (incidentally, it was always his lot to fight for causes before they became popular) he did not issue stuffy pronunciamentos about the infringement of personal rights. Rather he notified the prohibition authorities that in violation of their regulations he was going to appear at a specified time and place in New York City and mix near beer and malt extract, each of which was legal, defying the authorities to prevent these liquids, when combined, from achieving a high alcoholic content. He did this while news-reel cameras clicked. The story went throughout the country and its moral did not go unobserved.

When he wanted to have Congress do something about food profiteering he did not write a speech for the *Congres-sional Record* inserting conveniently the words "applause" and "laughter." Instead, he appeared one day in Congress with two lamb chops which he placed upon the Congres-sional desk and announced their price. The story aroused public opinion and Congress had to take action.

When he ran for Congress against Henry Frank and

Tammany, a few days before election, issued 50,000 circulars charging that LaGuardia was anti-Semitic, he did not issue pious assertions about his love of minorities. Instead he challenged his adversary to debate the subject, imposing only one condition: that both speak Yiddish. Mr. Frank, despite his origin, had not acquired mastery of that tongue as had LaGuardia, a former interpreter at Ellis Island. Frank failed to appear. LaGuardia had a one-sided debate and won a one-sided election.

When he was elected mayor and wanted to eliminate the slot machine racket, he did not issue formalistic statements against gambling. Instead, he appeared one morning in Magistrate's Court, acted as magistrate, convicted the manufacturers of the slot machines and freed the storekeeper. His announcement of the millions of dollars mulcted from citizens by this racket appeared on the front pages of the newspapers. The stores had to throw out the machines.

Indeed, LaGuardia even dramatized the fact that a mayor, if he is active, will make mistakes and that no higher standard should be expected of a public official than of a president of any other large corporation. So when his attention was called to an appointment which he had made which had not worked out very happily, his answer was, "When I make a mistake it's a beaut."

Illustration could be added to illustration, but the point is that LaGuardia did not hesitate to use the art of dramatization in order to obtain public support for decent government, thus enabling him to defy political machines and remain mayor for twelve years. He was a jumbo banner—a 24-sheet—a 22 by 28—a 40 by 60—a herald—an insert—a streamer—a broadside—a billboard—an electrical marquee—and a teletype news flash—all rolled into one. It is good once in a while to see the showmanship method used to overcome demagogues and to arouse the public against scoundrels. Al Smith practiced the art brilliantly. LaGuardia was its most recent exponent.

CHAPTER 31

Five Women

EDNA FERBER
DOROTHY FIELDS
MARIAN ANDERSON
BERNICE FITZ-GIBBON
ELLIN BERLIN

WHEN GREEK civilization dominated the western world there was a myth about the creation of the world and of man which differed from the story in the Bible.

The Greeks believed that originally there was no earth, water or air but that there was an inchoate mass over which reigned a Greek god called Chaos. Then the earth was separated and the Greek god Terror presided over it. Thereafter man was fashioned in clay and the spirit of life was blown into his nostrils.

The Greek gods proceeded to create woman. Jupiter called all the gods together on Mount Olympus in solemn conclave. There they fashioned a woman. Then each of the gods bestowed upon her a special gift. She was called Pandora, the gift of all the gods. Apollo bestowed upon her the gift of music. Minerva bestowed upon her the gift of wisdom and compassion. Mercury conferred persuasion. Vesta bestowed upon her love of family and home. The Muses, Erato and Thalia, conferred upon her wit and lyricism.

This year five American women were awarded golden keys in token of their position as outstanding women in their respective endeavors. It is wise to honor women. They have a feeling of immortality because they produce life, whereas men have a feeling of frustration because they are unable to give birth to anything but ideas. The committee which made the awards may not have realized that there was an association between its choices and the Greek myth. But it must have been Apollo who conferred the gift of music upon Marian Anderson. It must have been Minerva who bestowed wisdom and compassion upon Edna Ferber, for men have sight but women have insight. Surely it was Mercury who gave the gift of persuasion to Bernice Fitz-Gibbon. Vesta must have given the love of family and home to Ellin Berlin, and the Muses Erato and Thalia must be responsible for the wit and lyricism of Dorothy Fields. When all these precious gifts are combined, it appears that the committee selected in five key women but one woman after all. Her name is Pandora.

CHAPTER 32

Maurice Rose

I SHALL NOT begin with his birth in Connecticut in 1890. I shall go further back on the theory of the noted educator who was asked, "When is the best time to begin the education of a child?" He said, "With the grandfather."

So I begin with General Maurice Rose's grandfather. He was a learned rabbi of extraordinary spiritual insight. His son, Samuel Rose, following in the tradition of the family, also became a rabbi and for ninety-one years served the community of Denver, Colorado, where he settled when his son Maurice was only three years old.

It is natural that with this environment Maurice Rose should have been prepared in his childhood for a spiritual career. He studied in the Talmud Torah and received a profound basic education in the Bible. Yet is it not extraor-

dinary that from this background, where the greeting was
the traditional Hebrew word *shalom,* meaning peace, there
should have emerged, in the words of General Eisenhower
himself, one of the foremost combat generals of the second
World War? I don't believe that this was merely some perverse trick. I should like to think that Maurice Rose in his
youth read the prophecy in the Bible that some day a great
sword would be forged to be placed in the hands of the
righteous with which to strike down the enemy of mankind.
For how else can one explain the fact that at the early age
of fifteen. Maurice Rose ran away from home to enlist in
the Colorado National Guard? He was of course mustered
out when it was discovered that he was too young. In 1917,
when the first World War broke out, Maurice Rose enlisted,
was sent to Camp Funston, Kansas, for officer's training and
was graduated as a second lieutenant. Then he went overseas
to engage in thirteen months of hard combat. He distinguished himself by his extraordinary bravery and was decorated after being wounded.

At this time a great tragedy struck the home of Rabbi
Rose. In 1917 on a Friday night while Maurice's mother was
saying the benediction over lighted candles, a telegram was
received from the War Department advising that Maurice
Rose had been killed in action. A wave of sympathy for the
household swept the community. Rabbi Rose and his family
sat in mourning for a week, the traditional *shivah.* Then, at
the end of the week, when the formal bereavement had
ended, a miracle occurred. A courier announced that
Maurice Rose was not dead, that he was alive and would
soon return to his family.

When Maurice Rose returned a young hero, he did not
wish to be mustered out like millions of other soldiers. He
chose instead to re-enlist and to make the army his profession.
Somewhere in the recesses of his mind there must have been
a consciousness that the great sword of righteousness was
still to be forged to strike down the enemies of civilization.
He specialized in mechanized tank warfare, thus demonstrat-

ing a foresight which very few military men in those days possessed. So for twenty-three years he studied the arts of tank maneuver and mechanized warfare. He grew to full maturity, six feet, two inches tall, a handsome soldier, self-confident in his specialized knowledge, daring and beloved by his men.

Then, in 1941, when the dark clouds of treachery blotted out the sun over our beautiful country, he was ready, a mighty sword in his hand. By that time he had become the executive officer of the First Armored Division, stationed at Fort Benning, Georgia. He was sent to North Africa, where he distinguished himself immediately by his courage, resourcefulness and skill. He was always at the front of his troops. I shall tell you only one of many incidents about him. On one occasion his tank corps was under an artillery barrage. A shell exploded near him, and he and five of his men were wounded. All were placed on stretchers to be taken to the hospital behind the lines. But he regained consciousness before he could be removed and he insisted that the shrapnel be removed from his shoulder then and there so that he could continue to lead his men into battle. Upon his unwavering command, the shrapnel was removed and he was permitted to lead his men to victory. These were no heroics on his part; as he put it simply, "I must be up front so that I will know what to do."

Later he led the attack in Sicily, where it fell to him to give the terms of unconditional surrender to General Beroweitz, the Nazi commander of the opposing forces. Then came his great achievements in Normandy. Eisenhower and Marshall have both stated that he was one of the foremost combat officers and most responsible for the great breakthrough in Normandy. He drove the Nazis before him like a fury.

I make no pretense. No other inspiration was necessary for General Rose's achievements than his devotion to our beloved country. Yet I can't help but feel that in the complexity of his feelings, which expressed itself in a unique personal recklessness and dauntless spirit, there must have been the realization that the Nazis had killed six million European Jews. Somewhere in his mind's eye, there must have been the picture of patriarchial Jews, their wives and children, for whom his father had prayed, being crowded into boxcars and lime poured over them, so that their faces were eaten away and they arrived at their destination standing corpses. Somewhere in the recesses of his mind, he must have filed the picture of Borosov, a town near which his grandfather was born, where thirty thousand Jewish men, women, and children were lined up by the Nazis, forced to dig their own graves, mowed down by machine guns, and then buried even though some of them were still alive and the graves heaved! Somewhere in the back of his mind must have been the recollection that his heroic forebears, the Maccabeans, did not consider their victory against overwhelming odds to be a miracle. For God's law provided that when a people's culture has been assailed and they are willing to lay down their lives for it, God will deliver "the strong into the hands of the weak, the many into the hands of the few, the impure into the hands of the pure, the wicked into the hands of the righteous, and the impudent into the hands of the lawful."

Yes, to him was given the sword of righteousness with which to strike down the Nazi beast. Justice moves in curious ways its wonders to perform. A remarkable destiny dictated that General Rose should have been the first invading general since Napoleon to set foot on German soil; that he should have been the first soldier of the Allies to capture a German town; that he should have been the first soldier to smash the allegedly impregnable Siegfried Line and thus make possible the inundation of all of Germany by the Allied troops.

Then came March 31, 1945, a fateful day. Once more he was actually in front of his troops, inspecting the ground upon which the tank battle would be pitched. He was trapped by a Nazi tank unit. Instead of being captured according to the rules of warfare, he was brutally murdered by the Nazis.

A wave of horror and indignation at this atrocity swept the United Nations. In Denver, Colorado, Maurice Rose's parents for the second time sat *shivah* and mourned the death of their son. There was no venom in the heart of Rabbi Rose. When asked for a statement, he said, "No man dies too young who dies to protect the liberty of our country." This was practically the last statement of this patriarch. Shortly thereafter, he died and joined his son.

But now for a second time a miracle has occurred. America has heard that Maurice Rose is not dead. He is alive. No, this time it is not an error on the part of the War Department; it is a miracle created by the affection and love of his soldiers and his fellow citizens. They have raised more than $700,000 to erect a Maurice Rose Hospital in Denver in his honor. He will live on through this monument of healing. Now that the sword of righteousness has done its duty in striking down the evil-doers, it will be turned into a scalpel of mercy. All who have contributed to this monument are participating in the new miracle. This is our lasting tribute to a great American.

CHAPTER 33

Alben Barkley

THE SENATE has given us our foremost statesmen during emergencies. We shall never forget William Pinckney, Senator from Maryland, who said, "The free man is he who does not fear to go to the end of his thought." Nor Daniel Webster, Senator from Massachusetts, who said, "A constitutional statesman is a man of common opinions and uncommon abilities." Nor John C. Calhoun, Senator from South Carolina, who said, "Those who expect to reap the blessings of freedom must, like men, undergo the fatigue of supporting it." During the greatest emergency in our history, fate decreed that we should have a great leader in the Senate. He was a worthy successor to the distinguished statesmen who have graced our senior deliberative assembly.

Senator Barkley has been engaged in political activities for many years and yet I cannot call him a politician. He knows that there are two sides to every question, whereas a politician thinks there are two sides to every office, an inside and an outside. The politician knows that the unborn have no votes and, since posterity can do nothing for him, he does not see why he should do anything for posterity. Senator Barkley is concerned with the future as well as the present. The politician thinks that in a political discussion, heat should be in inverse proportion to knowledge. Senator Barkley realizes that reason must predominate in argument. Surely he does not fit Cato's famous couplet about the politician who "makes his own little laws and sits attentive to his own applause."

Senator Barkley is a progressive, not because he is always ready to move, but because he is a man who knows where he is going when he moves. I believe he understands that the art of statesmanship is to change a nation from what it is into what it ought to be.

CHAPTER 34

Ted Lewis

TED LEWIS is not merely a man. He is an institution. It is a remarkable institution. It has hands, supple, graceful hands which curve like a snake-charmer's to project you into the world of relaxation. This institution has a black instrument in its mouth from which emanate high, always incredibly higher, notes. The head of the institution leans

back and the instrument sprays the air with joy. This institution has legs. They are bent legs, probably because of the
weight of the music above. If I were not wiser I might say
they are bandy legs. But these legs move rhythmically. They
seem distorted, as if you were looking at them through
water. This institution has a hat. It is a high hat. But it is not
prosperous and silky; it is battered and broken. Yet it sits
defiantly and jauntily upon the top of this institution's head
as if to say, "I have seen better days but I am very content
with my lot."

Occasionally words come out of the mouth of this institution. They haven't much meaning. For example, I have
never heard anyone ask this institution a question and yet it
is constantly saying, "Yes suh!" It implies that it is being
asked whether it is deliriously happy and there is a constant
affirmation. Sometimes, as if continuing this one-sided conversation, it asks a question, "Is everybody happy?" Then,
without waiting for an answer in this one-sided repartee,
the hat becomes jauntier, the wrists become more supple,
the instrument reaches higher tones of joy, and the legs
wave rhythmically, as if to give assurance that the answer
must be "Yes."

He expresses our aspirations for escape from worry to a
world of joy, music and romance! This is the reason why
Ted Lewis has for thirty years been a leader in his profession.
This is the reason why, although vaudeville is supposed to be
dead, he continues to be engaged fifty-two weeks each year.
This is the reason why he is an institution.

Have you illness in your family and are you worried?
Well, look at that hat. It speaks to you. It says, "Happiness
or unhappiness depends on *how* you meet events, not on the
events themselves."

Have you had business reverses and have they caused you
anxiety? Well, look at that clarinet. It speaks to you. It says,
"Happiness depends not on how much you have, but on
how much you enjoy!"

Have you lost money in the stock market and are you

depressed? Well, look at those gracefully curving fingers.
They speak to you. They say, "A laugh is worth a thousand
groans in any market."

Are you lonely and therefore despondent? Well, look at
that twirling stick. It speaks to you. It says, "To have joy
you must share it. Happiness was born a twin."

Are you unnerved by the barbarities and cruelties of war,
by the helplessness of refugees, by the bickerings among
the victorious nations? Well, then look at those legs. They
speak to you, too. They say, "There are two rules for being
happy. One is never to vex yourself about those things which
cannot be helped; the second rule is never to vex yourself
about those things which can be helped." We will resist to
the bitter end the forces of darkness around us, but we can
best resist them if there is optimism in our hearts and joy
on our lips.

And so, our despondencies, our fears and our anxieties
are removed by that dauntless, gay and musical figure, Ted
Lewis. For he, "Doc" Sunshine, knows that a sunbeam can
pass through a hundred bosoms without losing a particle
of its ray. Indeed, if it meets a responding heart it will reflect itself two-fold, as from a convex mirror.

Because he transports us by a process of self-hynotism into
a happier realm, Ted Lewis has become an institution. And
now, after a quarter of a century of asking us, "Is everybody
happy?" he is entitled to an answer. Yes, we are happy for we
have always known that there is happiness in duty, but it is
you who have reminded us that there is also a duty to be
happy.

CHAPTER 35

Harley M. Kilgore

DEMOCRACY IS a substance, not a form. It is a philosophy which adjusts itself to changing conditions. The best evidence of the virility of our democracy is the manner in which it has developed to cope with the complexities of modern life. There was a day, for example, when the two chief requirements of a United States Senator were distinguished bearing and eloquence. But today a United States Senator is required to be a specialist and so democracy has developed a new technique. It is the Senate investigating committee. I should like to call it a scientific laboratory for fact finding. It has come into high estate, and is not regarded like the old committees which kept minutes but wasted hours.

These committees came into vogue only at the turn of the century because of the necessities of modern complex government. The Senate and the country had to have the facts. You may remember Senator Thomas Walsh's investigation which resulted in the exposé of the Teapot Dome scandal. You may recall the Senate Banking Investigating Committee, of which Judge Ferdinand Pecora was counsel, which resulted in the Securities Act of 1933 and the Securities and Exchange Act of 1934. You may recall Senator Hugo Black's investigation of public utility lobbyists, which resulted in the Registration Act of 1935. You may recall the Senate Banking Investigating Committee whose work resulted in the Investment Company Act of 1940. Surely you will recall Senator Truman's committee investigating frauds and incompetence in the war effort, of which committee Senator Kilgore was a brilliant member. Public recognition

of its fine work resulted in a unique expression of confidence
by the American people in its chairman.

And now there is Senator Kilgore's committee dealing
with the German problem. Already its revelations have made
a substantial contribution to public information. Its work
is in the best tradition of the new technique of democracy.
It is not too much to say that the work of this committee
may do much to save the next generation of Americans from
destruction. To be a chemist one must study chemistry; to be
a physician or a lawyer one must study medicine or law;
to be a politician one must study the public interest. I hope
the public will give recognition to the head of a new laboratory of fact finding: Senator Harley M. Kilgore!

CHAPTER 36

Sidney Hillman

THERE HAVE BEEN several great figures in the
history of American labor. Uriah Stephens, a poor Phila-
delphia tailor, organized the Knights of Labor in the 1870's.
This was the first labor organization in the United States.
It was a secret society with secret rituals, for in those days
labor activity was not publicly accepted. The Knights of
Labor grew to a membership of three quarters of a million
in 1886.

Then another gigantic figure in labor history strode upon
the horizon. He was Samuel Gompers. He broke away from
the Knights of Labor with his Cigar Makers' International
Union to organize the American Federation of Labor. He
led American labor for thirty-six years. Those were the days
when the right to strike and to picket had to be won in
crude combat and when the demand for an eight-hour day
seemed very radical. Gompers despised political action. "Put

not your trust in politicians and political action," he often said.

In 1893 another great labor leader entered the scene. He was Eugene V. Debs, who organized the American Railway Union in Chicago. He was the first to associate labor rights with political action and when he ran for president in 1920 he polled a million votes.

After labor had stormed the ramparts of its elementary rights and had won them, there followed a legislative era led by the LaFollettes, the Norrises, the LaGuardias and the Wagners. Then the stage was set for a new kind of labor leader, one who could abandon the rough-and-tumble tactics and apply statesmanship to the new high estate in which labor found itself.

It fell to Sidney Hillman to fulfil this new great role. As early as March, 1912, he brought the "impartial chairman" idea into labor relations. It was a revolutionary technique for it made strikes unnecessary by substituting judicial decision for economic force. It was Hillman who developed Judge Brandeis' idea of a preferential union shop. In the 1920's he smashed racketeering within his union. Labor disgraces no man, but some men have occasionally disgraced labor.

His Amalgamated Clothing Workers of America was the first union to lend large sums of money to employers to aid them in distressing times. It was his union which organized two of the first four labor banks in 1922 and 1923; and it was he who pioneered in the creation of production standards as an aid both to management and labor.

Then came national and governmental recognition of his activities. He was appointed to the Labor Advisory Board of the NRA by President Roosevelt. In 1936 he organized the Committee for Industrial Organization. Most important of all, when President Roosevelt in May, 1940, foresaw that production would ultimately win the war, he appointed a National Defense Commission composed of Stettinius, Knudson and Hillman. There followed the great miracle

of American production which overwhelmed the foreign
tyrants.

In the excitement of the emergency, perhaps we did not
realize the full significance of the partnership between labor
and management on a national scale. We preserved democracy because the reputedly natural enemies, workers and
employers, learned that they were after all citizens of one
nation whose safety and prosperity safeguarded their mutual
welfare.

Ever since then, Hillman has been the symbol not only of
the strength of labor, but also of its responsibility. Dema-
goguery and recklessness were not in his arsenal. He scorned
John L. Lewis' methods because they were deliberately designed to arouse passion and ill feeling, the better to attain
an objective. He particularly disapproved Lewis' reckless
disregard of the nation's welfare and of his exploitation of
national peril to win a victory for his miners' union. Such
special pleading had its temporary advantage, but it injured
the cause of all labor.

In general, Hillman decried strikes as wasteful and injuri-
ous to the economy of the nation. He employed the industrial court with an impartial chairman acting as judge to
avoid industrial warfare. How well he succeeded can be
gleaned from the fact that in fifteen years there has not been
a strike in the garment industry. Even during the post-war
wave of strikes, the most notable exception was this huge
industry which went its peaceful way through arbitration
of disputes.

However, he sought to make labor a political power too.
This made him an open target for attack in the political
arena. Thus he was suddenly lifted out of the comparative
calm of union leadership to the fierce combat of national
politics. But he had learned in early union struggles that
you do not get rid of your temper by losing it. He preserved
a calm and almost philosophical attitude toward vitupera-
tion, which diminished its effectiveness.

When Bevin and Molotov were exchanging violent words

at the London conferences. Hillman shook his head dolefully and said, "International disputes must be settled in a friendly way. It must be done by arbitration, and this I know something about. You can't have the disputants making public speeches at one another. They must conduct conferences privately and without fear that a concession will be blown up by the press to be a surrender. The trouble with international conferences today is that they use the Lewis demagogic method (he never missed a chance to denounce Lewis) instead of the Roosevelt method of 'give and take' to preserve peace."

Experts in international affairs have stressed this point. The Wilsonian ideal was to have "open covenants openly arrived at," but there are considerations of expediency which challenge this method. A significant analogy is that of the editorial board of a newspaper. It meets to determine policy. There are sharp differences of opinion. When the private debate has been resolved, the editorial expresses the view which prevailed at the argument. The newspaper has spoken its collective mind. Often its position may greatly affect public opinion and governmental conduct. But the readers are not admitted into the inner sanctum to learn about the struggle which took place in reaching the editorial position. If such internal debates were reported for all to read, there would often be confusion rather than clarity. Similarly in large business affairs the board of directors resolves within its own group the differences which may exist, no matter how acrimonious. The decision represents a unified expression in the company's name.

It is not necessary to revert to secret diplomacy. Merely the preliminary conferences should be held off the record. When agreement has been reached or for that matter when disagreement is unavoidable, the public should be fully informed of the respective positions of the parties. Then public opinion can properly bring its decisive weight to bear upon the issues. The democratic process is enhanced thereby. Full play is given to the possibility of compromise and agreement without the embarrassment of national passions. Then the announcement of unity can receive the blessings of public approval; or the announcement of disagreement can be subjected to the pressures of mass judgment. It is unnecessary purism to insist that even the bickerings and oft-times intemperate processes of original search for common ground should be submitted to the public ear.

No one who has participated in an ordinary business conflict among executives can fail to be impressed with the part that personal egoism and pride in opinion play in freezing mental attitudes. Few men can rise above their own mistakes while under fire. Lawyers who guide such conferences know how important it is to prevent a position from being taken too early for, once announced, the possibility of receding from it is often insuperable. A tactful interpolation which assumes that an opponent's position was never different and therefore does not require concession, will often save the day. Many businessmen, like other negotiators, are less concerned with the point they yield than with the face they lose in yielding it. This proposition is often exploited in reverse. An adversary will deliberately ask for more than is expected in the hope that by magnanimity in withdrawing the request an obligation of reciprocal "large-mindedness" will be created. No matter how expressed, the point is the same. It is the recognition that agreement is best reached in negotiation when neither side suffers a "defeat." This point is magnified tenfold when an audience is present which has an interest in the dispute. Then the danger is greatest of posturing, of cheap displays of loyalty by being uncompromising and of name-calling and wild accusation to please the combative instincts of the audience. In short, such conferences are likely to degenerate to the lowest common denominator of self-interest and bias.

Hillman knew how necessary it was for union representatives to be unfettered by such restrictions. It was sometimes impossible to serve the workers best when shop committees sat as spectators at the negotiations. Then a satiric barb at the employers would be rewarded by appreciative laughter and applause which would put a higher price upon besting an adversary with cleverness than upon coming to agreement. Often the public sessions were bitter while representatives suggested, in private discussion, that concession would be made "if the excuse for it" could be created.

Lawyers customarily begin conferences of opposing factions by announcing that all discussions are "without prejudice," that is, that they are off the record and that no one will ever mention in court or otherwise what was said. The inhibitions having been thus removed, the litigants will say what is really on their minds. They will not be as wary about making admissions or revealing their objectives. The conference can therefore come to grips with the real issues.

International conferences require all these aids. A terrible handicap is placed on statesmen when we report their every word through the press of the world. All comments must then be guarded lest they be misinterpreted or misunderstood or, sometimes, lest they be correctly understood. For it is important that a nation be encouraged bluntly to state its selfish demand without fear of public exposure, rather than be compelled to adopt a hypocritical public pose of pursuing principle.

We do not think off-the-record press conferences with our President are undemocratic. There are cautions which must be adopted even in disclosing information to our newspapermen. We ought not think that preliminary off-the-record talks in the international sphere are wicked connivings. It is one thing to keep the public in the dark as to what their representatives are agreeing to. It is another to aid the process of agreement by encouraging private talks, free from extremisms of nationalism, patriotism, prejudice and suspicion.

In the final analysis, Hillman's greatest contribution will be found to be the recognition of these facts in labor negotiations. It led to the outlaw of economic war; substitution of arbitration for strikes; recognition that force is not a proper criterion, whether it is in the employers' hands or in the employees' hands; subordination of "class struggle" between the employers and workers to the welfare of the nation; recognition that in the preservation of democracy and the general prosperity of all lies the real safety of unionism and the workers.

A skeptic once said that another man's money is capital and that trying to take it away from him is labor. In the new era of capital-labor relationship we will recognize the profundity of Lincoln's belief that there can be no capital without labor and that harmony between them is essential to the preservation of both.

CHAPTER 37

Jack Benny

MOST VILLAINS on the stage or screen are sweet and gentle people in real life. This paradox holds true of radio comedians. Take, for instance, Jack Benny. The radio Jack Benny walks with long steps in order to save shoe leather. The radio Jack Benny differs from a canoe because a canoe sometimes tips. The radio Jack Benny inspired the slow-motion picture when the inventor saw Benny reaching for a check. The radio Jack Benny looks over his glasses in order not to wear them out The definition of silence as given on the radio is Jack Benny whistling for a cab. The radio Jack Benny would rather be tight than President. He has pernicious anemia in the seat of his ambition. The radio Jack Benny does not spend money to restore his hair. He sells his brush and comb.

But the real Jack Benny is a generous and warm-hearted American. The real Jack Benny toured the Mediterranean and Pacific areas for the U.S.O., once performing for an hour and a half in a temperature of 140 degrees. The real Jack

Benny has been given an award for his service to the betterment of race relations. So there are two Jack Bennys, and
we revel in his split personality.

CHAPTER 38

Robert E. Sherwood

SINCE THERE IS always a great man behind a
great pen, it is not surprising that great writers have repeatedly abandoned mere literary pursuits to fight for great
causes.

John Milton believed in liberty. He interrupted the writing of *Paradise Lost* to fight bigotry and tyranny, and joined
the Puritans in their struggle against the Stuart monarchy.

Tom Paine believed in liberty. After writing the pamphlet
Common Sense he joined George Washington and his struggling army on their retreat from Fort Lee. His unshod feet
left blood stains on the snow.

Walt Whitman believed in liberty. At the age of forty-two,
he gave up his writing to become an army nurse in the
Civil War. His biographers report that he nursed more than
100,000 wounded soldiers before returning to his poetry.

You will recall Lord Byron, whose dreamy poetic work
about Childe Harold still stirs visions of his sensitive pale
face, gray eyes and brown curly hair, who sailed for Greece
to fight for her freedom, and who died at the early age of
thirty-six uttering the sentiment, "If Greece should fall I
would bury myself in the ruins."

You will recall Voltaire, who toyed good-naturedly with
his enemies. When he fought the medical profession, he said:
"A physician is a person who pours drugs of which he knows
little into a body of which he knows less." His attitude
toward his adversaries was summed up in his statement that

he had only one prayer: "O God, make my enemies ridiculous," and he claimed God had granted his request.

Yet when Voltaire, while in Italy, learned that Jean Calas had been killed on the rack on a false charge that he had murdered his son for turning Catholic, he devoted his life to freeing the family of Calas from persecution. He became a furious fighter, detested by the mob, but he won posthumous justice for Calas and his family. When Voltaire died there appeared on his tombstone no mention of his great works as a writer, but the simple inscription: "The Defender of Jean Calas."

There was Emile Zola who was so timid a man that he shed tears when he saw blood from a scratch and who writhed in agony when his pet cat was ill. Yet this great artist at the age of sixty, retired, rich with honors as well as money, suddenly turned into a demoniacal fighter against the injustice to Dreyfus, risking his own life. He was burned in effigy. Crowds stormed his home and threw rocks at his windows. He was humiliated and debased at the trial but he persisted, saying, "He who suffers for truth and justice, becomes august and sacred." He died not merely a great writer but, as Anatole France said, "He was a moment in the conscience of mankind."

There was Tagore, a great poet, born of aristocratic family, whose piercing black eyes and white silken beard gave him a Christ-like appearance; a man whose sensitivity can be judged by his statement, "Every child proves that God is not discouraged with Man." Yet when he determined to fight for India's independence, he threw aside his poetic pen, surrendered the knighthood which had been conferred upon him by England and fought to the end, dying with the statement, "O God, give me the strength not to bend my knee before insolent might."

In our day another great writer, playwright and screen writer, three times a Pulitzer Prize winner, abandoned his literary ivory tower to become chief of the Office of War Information. Here he learned that we can send a message around the world in one-seventh of a second but that it takes months to get an idea through one-quarter of an inch of the human skull. He also acted as collaborator with a great President in some of the greatest war documents ever written. Just as Milton wrote that he "left a calm and pleasing solitariness to embark in a troubled sea of noises and disputes"; just as Tom Paine wrote, "These are times that try men's souls"; just as Walt Whitman wrote "Where liberty draws not the blood out of slavery, there slavery draws the blood out of liberty"; so Robert Sherwood believes that where democracy does not draw the blood out of bigotry, there bigotry will draw the blood out of democracy. Robert E. Sherwood is America's most prominent emigré from the ivory tower.

CHAPTER 39

Belle Baker

IT IS CUSTOMARY in describing an author to relate his life to the books he has written. If one describes a composer, the description can be based upon the symphonies he has composed. I shall describe the life of Belle Baker in terms of the songs she has sung.

Rag-Time Rosy. This is the period of her life when she is ten years old. She is dodging truant officers, selling newspapers on the East Side, and pulling threads in a shirtwaist factory to support an impoverished mother. But such are the vagaries of life that upon this strange little girl with huge black eyes an extraordinary gift has been conferred, one which is given to only one in millions. She has a voice and she warbles all day. The men in the shop wag their bearded heads as they hear her sing and say, "That little girl is incomparable." For they know that although God gives speech to most, he gives song to only a few.

*Alexander's Ragtime Band. How I Wish Again I Was
in Michigan Down on the Farm.* This is another period in
her life. These songs were written by a frail young man from
whom torrents of melodies have poured which will roll on
through time, Irving Berlin. These songs represent the period when she sings twelve times a day in the Waco Moving
Picture Theatre on Stanton Street on New York's East Side.
She receives twenty-five dollars a week.

One evening Jacob P. Adler sees her perform and her
vocal velvet splashes over him. He is impressed not only by
the fact that her voice seems to come from her heart rather
than from her throat, but also by the fact that she is an
actress. She pours her emotions into her song. He takes the
little girl by the hand and leads her out of the theatre to
put her on the Yiddish stage. She plays the part of a small
boy in the Yiddish drama *The Homeless.* The audience is
deeply stirred by her and they whisper to one another,
"What is that child's name?" "Belle Baker," they are told.
"Well, well, she is incomparable!"

Blue Skies. He Is a Devil in His Own Home Town. Now
her talents flower into full bloom. She creates a new style of
singing, combining acting and emotion with personality,
ease and grace. She rockets to fame and fortune. Throughout
the United States billboards now announce the prophecy of
the East Side, "Belle Baker, the Incomparable!" She breaks
all vaudeville records, playing 242 consecutive weeks in
vaudeville theatres. Audiences say: "Belle Baker, the Incomparable!"

Then she develops another facet of her talents: *Put It On,
Take It Off, Wrap It Up, Take It Home. Cohen Owes Me
Ninety-Seven Dollars. Whoops, My Dear.* She learns how to
rest between songs by giving characterizations and telling
stories in dialect. Sarah Bernhardt stands in the wings of the
Palace Theatre to watch this girl transport an audience
from tears to hysterical laughter and then, within a moment,
sing an emotional ballad and turn the audience back to
tragedy. Between tears of laughter and of joy, the people

mutter to one another, "Belle Baker, the Incomparable!"

Eli, Eli. As a child she heard this Hebrew chant on the East Side. Now she decides to sing it to strange audiences who do not understand either the words or the melody. But they are stirred and moved for now it is not Belle Baker singing, but the Jewish people expressing their lament. Now she is a missionary singing for her people. "True singing," Carlyle said, "is of the nature of worship. A song will outlive all the sermons in the memory."

My Kid. Ten Little Fingers, Ten Little Toes. Her son is born on Christmas Day, her own birthday. Later when she sings at the Palladium in London (where she enchants the Prince of Wales with her talents), she need not sing *My Kid;* she can sing *Little Man.* Today he is a composer in his own right.

But tragedy strikes Belle Baker. Her husband, Murray Abrams, the noted composer of popular songs, dies suddenly. Now the song is *Don't Take My Loving Man Away.*

She becomes a motion picture star, a radio star, and a Ziegfeld star in the musical comedy *Betsy.* She sings to one hundred thousand in the cold Hollywood Bowl and turns it into a seething cauldron of emotion. We can think of her still as the artist who always lived up to her billing: "Belle Baker, the Incomparable."

CHAPTER 40

Spyros P. Skouras

I BELIEVE that the spiritual ancestor of Spyros Skouras was Pericles of Athens. In 459 B.C., Pericles presided over the Golden Era. He did not believe in conquering nations and enslaving people. He practiced tolerance and love of neighbor. It was Pericles who organized the first United Nations. He called it the Hellenic League. He was a patron of the arts. The magnificent Parthenon was constructed by him. Due to his encouragement, the theatre flourished as it has not done since then. Sophocles, Aeschylus, Aristophanes and Euripides were his contemporaries.

Now Spyros P. Skouras, in his own humble way, has strived to give aid to his brave but stricken Greek people. He has bridged the gap between the old world and the new, for in this country he has been a leader in the work for tolerance and understanding. He is like the farmer who, before sunrise, was walking across a meadow and saw through the mist a monster on the hill beyond. He was alarmed but drawn on by curiosity. As he drew nearer, the distortion disappeared and he realized that the monster was only a man. No longer afraid, he approached the stranger and found that it was his brother! So Skouras has been supporting tirelessly every cause which leads us to understand that the monsters we see through the mist of intolerance are really our brothers. A bias recognized can be a bias sterilized and he has labored through his own efforts and such motion pictures as *Gentleman's Agreement* to clear the minds and thus the hearts of our fellow citizens. It is fitting that he should be the head of one of the great art industries of our time, the Twentieth Century-Fox Film Corporation, for he thus combines the tradition of Greek art with the proficiency of modern business.

I do not know what the middle initial of his name stands for. If I did, I am afraid that I might not be able to pronounce it; but I should like to insert a middle name and call him Spyros Pericles Skouras.

CHAPTER 41

William O. Douglas

"THERE IS in each of us," said the immortal Cardozo, "a stream of tendencies which gives coherence and direction to thought and action. Judges cannot escape that current any more than other mortals.

"All their lives forces which they do not recognize and cannot name have been tugging at them—inherited instincts, traditional beliefs, acquired convictions—and the resultant is an outlook on life which when reasons are nicely balanced must determine where choice shall fall."

One can understand Justice Douglas' opinions only by knowing something about his background. His father was a traveling Presbyterian minister. After he died, his impoverished widow took her three small children to Yakima, Washington. As a boy, Bill Douglas ran errands, mowed lawns and worked in the neighborhood grocery store to help support his family. On his graduation from the local high school he was awarded a scholarship to Whitman College at Walla Walla, Washington. By working in a jewelry store, waiting on tables, assisting a janitor and working as a fruit picker, he managed to keep himself in college and support his family at the same time. He graduated with the highest honors and with the esteem of the student body which elected him its president. Then he started for New York nursing Chicago-bound sheep. It was a haggard tramp-like figure with twelve cents in his pocket who entered Columbia Law School some weeks later. He graduated second in his class and joined a leading law firm. In 1927 he resigned from active practice and became a teacher in Columbia Law School. When President Butler appointed a new dean without consulting the faculty, he resigned. He joined the Yale faculty and later became Sterling Professor of Law.

In 1936, as a result of his studies in bankruptcy, he was appointed to the Securities and Exchange Commission. At his first press conference he said: "What kind of a bird am I? To tell you the truth, I think I am a pretty conservative fellow of the old school—the kind who can't get away from the idea that simple honesty ought to prevail in the business world. I think the S.E.C. in the role of investors' advocate can do a great deal to preserve and revitalize the capitalistic system upon truly conservative standards." As a reward for his tough mind and gentle heart, he was appointed to the United States Supreme Court, the youngest justice in 125 years.

It is against this background that a proper evaluation can be made of his opinions. When the Jehovah's Witnesses case came before the United States Supreme Court involving the constitutionality of an ordinance requiring all canvassers to have a license, he wrote:

"Freedom of religion is not merely reserved for those with a long purse."

(Follett v. McCormack, 321 U.S. 573)

In another case involving the rights of a Japanese-American, he wrote:

"Loyalty is a matter of mind and of heart, not of race. That indeed is the history of America. Moreover, guilt is personal under our Constitutional system. Detention for reasonable cause is one thing. Detention on account of ancestry is another."

(Hiraboyashi v. U. S. of America, 320 U.S. 81)

In another case involving a Seventh Day Adventist who refused to bear arms but was willing to be a non-combatant, he wrote:

"The effort of war is indivisible; and those whose religious scruples prevent them from killing are no less patriots than those whose special traits or handicaps result in their assignment to duties far behind the fighting front."

(*Girouard v. U.S.*, 328 U.S. 61)

When a question was presented involving the right of the Postmaster-General to censor publications, he ruled:

"What is good literature, what has educational value, what is refined public information, what is good art, varies with individuals as it does from one generation to another. There doubtless would be a contrariety of views concerning Cervantes' *Don Quixote*, Shakespeare's *Venus & Adonis* or Zola's *Nana*."

(*Hannegan v. Esquire, Inc.*, 327 U.S. 146)

In a case involving Mann Act prosecutions against certain polygamists, he wrote:

"These polygamous practices have long been branded as immoral in the law. Although they have different ramifications, they are in the same genus as the other immoral practises covered by the Act. . . .

"Whether an act is immoral within the meaning of the statute is not to be determined by the accused's concepts of morality."

(*Cleveland v. U. S.*, 329 U.S. 14)

When the constitutionality of a sterilization statute for habitual criminals came before the United States Supreme Court, Justice Douglas wrote:

"We are dealing here with legislation which involves one of the basic civil rights of man. Marriage and procreation are fundamental to the very existence and survival of the race. The power to sterilize, if exercised, may have subtle, far reaching and devastating effects. In evil or reckless hands it can cause races or types which are inimical to the dominant group

to wither and disappear. There is no redemption for the individual whom the law touches. Any experiment which the State
conducts is to his irreparable injury. He is forever deprived of
a basic liberty."

(Skinner v. State of Oklahoma, 316 U.S. 535)

These are a few of many illustrations proving that Justice
Douglas serves the concept that the law is a silent magistrate
but the magistrate is a speaking law. Sympathy without
judgment is like wine without water, apt to be intoxicating.
But judgment without sympathy is like water without heat,
destined to be ice. Justice Douglas combines sympathy with
judgment in nice balance.

CHAPTER 42

Sholem Asch

A FINE ARTIST is one who makes familiar
things new and new things familiar. Sholem Asch is a fine
artist. An original writer is not necessarily one who imitates
no one, but one whom no one can imitate. Sholem Asch is
an original writer. A great dramatist belongs to the literary
caste of perpetual priesthood because he puts his head and
his heart into his work. Sholem Asch is a great dramatist. A
forceful writer is one whose thoughts breathe and whose
words burn. Sholem Asch is a forceful writer. His language
is Yiddish but he has been translated into more than twenty
other languages and his art is therefore universal.

There have been other great Yiddish writers. Mendel
Mache Seforum is called the Jewish Cervantes. Sholem
Aleichem is called the Jewish Mark Twain. Sholem Asch,
I believe, will be known as the Jewish Dickens.

George Eliot once said: "The Jews are among the aristo-
crats of every land. If a literature is called rich in the posses-

sion of a few classic tragedies, what shall we say to a national tragedy lasting for fifteen hundred years in which the poets and actors were also the heroes?" Sholem Asch, author of *Three Cities, Uncle Moses, Motke the Vagabond, The Nazarene* and *The Apostle,* is the poet, actor and hero of his works.

CHAPTER 43

Kurt Weill

KURT WEILL was a *wunderkind.* At the age of ten he was composing operas and performing for princes and dukes. He became a prominent student at the Berlin Conservatory and there endless melodies flowed from him. He wrote *The Three-Penny Opera, Mahogany, Anna, Anna* and many other notable works. Since coming to this country he has composed the music for *Johnny Johnson, The Eternal Road, Knickerbocker Holiday, Lady in the Dark, A Flag is Born, Street Scene* and many other musical plays.

It is a conventional theory that a musician should have long flowing hair and a profound, mystic face. However, nature seldom conforms with our idealized patterns. Weill is short and bald and wears thick eyeglasses. But his face and voice register a sweet gentleness and give an overall impression of delicacy. This extreme sensitivity is the key to the torrents of melody which flow from him. It is as if he were attuned to sounds which ordinary men do not hear. Take a quart of nature and boil it down to a dram and you have art. Weill boils the turbulent sounds of the world down to a dram of melody and presents it to us. Thus we get a glimpse into the mysteries of creativeness. Weill reproduces what he hears in the inner mind. Only when it has been translated by him into the more familiar idiom of music are we able to hear it too. The augury is bright that for a long time he will continue to compose music as elegant as simplicity and as warm as ecstasy.

CHAPTER 44

Stephen S. Wise

IT IS IMPOSSIBLE for contemporaries to meas-ure the stature of a gigantic figure in their midst. Time is equivalent to distance in such matters and with the perspec-tive of a distant view it is possible for posterity to render a proper verdict. I therefore ask you to transport yourself in imaginative flight to March 17, 2024. It is an extraordinary day. In more than thirty countries of the world there are celebrations of the one hundred and fiftieth anniversary of the birthday of Dr. Stephen S. Wise.

Palestine, which is now an independent Jewish common-wealth, has declared a national holiday. In a ceremony in the capital, Tel-Aviv, the President recounts Dr. Wise's historic role in Zionism. When he was but twenty-four years old he worked with Dr. Herzl, who fondly remembered him in his memoirs. He founded the American Zionist Organiza-tion. He won President Wilson to the cause of Zionism and the Balfour Declaration. The President concludes the ad-dress by pointing out that just as the American nation reveres Jefferson, Washington, Franklin and Adams, so Pales-tine will always remember its four founding fathers—Herzl, Weizman, Brandeis and Wise. At the end of the ceremonies a statue is unveiled which is the bronze image of the classic figure of Dr. Wise. On its base are inscribed the words: "Not unlike Moses, he carried the burdens of his suffering people."

In the United States, too, there are celebrations marking the event. In Paris it is recalled that Dr. Wise inspired the founding of the American Jewish Congress and the World Jewish Congress in which Jews of thirty-nine countries pledged themselves to fight discrimination laws against Jews everywhere and to foster the Bill of Rights for Jews all over the world. One speaker refers to the magnificent address which Dr. Wise made in October, 1950, before the United Nations, which is now required reading for all Jewish students in Palestine and other countries. In it appears this now famous passage about the pioneers in Palestine: "You have lived through a thousand deaths—nothing has killed your spirit. Like the earth's central fire, it may be smothered for a time; the ocean may overwhelm it; mountains may press down but its inherent and unconquerable force will heave both the ocean and the land, and, at some time or other, in some place or other, a volcano will break out and flame to heaven. Your spirit has broken out and flamed to heaven and now the whole world sees its beacon light."

There is a special celebration under the auspices of the Jewish Institute of Religion founded by Dr. Wise one hundred and two years earlier. There are now more than thirty such institutions training young men for the rabbinate. Most of these institutions are named after the original founder, and the young men who are graduated from them model their careers after their idol. The president of the institute makes the significant point that Dr. Wise has had more disciples than any other leader in the history of Judaism. "One is indebted to his father for living," he says, "but to his teacher for living well."

The most impressive ceremonies take place at the Free Synagogue, which is now a great marble temple in the heart of the city of New York. There the governor of the state of New York refers to the fact that Dr. Wise founded the Free Synagogue one hundred and seventeen years ago upon the theory that religious attendance and contributions should be voluntary. "No dues and no pews" was the principle of the Free Synagogue at the old Carnegie Hall where Dr. Wise preached for more than sixty years. His desk, which for almost three quarters of a century was the focal point of the complex problems of Jewry all over the world, is now a shrine in a wing of the temple.

The President of the United States in his message to Palestine points out that Dr. Wise was the poet and hero of the Jewish people, for "he who builds a church in his heart and carries it with him everywhere is holier than he who visits a one-day house of prayer."

The Chief Rabbi of Palestine in an address which is televised to most of the countries of the world refers to the Jewish custom and ritual which provides that one must stand when he rends his clothes in the presence of death. This symbolizes courage in the presence of disaster. When Dr. Wise was distressed at the murder of six million of his brethren, he stood upright and raised a prophetic voice in soul-searing torrents of denunciation. Like coruscating cascades of burning lava, his words consumed all before him. Wises are born to rule empires. The Jews offered him only a pulpit but he made of that pulpit a flaming platform of righteousness and spirit around which his people huddled to receive sustenance and warmth.

The chief rabbi concludes: "Dr. Wise had a dramatic personality. It was the drama of life of the Jewish people incarnate and alive. It had the shadow of tragedy. It had the lightning of wit and humor. It had earnestness and saintliness. It had, above all, heroic moral intransigeance which would not bend the knee to an injustice. He was never proud nor aloof nor ever divided from his fellows except by his gifts and his grace."

At the Hebrew University an author who has written one of the fifty-two biographies of Dr. Wise tells his audience: "While Dr. Wise's name is now universally revered, a careful study of his life reveals that during his own lifetime he was by no means entirely free from criticism. Like Lincoln and Roosevelt, he was the subject of much bitterness and resentment but," continues the author with a flicker of a smile barely discernible, "even our best researchers do not now remember the names of any of his detractors. Their names are buried in oblivion while his name lives on lustrously."

The President of the United Nations, which has evolved into a world government, sends a message of commemoration to the Jews of the world in honor of the one hundred and fiftieth anniversary. He undertakes to describe Dr. Wise's oratory which moved and electrified audiences as if they were struck by some tremendous force. "His eloquence was vested with the conquering power of the prophets of Israel. The thundrous tone of Isaiah, the melodious accents of Micah, the furious indictments of Jeremiah poured fourth from him in majestic organ tones." Oratory is the flashing eye underneath the philosopher's brow. He possessed both.

As the audience departs from a celebration in Prague, a fourteen-year-old boy is heard to say to his mother: "What a wonderful thing it must have been to live back there in 1948 and to have had the chance to see this man in the flesh and hear him speak. What a thrill that must have been!"

Well, we are not privileged to live in the happier and more peaceful days of Jewish equanimity in the year 2024, but we have the privilege of seeing and hearing on his seventy-third birthday, the distinguished American, the great leader of his people, Dr. Stephen S. Wise.

CHAPTER 45

Maurice Maeterlinck

WHENEVER WEIGHT is given to paper rather than to scrap iron, man reveals his sensitivity. The scroll known as the Magna Carta will be cherished for centuries after the armies which marched across Europe have been forgotten. The scroll known as the Declaration of Independence will live in men's hearts long after they have stopped hating Hitler and Mussolini. And the writings of Maurice

Maeterlinck will lift the hearts of men centuries after cities which have been destroyed have been rebuilt.

Not being a physician I cannot authoritatively discuss the distinctions between the body and the mind, though I know that one must let light into the mind if the body is to be healthy. But I would rather seek the refuge of evasion which a student is reputed to have taken when he gave the following definitions:

> What is mind?
> No matter.
>
> What is matter?
> Never mind.
>
> What is soul?
> It is immaterial.

Maurice Maeterlinck has combined body and mind to create soul. Very few people know the proficiency of his body. In his youth he boxed with Kid McCoy and later gave an exhibition with Georges Carpentier. Indeed, McCoy said that he had never before met a poet but after boxing with Maeterlinck he had a new respect for poetry. I can hardly think of a more difficult task than bringing such appreciation to Kid McCoy.

But Maeterlinck has also written of the souls of men pleading for recognition. He has lifted impenetrable veils so that the human eye might see greatnesses beyond, theretofore reserved only for the dead. He is a man of extraordinary contrasts. His *Life of the Bees* proved him a great naturalist, and his *Pelleas and Melisande* proved his quality of spiritual mysticism. He looms as one of the great literary figures of our era. The Nobel Prize, awarded to him in 1912, was an inevitable recognition of his stature.

I think there is prophecy even in his name for "Maeterlinck" is derived from a Flemish word meaning "to measure" and "Maeterlinck" undoubtedly means "measurer" or "distributor." Yes, distributor of joy and hope. Just as the firefly lights up when it is on the wing, so the human mind lights up when it is in action. The mind of Maeterlinck sets all our minds and aspirations to soaring flight; our intellects light up and perhaps also there is a divine spark.

In his youth his great ambition was to be a doctor, but since it was the custom of his country that the oldest son should be an *avocat,* he studied, as he describes it, "the vainest of all professions." Yet I do not consider this a slur on my own profession. For perhaps his training developed his clear-thinking and the faculties which are responsible for his great works.

Now in his eighties, Maeterlinck continues to create. He is like the workers in a bronze factory who make the panels of massive doors. They clean surfaces, trim edges, fill in cavities, smooth and polish over and over again. When asked by a visitor, "Are you never through?" they reply, "We are not finished as long as they let us keep at it. We stop when they take the panels away." So a true artist, year after year, cleans, shapes, smooths and polishes his work until he is taken away. Only then does he stop. Robert Browning wrote two lines which appropriately describe this artist:

> God is the perfect poetry
> Who in his person acts his own creations.

Maeterlinck is the representative of man's perfect poetry to whom generations yet unborn will owe a great indebtedness for the beauty he leaves to them as a heritage.

CHAPTER 46

Modern Minute Men

EDGAR ANSEL MOWRER

JOHN ROY CARLSON

FRANK KINGDON

WILLIAM SHIRER

REX STOUT

GEORGE FIELDING ELIOT

DOROTHY THOMPSON

IN 1775 Robert Newman hung a lantern on a church steeple and Paul Revere began his journey of eighteen miles through Lexington and Concord to warn Americans that the enemy was here. That incident has been symbolized and immortalized in American history. But there have been other Paul Reveres who have knocked with their pens on the doors of their countrymen and warned them that the enemy was here.

France had its Paul Revere. He was Zola. He warned his countrymen that corruption would destroy the French Army. If the French had taken his lesson permanently to heart, France's army might not have been internally disrupted in 1940 and Marshal Petain, who testified against Dreyfus in Zola's day, would not have been its leader. Zola knocked on the doors of his countrymen and said: "Truth is on the march and nothing can stop it."

England had its Paul Revere. He was Churchill. In 1932 Churchill wrote: "All these bands of sturdy Teutonic youth marching through the streets and roads of Germany with the light of desire in their eyes to suffer for their Fatherland, are not looking for status. They are looking for weapons."

This country had its Paul Revere to warn us against

Japan. His name was Homer Lea. In 1909 in his book *The Valor of Ignorance* he wrote: "The United States and Japan are approaching, careless on the one hand and predetermined on the other, that point of contact which is war." He predicted with remarkable vision, upon maps, the very places that Japan would attack.

Even Germany has its Paul Revere. His name is Friedrich Wilhelm Foerster. When his own people would not listen to him, he warned the French and the English that Germany, even under the Republic, was arming for another war. He said, "If you don't use your eyes for seeing, you will use them for weeping." Such is the suicidal tendency of the human race that we preferred to use our eyes for weeping.

Fortunately we have had a whole series of modern Paul Reveres who have knocked on the doors of our countrymen with their pens and warned them of the danger in their midst. The influence of a bigot is like the pupil of an eye: the more light you pour on it, the more it will contract. These Paul Reveres have cast piercing lights upon the bigots and caused their influence to contract. Love of country is like love of a woman: he loves her best who bestows the greatest good upon her. I nominate as modern minute men Edgar Ansel Mowrer, John Roy Carlson, Frank Kingdon, William Shirer, Rex Stout, George Fielding Eliot, and at least one lady, Dorothy Thompson.

CHAPTER 47

Jonah Goldstein

A MAN who works with his hands is a laborer; a man who works with his hands and his brain is a craftsman; but a man who works with his hands and his brain and his heart is an artist. And Judge Jonah Goldstein, beginning in humble position with his hands, and then adding his brain, and his heart, has become a judicial artist.

Judge Goldstein has a characteristic mannerism which has always fascinated me. He takes a long pause after a sentence and at the same time holds you transfixed with his blazing black eyes. Sometimes the sentence is a question. There is a long pause and those eyes pin you with your back against the wall for a long time, the eyes becoming question marks. Sometimes there is just a pause in the middle of a sentence and the eyes hold you as if he had put his hand on your lapel, the eyes becoming a dash. Sometimes the eyes are a semi-colon, but most often the eyes are exclamation points. So it is a terrifying experience to talk to the only man I know who uses his eyes as punctuation marks.

But that isn't the only unusual characteristic of Judge Goldstein. It is very difficult to describe him because he isn't just one man. He is a whole series of men. There is, of course, Goldstein the Jew. He is the man who discovered that at Randall's Island the delinquent youths in the House of Refuge didn't have a rabbi to perform services, so he took his prayer shawl and his prayer book and went there and acted as a rabbi. He is the man who organized the Jewish Big Brother movement, who is a trustee of the Joint Distribution Committee, who went to Europe in 1922 for that organization to take care of the relief of the Jews, and to Palestine in 1929 to organize and investigate the question of riots. He is a man who is immersed in a whole galaxy of charitable Jewish enterprises.

Judge Goldstein is a Jew, but then you cannot stop there. Judge Goldstein is a Catholic. He is the man who was the legislative assistant to Al Smith and participated with Smith in a myriad of Catholic charitable undertakings. He is a member of the board of the Holy Name Center for Homeless Men. In 1917, when the St. James Church put on a play about the Irish, it was necessary to have someone play the part of an English captain (of course, no self-respecting Irishman would play that) and they had to call upon Goldstein the Catholic to play the part. Opposite him was Jimmy Walker, the hero, and Al Smith, the villain, and Father Curry had to guarantee to Goldstein that he wouldn't be lynched after the performance.

There you have Goldstein the Jew and Goldstein the Catholic, but that is not all by any means. Then you have Goldstein the Protestant. When the Cathedral of St. John the Divine set up a Legal Aid Panel under Dean Gates to aid Protestant juvenile delinquents and to lead them into the proper path, they called upon the Protestant Goldstein to act as one of the counsel to their Legal Aid Panel. He has participated in hundreds of benevolences for Protestant charitable organizations and societies.

But that is not all. Then there is Goldstein the Negro. When he was a young practicing lawyer he hired young Negro legal clerks in his office, some of whom have since graduated to judgeships. He is a member of the board of the Mayfield Day Nursery for Negro Children and participates in numerous Negro charitable activities in this city.

To him being a Protestant, Catholic or Jew is just a different way of voting for God. Jonah Goldstein practices universality of religion. But perhaps you think you have run out of your Goldsteins. By no means. Then you have Goldstein the doctor. He is the man who suggested that there should be legislation to obtain physical and medical examinations for juvenile delinquents, because he discovered one day that a juvenile delinquent who was constantly losing his job was ashamed to tell anybody that he had epileptic fits. He is the man who finally obtained, in 1934, legislation for the establishment of a Domestic Relations Court with psychiatrists and psychologists as part of the court staff. Every reform begins as a private opinion and a good many of Judge Goldstein's private opinions have become legislative reforms. So there is Goldstein the doctor. But that is not all.

Then there is Goldstein the lawyer and the jurist, for he knows that God created law before He created the universe. He is the man who reformed the criminal courts system by taking the problems of domestic relations out of the Magistrate's Courts and transferring them to a newly created Domestic Relations Court. He is now judge of the highest criminal trial court in this state.

Then of course there is Goldstein the engineer of human relations and Goldstein the author, who wrote *The Family in Court,* now a standard work, and Goldstein, recent candidate for the mayoralty of the city of New York.

In Brazil there is a unique custom. Every professional man wears a ring which identifies his profession. A doctor always wears an emerald, a lawyer a ruby, an engineer a sapphire, a psychiatrist a topaz. I often think that it is fortunate that we do not follow that custom in New York because if we did, Jonah Goldstein would be the most bejeweled man in the city of New York. Instead of singing *East Side, West Side,* he would probably be singing about rings on his fingers and rings on his toes.

Well, is he Catholic, Protestant, Jew, Negro, doctor, lawyer, engineer or author? He is none of these and he is all of these, for he is Jonah Goldstein, American!

CHAPTER 48

Moss Hart

WHEN I THINK of all the arts which a playwright must possess, I am awed. A playwright must be a man of letters because drama is what literature does at night. A playwright must be a historian because playwrights are the moons of literature. They reflect light received from the ages. A playwright must be a preacher. He must not only make imaginary things seem real but he must make real things seem imaginary. A playwright must be a poet who writes exquisite expressions of exquisite impressions. A playwright must be a businessman who arranges finances on the theory that the riches of a play increase as they are consumed. A playwright must be a psychologist for he cannot solve the dramatic problem unless he understands the motivation of the characters he has created. Even then the dramatic work may represent all work and no play.

However if you combine all of these—the man of letters, the historian, the poet, the businessman, the psychologist— and add the wit and graciousness of this particular playwright, you have a composite picture of Moss Hart.

CHAPTER 49

Frederick W. Foerster

HE IS a great German and therefore, of course, has had to run away from Germany or, to put it more accurately, Professor Foerster did not run away from Germany; Germany ran away from him. Recently he and I presented the same view at a small dinner gathering of important German ex-leaders. They were apologizing for Germany, and one said that Germany did not cause the war; that after all England and France had declared war on Germany. I shall never forget Professor Foerster's answer. He said, "All of you distinguished German liberals and Social Democrats seem to think it your duty to the fatherland to apologize for certain German conduct and to make the best case for her that you can. I think you are wrong. Knowing what my country and my people have done to the world in two world wars, how they have ravaged Europe and killed millions of people, and that they are plotting to do so again in a third world war, the least I can do to make amends for my country and my people is to warn the world against them." This statement measures the heroic stature and courage of the one German who has told the truth about Germany.

If one were to define a prophet as a man whose understanding of existing forces is so keen that he can foresee their inevitable development, then Professor Foerster is the true prophet of our generation. In 1927 he knew that the German Republic was only a screen for the militarists. He knew that Germany was like the character in Dostoevsky's *The Brothers Karamazov* who is bound by fate to commit murder. "Germany," he wrote, "is drawn irresistibly, as if accursed, toward new and even greater crimes. This is because the preceding crimes have not been recognized and atoned for as such. The German people drift toward crime because they are composed of a hundred wolves and a hundred thousand sheep, the sheep joining faithfully in whatever the wolves propose, and at the present they are kept busy fighting the 'lie of the wolves' guilt,' an occupation they will endure until the moment the wolves jump at their throats and their neighbors' throats."

His understanding of the German people was so profound that it enabled him to predict in *Die Menschheit* of July 8, 1927: "This much should at least be clear to us. The masters of Germany today need peace and want peace, but only in order to prepare for war and to be armed upon a date which will be decided by the weakness of her neighbors. That day will fall anywhere between 1933 and 1938." Thus he foretold precisely the ascendency of Hitler to take over openly that which had been prepared for him, and the consequent attack upon the world.

Foerster's record for accurate analysis should add special weight to his present view that the Germans are unregenerate and that, far from being contrite, they are planning a third world war. His usual detractors are berating him again. Those who seek a firm, victorious control of Germany (to counteract German psychology which Foerster once described as "a mentality which will not yield until it has found its master; the more generously it is treated, the more it dismisses its foe as weak and cowardly") are accused of being vengeful. Contented slaves are the most dangerous foes of liberty, and the Germans are happy to be ruled with

an iron hand. They are slyly taking advantage of the rift
between the victorious Allies and we, with maddening astigmatism, are proceeding once more to build up a totally unre-
formed enemy. I say "we" referring to the democratic gov-
ernments and to Russia who are already in a race to acquire
German military strength, not realizing the certainty that
German arrogance and militarism will seek to make both
victims when "Der Tag" arrives.

The German problem is round like the world. If one
sails stubbornly in the same direction, he seems to reach the
starting point all over again. We have had two world wars
waged by Germans in the last thirty-four years, and we are
risking a third at her hands. Foerster could do no better in
such a cycle of events than to repeat today what he wrote
in 1920. Listen to him:

"It is no disgrace to a nation that she has fallen into
serious error. What does dishonor a people is refusal to
acknowledge its error and guilt. . . . This is the core of the
German guilt, and this is what for our own sake we ought
to recognize without reserve and without excuse. I won't
subtract a farthing of that German indebtedness. It is not
for nothing that I have been watching and pursuing that
evil spirit ever since I first encountered it in high school,
where I became acquainted with its disdainful talk of dis-
regarding the highest hopes of man, its haughty renuncia-
tion of the fine true Germandom of the past, and its narrow
corporal's horizon.

"All my books are dedicated to the task of softening this
swollen, oppressive and short-sighted egoism and to bring
the German soul from State-worship back to humani-
tarianism.

"I know that new German evil from the core, being myself
a Berliner and a Prussian. You will not fool me with all
your lying about 'those others,' my dear countrymen. I know
'those others' and I know 'us' too. I leave it to those others
to recognize and extirpate their own sins. I am a German,

fearful for Germany. I am anxious to save Germany from Prussianism, and be assured, you won't get rid of me! In vain is your continued buying of whitewashing literature; in vain do you clamor for the opening of the Allies' secret archives. All is in vain. The truth is not imprisoned in Allied archives, but in the secret archives of your conscience. Only there can you learn precisely what had to happen, and what is going to happen again, if you do not recognize and confess in true spirit, with humility, with truthfulness and with honesty your formidable apostasy from God." Yet even today where can one find a German with a guilt-edged conscience? It was Hegel who said, "We learn from history that we learn nothing from history."

Foerster's father was a descendant of Von Moltke, the Prussian general; his mother, of Alexander von Humboldt, the great German democrat. Thus Pan-Germanism and democracy clashed in his house. When he was a boy he heard the Junker generals arguing fiercely in the room below. Once Bismarck was there. His mother, shrewdly aware of the conflict, used to comment upon Frederick's aquiline nose, "Say you have Von Moltke's nose but turn it in the Humboldt direction." How truly that sensitive nose has pointed toward peace and justice.

In a nation seething with nationalism, he dared to write and speak of Christian ethics and international morality. When, as early as 1895, he savagely attacked the Kaiser's saber-rattling speeches, he was sentenced to "fortress custody" for three months. He describes this as "honorable imprisonment." He became a foremost authority on education and received international recognition for his books on ethics and pedagogy. He could have lived with honor in his own country, where he had become professor of philosophy at Munich University. But he chose to make learning a road to a better world, not a sheltered art. So, in the very midst of the first World War, he denounced German militarism and demanded that Germany "abandon national egoism and join a new European cultural order." The philosophy faculty protested. There were riots at the university. He had to resign.

However, after Germany's defeat he was recognized as one of the few Germans who were trusted by the Allies and was appointed ambassador at Berne, Switzerland. Having become plenipotentiary for the new German Republic, he returned to Munich University and, while sailors guarded the doors with machine guns, he made an historic speech pleading with the Germans to confess their guilt and accept democracy and peace in their hearts. The German nationalists marked him for death, but his friend Colonel von Sonnenburg warned him and on a half hour's notice he fled from Germany and saved his life, only to continue the fight from France.

His military friends had revealed to him the precise facts of secret rearmament. Part of the Pan-German conspiracy was for Stressemann to appear before the League of Nations and insist that since Germany had disarmed, other nations must do likewise. Thus German militarists would double the effectiveness of their illegal military preparation.

Foerster printed a pamphlet disclosing the exact details of Germany's rearmament. On the very day that Stressemann was to address the League of Nations and make his hypocritical plea, Foerster (with the magnificent connivance of Briand) had placed on the desk of every delegate the complete revelation of Germany's deceit. Stressemann was as infuriated as he was frustrated. *"Canaille!"* he screamed at Foerster.

There was a small group of German liberals led by Helmut von Gerlach who urged that Foerster be elected President of the Third Reich. How different world history would have been if this had happened. But there is little comfort in such rumination because if the Germans had been enlightened enough to elect Foerster, they would not have been the people who for a second time immersed the world in blood. Conversely, being the people they were and are, no Foerster could even cross the border into his own country. So it was. The Germans, hundreds of thousands of them, threw roses in the path of von Hindenburg and elected him President! He, the pure Prussian, the perfect Pan-German, the "iron" general (even though defeated) was their idol. He was the chosen representative of the new Germany in a free election!

Foerster, having failed to win over his countrymen, then traveled throughout the world to warn against their second attempt at world conquest. He was listened to respectfully, but he could not dent the disbelief of other people that Germany as a nation was still barbaric.

His was a voice in the wilderness. And today, even after a second World War, concentration camp horrors, Maidenek, Buchenwald, Auschwitz and all, the same refusal "to use our eyes to see" greets this prophet's new warnings.

Foerster is now seventy-nine years old. He is erect, clear-eyed, strong-toothed and resonant-voiced. He has ruddy cheeks and his energy is natural, not the by-product of nervousness. Like most courageous men he is gentle in mien. Even without his impressive beard, which rounds out a handsome face, he would be an effortless model of dignity. He has experienced the elation of a scholar and the suffering of a martyr. Both have fused in him a sense of integrity which shines forth and gives him the radiance of greatness. He is totally devoid of those elements of vanity and pride which often stand as obstacles in the path of even the purest thinkers. He is self-effacing when others can lead and boldly assertive when he must carry the burden. As a lonely—I might say, *the* lone—German spokesman for German repentance and reform, he has been in a swirl of German nationalism, fighting valiantly against the accusation that he was a "traitor" for telling the truth. Yet his views are untouched by passion, self-justification or emotionalism which may turn him even a degree off the course of principle. I nominate him as the great German hero of our era.

CHAPTER 50

Billy Rose

WHEN ONE ACTOR looks into a mirror, that is a love story. When two actors appear on the stage, that is a crime story. Each is trying to steal the show. When one hundred and fifty actors appear on the stage, that is a Billy Rose spectacle. Rose has an extraordinary advantage over all other people. When he wants to see a spectacle, he produces one. One has the impression from him that his plays are always successes. It is only the audience which is sometimes a failure. Even his critics can say no worse than that nothing succeeds like excess.

His versatility is prodigious. He was the amateur shorthand champion of this country. He was a secretary to Bernard Baruch. He was a famous songwriter and the producer of *Jubilee,* the World's Fair Aquacade, and other enormous enterprises. As a nightclub operator he practices the principle that his "saloon" is a place where tables are reserved and guests are not.

A typical illustration of his resourcefulness combined with native talent is a series of advertisements he recently wrote in the newspapers. So piquant and arresting was the writing, that a syndicate offered him an attractive price to write a daily column. Now his comments, which formerly adorned his sales talk, are printed without charge and he receives an income from them. He is making hay with grass that grows under other people's feet.

His columns range from the very short story with the unexpected ending to sentimental vignettes about people and things. What distinguishes them is pungent phrasing. "Blowing the whistle on you" means reporting you to the authori-

ties. "She was pretty all over" means she had a beautiful
figure as well as face. "Not since jelly apples sold for one
cent" means 1910. "A four-kleenex cold" means a severe
cold. "A business man's fox trot" means a graceless dance.
"A low ceiling and high foreheads" describes a chess room.
"Dead end kid with a library card" means William Saroyan.
"A Welsh rarebit dream" means a nightmare.

Some writers have a keen ear for reporting dialogue. Rose
has a keen inner ear. He reports impressions in language
which has not been standardized by culture. The result is
a fresh and original slang which derives from the East Side,
the circus, the carnivals, Broadway and Main Street. His
writing drips colors of every hue. The print never seems
merely dark gray. It shimmers with odd expressions and an
occasional moving thought. Yet, though the style is unorthodox, the editorial values are based on Arthur Brisbane's
shrewd advice, "When you write, tell the people what *they*
think, not what *you* think." What better formula can there
be for "light reading"? His column, conceived by accident
and born in humble circumstances, will rise to affluence and
influence. It is the story of the self-made column by a self-
made man.

Men who pass through tragic times often mature and
grow in stature. In the past few years Rose traveled through
war areas. The sentiments and emotions which previously
expressed themselves in mere showmanship have now been
poured into relief causes. He has learned that to pity distress
is human, but to relieve it is godlike. The Polynesians have
an extraordinary custom. They exchange children at birth.
Then in later years if any amongst them is in difficulty, they
cry, "Help him—he may be your brother!"

Rose is assured a bright reception in the hereafter, for
when the angels measure the applicants, they do not put the
tape around the head but around the heart.

CHAPTER 51

Irving Lehman

THE PAINTER or the composer may think when he creates his work that it is the inspiration of the moment. Actually, it is the result of thousands of stimuli to which he has been subjected during his lifetime. Similarly, Judge Irving Lehman may have thought when he retired to his study in the evening to write his opinions, many of which have become landmarks in jurisprudence, that he did so out of his spontaneous reactions and current studies, but this was not so.

Actually, his opinions were written as far back at 1848, when his father and mother left Germany to settle in Alabama and enjoy the freedom and opportunity of our beloved country. They were written when he was a brilliant student at Columbia University, which later honored its distinguished son by conferring upon him a doctorate of laws in 1927.

They were written during his early childhood when he enjoyed an extraordinarily intimate and affectionate relationship with his brother which flowered to climactic fruition when he, as chief judge of the highest court of the State of New York, administered the oath to his brother Herbert as lieutenant governor on two occasions and as governor on four occasions. These must have been even more deeply moving to him than when he administered the oath of governor three times to Alfred E. Smith and twice to Franklin D. Roosevelt.

They were written when a passion for mutual understanding among different faiths caused him to become one of the three Jewish representatives on the Commission for Better Understanding, together with three Catholics and three

Protestants. They were written when his deep concern for
the unfortunate caused him to serve as president of the
Jewish Welfare Board for nineteen years. They were written
when his deep religious conviction induced him to serve for
nine years as president of Temple Emanu-El and when his
scholarly interests induced him to become a director of the
Jewish Theological Seminary. They were written when he
married Sissie Straus, the daughter of a noble man, Nathan
Straus, to share with her his work, his happiness and his
sorrows for almost half a century. They were written during
his intimate and soulful friendship with the immortal Benjamin Cardozo who, in the last days of his life, chose to live
with Judge Lehman, undoubtedly recognizing not only an
affinity of scholarship but also of spiritual breadth. These
constituted the conditioning of a great judge who poured
forth wisdom over a period of thirty-three years.

Here was a judge who knew that justice was truth in
action; who wore the weight of his learning lightly like a
flower; who was imbued with the sanctity of reason; who
knew that justice was represented as blind because a judge
must discard party, friendship and kindred; who knew that
to be free one had to be a slave of philosophy.

In certain cities of the Netherlands, cutters of precious
stones live in obscure little shops. All day they weigh on
their scales jewels so rare that one of them would suffice to
lift them forever from their poverty. But every evening
when they have returned the gems to their anxious owners,
they sit down serenely to supper. On the same table where
previously they had weighed another man's treasure without
envy, they spread their frugal meal. So lived Irving Lehman.
He decided enormous issues involving other men's treasures
and even their lives. After he had polished his opinions so
that they brilliantly reflected his wisdom and justice, he
retired to a simple life of learning.

CHAPTER 52

Ben Hecht

LIKE SO MANY other people, Ben Hecht is terri-
fied at speaking in public. An iron shutter drops across his
mind when he rises and this most articulate man finds it
difficult to utter a phrase. Microphones have made it possible
for singers with mild, soothing voices appropriate for intimate groups to be enjoyed by millions. It is unfortunate
that this discovery has not been applied to brilliant conversa-
tionalists like Hecht. Over a table he can regale you for
hours with fascinating descriptions of his hectic reporter
days in Chicago or his more recent escapades with motion
picture producers. He does not, like most story-tellers, rely
on skilful delivery or use of dialect and gestures. He leans
entirely on sharply-edged word pictures which are framed by
observations so analytical that you are torn away from the
story to reflect upon his own interpretation of it. Thus in
droll and matter-of-fact recitals there are conjured up most
exciting and hilarious images.

You see the Negro, convicted of shooting a policeman,
about to be hung. Though the condemned man's color has
changed to an unprecedented grayish blue, he appears to be
self-composed. The hangman puts the noose over his head
and the warden says, "Have you anything to say?"

"Not at this moment," is the quiet reply.

Or there is the occasion when Hecht and a reporter from
a rival newspaper are reporting a murder trial. The reading
public is hungry for the minutest details, so the two reporters
vie with each other in recording not only the mannerisms
of the defendant but every stitch of clothes worn by the important actors in this natural drama. Hecht and his rival

watch each other scribble to be sure that neither catches an incident which will make the story more complete.

On the climactic day the woman defendant is found guilty. To everyone's amazement she turns suddenly, seizes a sharp letter opener lying on the table and with two long leaps, bounds up to the judge's bench and plunges the knife into him with furious, repeated blows. The court attendants are so stunned that they stand frozen for a minute. Hecht is paralyzed. He cannot move his pencil. But across the table he sees the rival reporter writing frantically. Hecht tries to unloosen his arm, but he cannot. He stares at the defendant swinging the knife, but can record nothing. His misery matches his helplessness when he observes the opposing pencil moving faster and faster as its master's eye scans every wild movement of the murder in the courtroom.

In less than three minutes the scene is over. The defendant, panting hysterically, is pinned down by three attendants. The judge is carried out. Hecht's rival tears three sheets from his pad and hands it to a messenger to rush to the newspaper for a scoop. As the boy dashes by, Hecht, in desperation, snatches the sheets from his hand. They are fully covered with writing. But they contain only one phrase, repeated continuously: "She leaped up, she leaped up, she leaped up. she leaped up . . ."

"His brain was as paralyzed as mine," laughs Hecht, "but his hand kept writing."

On one occasion an Indian Yogi, turban and all, assured Hecht that if he would follow his advice he would live to be 150 years old and be in perfect health. "You can start now," replied Hecht. "I have a terrible cold. Can you cure it?"

"Of course," replied the Yogi. "In ten minutes, if you do as I say."

Consent having been promptly obtained, a bowl of ice-water was called for. "Now place your face in this water and breathe in and out only through your nose, and without swallowing any water," was the command.

This was no mean feat but Hecht obeyed, although not

without sputtering and coughing. When he was through his cold was gone! "This I must tell my doctor," he cried.

His physician was unimpressed. "Why, of course, if you freeze the nerves in your nose, the cold will seem to disappear. But it will return in a few hours. You can rub the tongue with ice before taking a bitter medicine and taste nothing, but you have not killed the sense of taste, only anesthetized it for a while. We get the same effect more easily by an injection." The cold did return, but the Yogi remained insistent upon his prowess.

The next evening the Yogi appeared with his female assistant, a lithe unpretty woman. Hecht was to receive instruction in certain exercises guaranteed to lengthen his life. The assistant stretched out upon the floor of Hecht's room and, while the Yogi explained her contortions, she moved her stomach muscles from side to side and then in circles, first clockwise and then counter-clockwise. Hecht leaned against his bed and ruminated, "This Indian, having failed with his ice-water trick, is now trying to get me with sex."

At that moment, Mrs. Hecht opened the door and took in the bewildering scene. The lady on the carpet was too devoted to science to stop her rhythmic movements. The Yogi demonstrated his quickwittedness. "You seem pale. You have a headache? Sit here," he said to his hostess and, leading her firmly to a seat, began to massage the back of her neck. His fingers were educated to every nerve end and as they pressed they seemed to release a cool spring from each nerve center. Mrs. Hecht insists he cured her headache and her husband is certain he avoided one.

Hecht's conflicts with motion picture moguls are likely to become legendary. To cite only one instance, he was entrusted to produce a motion picture for (let us call it) Superb Motion Pictures, Inc. After he had completed his task, the president of the company insisted upon making certain cuts, despite Hecht's violent protestations. The dele-

tions having been made, a test preview was arranged in a
suburb of Hollywood.

By resort to bribery and more ingenious methods, the title
and credits of the motion picture were changed at the last
moment without the knowledge of the studio executives.
That evening as the officers of Superb Motion Pictures, the
stars and publicity experts sat in the theatre to watch the
audience's reaction, the following title was flashed on the
screen:

SUPERB MOTION PICTURES, INC., PRESENTS
(TITLE OF THE PICTURE)
PRODUCED BY
BEN HECHT
BUT
MUTILATED AND RUINED BY
THE OFFICERS OF SUPERB MOTION PICTURES
WHO BEING ILLITERATE AND IGNORANT
HAVE NEVERTHELESS INSISTED ON TAMPERING
WITH THIS WORK

When the officials of Superb Motion Pictures fled from the
theatre, leaving the audience in gales of laughter, they ran
into pickets carrying signs which read:

THIS THEATRE IS SHOWING THE WORST MOTION
PICTURE IN HISTORY.
YOU ARE CHEATED IF YOU PAY ADMISSION.
DEMAND YOUR MONEY BACK.

The next morning a telegram informed the already ill
officers of Superb Motion Pictures, Inc. that unless the cuts
made in the motion picture were restored, thousands of
pickets would be hired to trail the picture to each exhibition.
Needless to say, these subtle tactics succeeded and the motion
picture was presented in its original form.

No matter how playful pranksters like Charles MacArthur,
Gene Fowler and Hecht may be, they are artists and there-

fore sensitive to injustice. Our troubled times have sobered them and sublimated their mischievousness into more productive channels. Hecht's greatest book was written only a few years ago. It was called *The Book of Miracles*. It is an appropriate title to describe also its author's talent, for Hecht can make words luminous by passing his hand over them.

In his book there is a story called "The Death of Eleazer" in which a rabbi, Eleazer, and a priest, Dominic, share an extraordinary and sensitive friendship. The priest's friends and the rabbi's friends cannot understand the bond which ties them together. But these two lifelong friends meet daily in the garden of the monastery and in the setting of flowers and birds which talk to them as well as to one another, their spiritual friendship reveals God to them.

Only a great artist could so epitomize the unity of Christians and Jews. Now Hecht has turned his mighty pen to right a great injustice. His plays *We Shall Not Die* and *A Flag Is Born* are political documents as an artist would write them. Hecht may some day be best remembered for his heroism in wielding an unconquerable pen against the callousness and cruelty of the human race.

CHAPTER 53

William B. Ziff

THERE IS an old superstition that any man who has a "Z" in his name is tinged with genius. Ordinarily I do not encourage superstitions but, in this case, due to considerable personal experience, I do not hesitate to recommend highly the accuracy of such a notion.

Usually a man who has achieved distinction excels in one particular sphere. Mr. Ziff has an enormous variety of avocations. But I believe that they have each contributed to his books. You may be surprised to know that Mr. Ziff is not only the author of a famous aviation book but is a horticulturist. He has the finest outdoor cactus garden in the eastern United States. Voltaire once said that a man should cultivate letters or his garden. Apparently Mr. Ziff finds no difficulty in doing both.

You may be surprised to know that Mr. Ziff in his earlier days was a portrait painter. Many men of talent have expressed themselves in diverse fields. After all, a painting is silent prose and, conversely, fine prose is painting with words. Perhaps this explains Mr. Ziff's ability to paint vivid word pictures in his books.

Or you may be surprised to know that Mr. Ziff has been a day laborer. He shoveled coal from box cars. He washed greasy dishes in restaurants. He has sold everything from flatirons to shoes. Of course I admire hard work. It fascinates me. I can sit and look at others performing it for hours. But now I understand the prodigious physical energy which Mr. Ziff puts into his many activities.

Or you may be surprised to know that Mr. Ziff is an authority on character analysis. I hope he has learned that men are loved for the bad qualities which they do not have rather than for the good qualities which they have. Someone once described character as what a man is in the dark. Mr. Ziff is the kind of man I should like to meet in a blackout.

Or you may be surprised to know that Mr. Ziff is an adventurer. He spent a half year in the Honduran jungle at the invitation of the government of Honduras, looking for a lost city. Probably he learned from this unique experience that the human animal is the most ferocious of all and is the only one that systematically preys on its own species. Or perhaps he has even learned that the human animal is the only one that blushes and the only one that has reason to.

Or you may be surprised to know that he is a publisher and editor of many technical magazines such as *Flying, Radio, Popular Photography* and others and that as editor he introduced the now revered Billy Mitchell to the public.

You will not be surprised to learn that he is an expert on aviation and international affairs: not the kind of an expert who knows more and more about less and less; not the kind of an expert who avoids the little errors as he sweeps to a grand fallacy; but the kind of an expert who builds a solid foundation of fact for an application of keen judgment. He has been the official guest of the British Air Ministry and is generally considered one of the best informed men in the new realm of aviation which literally is as deep and high as the sky.

We need not look askance at the fact that Ziff, a flier for only one year in the first World War, was considered an able military strategist during the second World War. Many of the great military geniuses of history have had no military training. Frederick the Great refused his father's advice to be a soldier. He was interested in art and music and carried on extensive correspondence with Voltaire. Yet he turned out to be the general who led the Prussians to victory in 1756. Caesar, as we know from his *Commentaries,* was a man of letters and without military training, but he nevertheless revolutionized military warfare of his day. Fabius Maximus, who defeated Hannibal, was a Roman consul with no orthodox or professional military training. Oliver Cromwell studied law and was a farmer, yet he became the greatest military strategist of his day.

So though I am not given to superstition, when I think of Ziff's versatility I am ready to subscribe to the notion that a "Z" in a proper name is a token of great talent.

CHAPTER 54

Molly Picon

SUDDENLY it occurred to me: That is why Molly Picon is the darling of the Yiddish theatre. She is the personification of her people. She represents their humor, their pathetic helplessness, their courage and tragedy, their love of song and gaiety and their versatile artistry. She is tiny, like her people. There are only ten million Jews in the world. Yet there is a dynamic quality in this infinitesimal segment of the world's population which focuses a dramatic spotlight upon it. Sometimes it is a green spotlight of world prejudice which seeks to place upon it the responsibility for all ills, as if this people could possibly be so powerful for good or evil. Sometimes it is the amber spotlight of appreciation for the unique contribution to science and the arts made by so small but so gifted a group. Yes, Molly is tiny but dynamic.

She is a wanderer, like her people. Few artists have traversed the world as she has, traveling 35,000 to 50,000 miles annually year after year. She has appeared in Russia, Poland, Rumania, Belgium, Switzerland, England, France, South Africa and South America. The Jew's home is everywhere. Molly's art has been everywhere. Zulu chieftains have feted her. King Ferdinand and Queen Marie of Rumania have ordered command performances. Students in Vienna have carried her home on their shoulders in triumph. But also, Nazis in the Berlin of 1931 insulted her and anti-Semites in Bucharest rioted against her. Like her people, she has been admired and hated. There seems to be just enough religion to make us hate one another, but not enough religion to make us love one another. Always she has been restless, an East Side girl building a European reputation so that she would be appreciated on the East Side.

She is a singer, like her people, for Jews sing even in prayer. The Talmud is read in melody. The cantor's musical supplications have become a unique art so developed in its virtuosity that it may be judged by rigid artistic standards. Molly possesses this highest gift of her people. Hers is not a great voice. Her alto tones shift in unorthodox manner to "head" notes in the higher octaves. But the transition is soothing. It is a sweet voice, a hearty voice. Its softness tugs at the heart. It creates moods and can bring forth laughter or tears instantaneously. When she sings one is not conscious of the voice. It is as if she were speaking in melodic rhythm. And when she talks it is as if she were singing simply. The secret of all artistry fundamentally is rhythm. Whether it is the pulsating speed of *The Rhapsody of a Working Girl* or the stately, tragic beat of *East Side Symphony* or the gay evenness of *In Meine Oigen Bist Du Schoen*, rhythm projects her sincerity and carries the listener along.

She is versatile, like her people. In different shows she has performed sleight-of-hand, walked a tight rope, and played eight musical instruments. But more varied still is the range of her characterizations and, above all, of the moods which she projects, from patriotic fervor to bouncing farce, from sensitive, tragic feeling to impish and whirling gaiety.

She is a gifted mimic; she can *be* her people. Her face is contorted before your very eyes into a toothless grandmother and her body, sagging ever so slightly, gives you the frail dignity of old age. Or she can be a tiny child, her voice becoming shrill and plaintive, her body restlessly young from embarrassed toes to wondering eyes. Or she can be a huge fat man. Her body then curves outward into an arch and her breathless, guttural tones give you the full impression of jowls and a voice choked by burdens of fat. Whether she is the stuttering idiot, Schmendrick, or the struggling mother and, later, gradmother in the Broadway drama *Morning Star*, her effects are modified by artistic restraint which heightens their veracity. Sometimes I think she is so utterly charming as a dancer and ingenue because she can mimic beauty and grace too. Shakespeare's words apply to her:

> To make the weeper laugh, the laugher weep,
> He had the dialect and different skill,
> Catching all passions in his craft at will.

Above all her talents, Molly is *becheint*. The word defies definition. Charming? Cute? It is something much more. It includes an ineffable quality which makes an audience sigh ecstatically, "Isn't she wonderful?" "She's a darling." If you asked why and the audience could explain it, that would be the definition. It is a winning quality which is irresistible. We hide our inability to solve such mysteries by using the word "personality." But what is that? If a critic could, like a chemist, break it down into its component parts, he would probably find artistic color, great sincerity, a sense of one-ness with the audience and affectations so invisible that they do not irritate but, on the contrary, give the illusion of natu-ralness and simplicity. Even then many factors would not have been isolated. But the results are always evident. Audi-ences adore her. They are as anxious to recognize her talents as if they felt pride in their appreciation as much as in her achievements.

She breaks down the barriers of resistance. Her comedy then seems funnier and her sense of tragedy more profound. She can disarm a listener in a few minutes, sometimes sec-onds. In this sense she literally captures an audience and its emotional responses then become full and uninhibited.

All this and more explains why this mite has shone in every theatrical realm and has received recognition from the most discerning critics of the English and foreign press as well as from the Yiddish press. Brooks Atkinson has written of her: "Once the idol of Second Avenue, more recently the darling of the world, she has the daintiness of a lady and the warmth of a street singer. She is a singer of songs about people and an honor to her profession."

She is the personification of her people's joy and tears, their song and dance, their versatility and charm. That is why she is their darling. They pay her tribute because she is a living tribute to them.

CHAPTER 55

Kenneth C. Royall

THERE WAS a day when pacifism was considered idealism and military preparedness was considered wickedness. But now we know that one sword keeps another in its sheath. A nation is not justified in defending itself with part of its strength when the whole of its existence is at stake.

However, it would be a mistake to think of the army merely in terms of a destructive military force. Today the army is a great reconstruction and educational organization. One million American soldiers took advantage of free educational programs in Europe. Two thousand unit schools were set up. Four million textbooks were printed under army auspices. There were ninety thousand army instructors. The stupendous sum of one and a half million books are shipped annually by our army to our soldiers overseas. Thus we use the great moral invader, knowledge. Upon few men in all history has so great a responsibility been placed as upon Kenneth C. Royall. As Secretary of the Army of the United States, he has become one of the most important military figures in the whole world. Yet in view of the army's record, I should like to think of him not as Secretary of the Army but as secretary of peace and education.

CHAPTER 56

Gael Sullivan

IN 1891 the distinguished archaeologist Wilhelm Dorpfeld discovered that the ruins of Troy were composed of nine layers, one Troy under another. They are now referred to by number, such as Troy 3 or Troy 5. Some human beings are composed of layers of talent. If you excavated Gael Sullivan analytically, you would find at least five Sullivans.

First, there is Gael Sullivan, associate professor of political economy and ethics at DePaul University. This professor is lost. Second, there is the Gael Sullivan who taught public administration at Loyola University. This teacher is lost too. Third, there is Gael Sullivan, the boy orator and college debater, who was later chosen by President Roosevelt to make an oration for him at the Herald Tribune Forum. This orator is lost. Fourth, there is Gael Sullivan, the organizer, whose activities ranged from making a relief survey for the conference of mayors to supervision of helicopter experiments. This organizer is lost. Fifth, there is Gael Sullivan, the business director, sought by many large firms in the United States for his demonstrated executive abilities. This business man is lost.

Two years ago all five of these Sullivans were found. They turned up in Gael Sullivan, the public servant. Why had they disappeared? Because as a professor he knew that knowledge may be planted in solitude but must be cultivated in public. As an orator he knew that there is no eloquence without a man behind it. As an organizer and business man, he knew that although one machine can do the work of fifty ordinary men, no machine can do the work of one extraordinary man.

In recent years the word "logistics" has achieved profound meaning. We are familiar with it thus far only as a military term. War has become so complex that the science of determining how many barrels of oil, guns, food and a thousand assorted items are necessary for a certain kind of operation and how many ships, trains or trucks it would take to transport them to the proper place at the proper time, has become more important than audacity or heroism on the field of battle. It was because General Eisenhower had proved himself in war maneuvers in this country to be a brilliant specialist in the science of logistics that he was designated Supreme Commander of the Allied Powers.

However, "logistics" is a word which need not be limited merely to military science. It applies to the arts as well. The motion picture producer is the logistics expert of the cinema; the producer is the logistics expert of the stage; the impresario, of the ballet; the publisher and editor, of literature. The science of politics, too, has advanced. New techniques have been adopted for the complex requirements of mass information and persuasion. Gael Sullivan has proved to be the logistics expert of politics.

So here are the lost Sullivans: professor, orator, organizer, business man—they are all represented in the executive director of the National Democratic Committee, Gael Sullivan.

CHAPTER 57

Helen Hayes

THERE IS a fable about a child who, when she cried, shed pearls instead of tears. A cruel stepmother beat her in order to obtain precious pearls. I sometimes think of artists in this light. They are sensitive to injustice and mean-

ness and, when a cruel world beats them, they cry artistic
pearls and we are enriched by their sorrow. Helen Hayes is
such an artist. She is not content to have reached the very
pinnacle of the most exacting of all arts. She does not use
the cloak of her artistry to shield her from the fierce winds
of current events. One does not hear from her, "After all,
I am an actress and my public is very diverse. I cannot take
sides in controversial matters."

Indeed those are the very matters in which she must take
part, for the same emotional driving force which makes her
slight body an irresistibly impressive figure and etches every
word and gesture with fiery outline, also causes her to rebel
against injustice and intolerance. So she stumps against the
re-election of Hamilton Fish and lends the magic of her
name and presence to charitable enterprises and to democratic forces everywhere. She does not recognize the distinction between the message cast comfortably across the foot-
lights and the message which must be projected across the
lecture platform and the dais. Her interpretative touch trans-
forms make-believe of the stage into reality. She does not
find it difficult, therefore, to transpose her effort to the world
of reality itself.

Yes, if art is the essence of nature, then no true artist can
shy away from life while busying herself with mere imagery.
This Helen Hayes understands intuitively. It automatically
drives her to open the sheltering door, as Nora does in
Ibsen's *A Doll's House,* and walk out into the turmoil of the
world.

I have chosen to appraise Helen Hayes as a noble person
rather than as an actress because her consummate artistry,
ranging from characterization depicted through the subtlest
gesture to comedy built upon exquisite timing and charm
is now accepted as the highest standard of our theatre. She
has transcended the limitations of the theatre. As Santayana
said: "The artist is a dreamer consenting to dream of the
actual world."

CHAPTER 58

Sol Bloom

ON HIS seventy-seventh birthday Sol Bloom is agile, cheerful and without a gray hair on his head. How does one explain the mysteries of youth preserved? There are two seas in Palestine. Both come from the Jordan and yet they are completely different. One is the Sea of Galilee, whose water is pure and fresh. Fish abound in it. Beautiful foliage adorns its banks. Brilliantly-hued birds hover over it. The other sea is the Dead Sea. Its water is stagnant. The air hangs heavy over it and birds shun its surface. Both seas come from the same river but the difference between them is that the Sea of Galilee permits its waters to flow out just as they flow in. The Dead Sea hoards every drop it receives.

People can be of two kinds, too. For every honor conferred upon Sol Bloom, for every authority vested in him, he has poured forth in equal or larger measure kindliness, generosity and service. So he remains fresh, pure in spirit and youthful despite his years. Although he was cast by events to be the legislative agent of the immortal Roosevelt during the days when the arms embargo was being lifted, the Selective Service Act was being passed and other historic measures were being taken which enabled the United States to pass through the holocaust safely, that is not what Sol Bloom is distinguished for. It is the simple quality of kindliness expended lavishly on thousands of individuals which has endeared him to so many people. His is the statesmanship of the "little favor" rendered honorably and with compassion for those in need. On such generous acts he has built a monument of good will.

CHAPTER 59

Franklin D. Roosevelt *

THOSE TERRIBLE WORDS, "Roosevelt is
dead." They are sharp words with piercing edges. They stab
the heart. They cause numbness and disbelief. His voice,
it will never spill music over us again. His smile, it will
never warm us with its radiance. Our shock dissolves into
tears. We cry unashamedly. Not for our Commander-in-
Chief; not even for our President. For him we would have
only deep sorrow. We cry for our personal friend, for a near
and dear member of our family; that is what he was to each
of us.

And then we see his noble widow emerging even greater
in her tragic grandeur. There she stands at the grave clutch-
ing the flag which has been taken from his coffin as it is
lowered forever underground. When the military ceremony
is over and everyone has gone, she returns alone to stand
over the grave in a long, silent and final farewell. We stand
with her, all of us. Prayers emanate from our hearts for him
and for her.

Throughout the war, homes had been darkened here and
there by news that henceforth a gold star must substitute for
the presence of some beloved son. But now our whole nation
is suddenly old with grief. We have all lost a father and
America has lost its greatest son.

It is a national tragedy. But of what nation? Not only
America but England also sorrows in equal measure. Its

* This was written a few days after his passing. It attempts to record the
wave of sorrow which inundated the world and evoked an emotional evaluation undiluted by the passage of time.

Such an appraisal may be a contribution to the more objective judgments
which future historians will render.

humblest worker and its heroic Prime Minister sob for England's loss. They have recognized the greatest of English characteristics in this American, unconquerable persistence and love of liberty. Gratitude is the memory of the heart. And England's heart is filled with memories of her rescue by him who loved liberty. The people of England know that adversity is sometimes the rain of spring. A merciful rain fell upon them in their most desperate hour and now a harvest of friendship and love for our President—yes, for their President, too—makes them equal mourners.

And in France the simple farmer leaves his plow untouched. He sits with bowed head in his liberated home, sharing with his wife and hushed children this new loss for France. They admired the great French qualities of the President, his gaiety akin to courage and his graciousness akin to humaneness. Joy and courage make a handsome face, and what artist would have conceived a nobler one? It bore grim determination highlighted by wit and made forever young by enthusiasm. The heart of France is heavy and tears consecrate his memory. The French people, too, have lost a President.

And over the vast plains of Russia a winter of grief suddenly envelops the people. Millions of peasants and workers bow in despair before their great loss. They understood the President's indomitable will in overcoming disaster. They understood his leadership which encompassed military gifts as well as statecraft. These were Russian qualities and, since he embodied them, he was one of them. Not the learned, but the one who suffers most, is wise. He knew suffering and he worked that others might never have to endure all that they could learn to bear. He knew how to turn helplessness into hope. He infused the world with his spirit. He, who could not stand, raised a stricken America to her feet in 1933 and a shattered Europe to her feet in 1944. The Russian soul is draped in black. Russia has lost a President, too.

And so has China. Word spreads to the farthest corner of that ancient land that the great American has slept away. In millions of families there is the painful silence of personal tragedy. The Chinese understood and recognized the great man's endless patience. It is the philosophy of their ancestors. Patience, in time the grass becomes milk. They understood his simplicity. They knew that a truly great man never puts away the simplicity of a child. He was their idol, their friend. Yes, their President, too.

For the first time, all the peoples of the world are united in sorrow. Never before has the death of a statesman of one nation been so profoundly and intimately felt by all civilized nations. It is a new phenomenon in international relationship. His life was a bond of amity among the nations of the world. It was a triumph of personality which exceeded any in the history of statesmanship. He stormed the ramparts of national suspicion and transferred them into faith. Faith in humanity. Faith in neighborliness. Faith in one another. Faith in peace. The international structure to be built is a great mechanical adventure. He created the spirit which impels the builders. He inspired the people of the world to demand its successful consummation.

There are many echoes in the world, but few voices. His was the great voice of mankind. He will stand alone like some peak that has no fellow in the mountain range of greatness. He believed in deeds, not years; in thoughts, not breaths; in feelings, not figures. He counted time in heart throbs. One can say of him what Stanton said about Lincoln at the moment of his death, "Now he belongs to the ages; to all those who love strength, simplicity, gentleness and an unswerving devotion to a high cause."

This is our comfort. In this realization our burdened hearts will be joyous again. For in saying farewell to our President, we know that the ages will welcome him. Their peace will be his lasting monument. Its inscription will be written in the hearts of millions yet unborn: "To Franklin Delano Roosevelt, first citizen of the world."

CHAPTER 60

Albert Einstein

PROFESSOR EINSTEIN is not only the creator of the general theory of relativity. He developed the formula for Brownian motion, a phenomenon which revealed to physicists in the nineteenth century that even though an object is in equilibrium, its molecules are in constant unrest. He is also the discoverer of the law of photo-electric effect which has been used in the development of modern X-ray technique, the ultra-violet ray and the photo-electric cell. He developed Planck's quantum theory and first stated the general field theory which unified the mathematical concepts of electro-magnetism and gravitation. More recently he was a significant contributor to the freeing of atomic energy.

The question is often asked: "How is it that one who has devoted himself to such abstruse scientific subjects should have become one of the most popular figures in the world?" I suspect the answer is: One of the characteristics of genius is its power to light its own fire.

There are very few immortals in the world's history but they tower over their period. The wars which took place during their time are reduced to insignificance. Their fame transcends the turbulence of their day. Plato, Aristotle and Diogenes all lived in the same day. Diogenes, incidentally, had the great simplicity of Professor Einstein. It is said that when he saw a young child drink water with his cupped hands, he threw away the only utensil he had, a wooden bowl. Simplicity is often the mark of the great man who does not lose his child's heart. The wise man is like the ripening grain. The riper he grows, the more lowly he bends

his head. Do we remember today Plato, Aristotle and Diogenes or do we remember the silly wars of their day between
Persia and Greece?

The great Roman Empire was built by Caesar, the general.
Do we revere him, or Christ of that era? In the Middle Ages
there were many crusades. We wonder today of what use
they were. Do we remember Emperor Conrad III and Barba-
rossa, or do we remember St. Francis of Assisi, St. Thomas
Aquinas and Roger Bacon? Loyola and Torquemada wrote
their names in blood during the Spanish Inquisition. Do we
remember them, or Leonardo da Vinci and Copernicus of
that era? Sir Isaac Newton gained immortality in the seventeenth century. How many of us remember him and how
many of us remember the Great Rebellion or the terrible
civil wars in England and Scotland? Galileo and Shakespeare
were both born in the same year. Do we remember them,
or do we remember the Thirty Years' War which convulsed
the Continent during their lives? When we think of the
French Revolution do we remember with affection Marat,
Danton and Robespierre, or do we remember the philosophers Rousseau and Montesquieu?

And so, though it may seem extraordinary today to say so,
the two world wars through which this generation has
passed may to future historians be merely two more cataclysms in the process of mankind's evolution. But towering
above this century will be the majestic figure of Albert
Einstein. He will not pass into eternity for he is already
part of it.

PART IV

Looking Out the Window

CHAPTER 61

We Have No Alternative

ORDINARILY, I WOULD deem it my first duty to disavow the general compliments, and the obituary, which have just been read about me. I shall not do so, however, because your Chairman has such a fine reputation for accuracy that I would not insult him by suggesting that anything he said about me was not precisely true. Indeed, he also has a reputation for understatement. If I were hard pressed, I might confess to you that if it were not for that frailty he would have done me more justice.

It is good, on an evening like this, to share the dais with so many judges. In France, the identity of the lawyer is preserved by his costume. The French lawyer wears a gown with a red velvet collar. In England, the barrister wears a wig. In this country, democracy has denuded us, and we do not wear a gown or a wig, although we are sometimes permitted to wear our masks.

In any event, it is good on such an evening to catch the judges with their robes off; it gives us an external appearance of equality.

When you invited me to address you this evening, I had thought it was to be a meeting only of the members of the Bronx Bar Association and, therefore, I intended to address you on a subject of technical professional interest.

Then, I learned that this was to be a social gathering; indeed, as I now know, preceded by a cocktail party designed, I suppose, to dull the razor-sharp brains of many counsel here. I also learned that it would be an occasion which was to be graced by beauty other than that which can be found in a legal syllogism.

Therefore, I decided it would be wrong to talk shop, just as if you had a lady speaker—it would be wrong for her to talk shopping.

Instead, I choose this opportunity to address you on a subject which has pressed upon my mind, and is very dear to my heart. I hope you will find it appropriate, because it does involve the subject of international law. I assure you, though, it is a subject of profound interest to every person alive today, for it involves nothing less than the survival or extinction of the human race.

I do not like suspense, except in stories. When an associate of mine comes from the law court, I implore him to tell me the conclusion first, and then he can sit back and tell me, at great length, how he brilliantly bested his adversary. Therefore I shall state my conclusion first.

President Eisenhower should address the United Nations and propose a new Constitutional Convention to amend the Charter of the United Nations. Such procedure is authorized (United Nations Charter Section 109, Subdivision 3) at any time after ten years existence of the United Nations.

The calling of such a Convention to amend the Charter need be passed by only a majority of the Assembly, and seven members of the Security Council.

The objective would be to create an effective instrumentality for the preservation of world peace.

In making this proposal, I do not share the view of those who think that the United Nations is an impotent, helpless organization, which might mercifully be put to death.

On the contrary, to have a shelter where all the nations of the world can gather and listen to each other, and pass resolutions which at least have the moral grandeur of an international assembly meeting in democratic process, is the hope of the world. It is because, in our desperation, we reach forward to that hope and find it a mirage, that we must take steps to make it real.

In discussing this proposal, I shall drink heavily from the fountain of our Constitutional history. For there is a remarkably apt analogy of our own ineffective Constitution which was later revised to make it workable.

In 1776, when this country was founded, we drew the Articles of Confederation. They were so ineffectual that the Republic foundered. Eleven years later, in 1787, though there was no authority to do so, we called a Constitutional Convention. We transformed the Articles of Confederation into the Constitution as we know it today.

Notice even the similarity of the lapse of time—eleven years between 1776 and 1787—and it is eleven years since the United Nations Charter was drawn in 1945.

Why did the Articles of Confederation turn out to be inadequate? Chiefly because each of the thirteen States deemed itself to be an independent nation, and would not surrender its sovereignty to a Federal Government. Article II of the Articles of Confederation read: "Each state retains its sovereignty, freedom and independence."

This meant that the Federal Army was subordinated in effectiveness, to the State Militia. Massachusetts and other States had their own armies, while the Federal Army constituted only a token force. Notice the new United Nations token Army we have just founded for the Mid-East crises.

Under the Articles of Confederation, there was no effectual means to raise money. The Federal Government levied a tax of $8,000,000. Only $420,000 could be collected.

Congress consisted of one house, and each State had one vote, just as each country has one vote in the United Nations. Nine out of thirteen States had to assent to make possible a decision. This was equivalent to veto power.

Indeed, each State considered itself so much an independent sovereignty that it would not even yield to the Government the right to declare war or make peace. Georgia declared war on two Indian tribes, used its own Georgia army to win, and then made two peace treaties, ignoring the United States Government.

Four States—Maryland, New Jersey, Pennsylvania and Virginia entered into treaties with each other, without the consent of Congress.

Many States taxed imports across their borders. New York, for example, imposed a tariff on wood and cabbage which came from Connecticut.

There was no Federal Judiciary. There was no Supreme Court until 1787. When there was a dispute between the States, Congress would appoint a committee to determine it and, sometimes, the States would not even subject themselves to the jurisdiction of that Congressional Committee.

The result was that our Federal currency failed, our laws were unenforceable, and there was chaos in our Republic. This great and noble experiment in modern democracy almost collapsed during the first ten years of its existence.

When John Shay, a hero of the Revolutionary War, led an army in revolt, due to the desperate condition of farmers and debtors, the time had come for some radical measures.

Alexander Hamilton, practicing deception, got together the representatives of the thirteen States on the theory that they would make some minor amendments to the Articles of Confederation. Previously, in 1785, he tried to convene them, but only five States agreed to attend.

Then it was that out of a cauldron of fierce debate, resistance, and compromise the Constitution of the United States emerged.

What were the changes of the Articles of Confederation which transformed it, eleven years later, into the Constitution? As we analyze them, keep an eye on the present situation in the United Nations, because the parallel is striking.

First, we made possible, through effective taxation, the maintenance of a Federal Army to enforce the edicts of the Federal Government.

We changed the voting, so that representation was based on population. But we created a bicameral Legislature so that, in the Senate, each State would still have an equal vote with any other.

Finally, we created the United States Supreme Court over such protests as that of Mason, the delegate from Georgia,

WE HAVE NO ALTERNATIVE

who said: "I will not permit a foreigner from New York to determine the rights of the sovereign State of Georgia."

We think of our Constitution as an inspired work designed by great minds. So it is, but those who drafted it had misgivings, for they were compelled, by fierce opposition, to compromise their convictions.

Patrick Henry is often quoted, approvingly, for "Give me liberty or give me death," but listen to him, as the delegate from Virginia, oppose the Constitution: "I would rather infinitely have a king, lords and commons, than a government so replete with such insupportable edicts."

A Delaware delegate said: "We are told that although three large States form a majority of the people in the thirteen, yet these three States will never do any harm to the rest of the States. Gentlemen, I do not believe you."

Jefferson said about the Constitution: "There are, indeed, some faults which revolted me a good deal in the first moment, but we must be contented to travel on toward perfection step by step."

The delegate from South Carolina said: "What is liberty? The power of governing yourself. If you adopt this Constitution, have you this power? No. You give it into the hands of a set of men who live one thousand miles distant from you."

There were also predictions that the Federal capitol "would be a walled or fortified town with an enormous standing army to sally forth and reduce the people to submission."

Yet the new Constitution was adopted and, from a faltering Republic, a steady and powerful nation emerged.

How shall we now amend the United Nations Charter to transform an ineffectual symbol into the reality of international power.

First, the veto must be abolished.

Russia is guilty of many, many iniquities, and Communism is the shortest distance between the cradle and the grave, but let us not blame the existence of the veto upon

Russia. The truth is that the United States, as well as Russia, had to have the veto. Without it the Senate would not permit us to join the United Nations and "surrender our sovereignty" to foreign powers.

We did not join the League of Nations because of Article XIII, which was deemed to impinge upon our sovereignty. President Roosevelt, mindful of that experience, took the precaution of designing the veto, so he could say to the United States Senate: "You are not surrendering your power; you can always veto a decision which you, in your sovereign powers, deem should not be made." Thus, we were lured into the United Nations. But the time has come to eliminate the veto, which immobilizes any effective action. How, for example, could any judicial system operate if the losing litigant could veto a decision rendered against him? We can no longer permit the paralysis which the veto imposes on international conduct.

We might realistically take a new look at the outmoded notion of sovereignty. Sovereignty means free and independent choice of action. Have we real sovereignty with respect to taxation, or is it determined by Russian policy, and the necessities for defense? Have we real sovereignty with respect to our domestic program, or is it determined by what happens in the world about us, over which we have no control? Is it not true that sovereignty can actually be enlarged by each nation diminishing the extreme concept of its sovereign rights, and pooling it for the common good? The greatest sovereignty of all is that of the human being. We speak of the rights of nations, but who speaks for man, and his self-preservation?

The Charter of the United Nations should be amended so as to excise the veto, and subject all Nations to the will of the world assembly. Only in this way can sovereignty be preserved at all.

Second, we must amend the Charter so that voting power will be more representative. Today, twenty South American nations, representing seven per cent of the population of the United States, control forty per cent of the votes in Assembly. Russian satellites carry an artificial voting power. In dealing with Mid-Eastern crises, 24 Afro-Asian votes can defeat any resolution which requires a two-thirds assent.

I have no precise blueprint to submit on this difficult question, but let me suggest a few thoughts to stimulate a solution.

Would it not be wiser to have voting power which reflects four combined and weighted elements—population, industrial output, food production, literacy and education?

Such a yardstick for voting would more realistically measure the size and power of each nation.

To those idealists who believe that raw power should not be afforded so much consideration, I would commend Churchill's statement: "Only if you make a political organization which has an alignment between the reality of power and politics can you achieve an ideal ultimately . . . We may deplore, if we choose, that there is a difference between the strong and the weak in the world, but there is undoubtedly such a difference, and it would be foolish to upset such arrangements in order to try to attain immediately what is a hopeless ideal."

Third, we must create an International Supreme Court with power to enforce its edicts. The judges should be chosen as were those of the International Court of 1921; each country nominated one of its own nationals, and two from other countries. National partisanship was thus reduced to a minimum. This device had all the ingenuity which is attributed to the Greek generals who, after their victory over the Persians at Salamis, voted to select the best among them. Each general voted for himself, but each chose Themistocles as the second best. It was he who was declared the winner. It is possible to establish a tradition of impartiality, freed from national bias, just as we have achieved such a tradition in the United States Supreme Court, notwithstanding the dire prediction of State prejudice.

Finally, we must create a United Nations military force to implement its decisions.

There have been many cogent proposals for a world army. I submit only one: That each nation give twenty per cent of its military power to the United Nations, and the collective twenty per cents would be greater than any country's individual army.

The by-products of such an international military body would be to encourage genuine disarmament among the individual member states. We would not have to resort to such circuitous plans as air inspection—Russian planes flying over America, and American planes flying over Russia. On the contrary, United Nations representatives would have free access to all countries of the world, to every city, nook and cranny of them.

Would Russia continue to belong to a United Nations which had been so revised? The probability is she would. Self interest, rather than good faith, might compel her to. For Russia has always wished to be in contact with world opinion. She has always respected military and political power. Russia may want one world which is divided, but she does not want two worlds. I think she would fear to be outside the pale of international justice as organized in the United Nations.

However, let us suppose that Russia, and her satellites, chose to quit a veto-less United Nations. Would we be worse off?

Let us make a few comparisons of power:

The United States and the United Nations would have a production of 165,000,000 tons of steel, as against 50,000,000 tons for Russia, and her satellites;

$690,000,000,000 of gross national products, against $155,000,000,000 for Russia.

323,000,000 tons of oil production, against 68,000,000 tons.

58 percent of the world's total power consumption, against 19 per cent.

Our farmers are five times as productive, per man, as Russia's and her satellites'.

Our rate of increase of surviving population is twice as great as Russia's and her satellites'.

Another advantage to the free world would be that our military position would be improved by the cooperation of all members in the United Nations against any non-members. No longer would it be necessary for us to implore distant countries to afford us bases or sell our soul for such privileges. The United Nations would have the right to call upon every nation to make available sites for United Nations bases.

Even if Russia and her satellites withdrew from the United Nations, the possibilities of peace would be better than they are today.

I come, then, to the final inquiry: Is it possible to achieve this "Utopian" scheme, as many will call it? Shall we yield to the cynicism that one cannot hope to organize international society to stop war, because, by precedent, nations have always had war?

The answer—and I ask you to note it deeply in your hearts —is that we have no alternative. We have no alternative!

The peoples of the world are not fully informed concerning the power of annihilation which now exists. The bomb at Nagasaki had 20,000 tons of T.N.T. power, and today there are hydrogen bombs of 10,000,000 tons of T.N.T. power. Indeed, we have had to coin the word megaton to measure a million tons of T.N.T. power.

The fallout destruction of one such ten megaton bomb could extend to 100,000 square miles—twice the area of the State of New York.

We have no alternative!

We have now learned how to make hydrogen bombs of limitless power because we case them in U-238, a uranium isotope easily created.

Scientists now tell us we can combine a hydrogen bomb with cobalt, a common ingredient available cheaply which has the characteristic of becoming radioactive, and floating for long periods in the air currents, until it descends to lay waste to vast areas. Indeed, it is no longer an imaginary concept, that we could destroy not only all human life on this earth, but every insect, invisible microbe and every blade of grass and vegetation.

We have no alternative!

Even hydrogen bombs give only a glimpse of the potential horror! It is now possible to wage biological or germ warfare. Without use of intercontinental missles an enemy can destroy, selectively, the complete cattle or wheat supply of another nation, not to talk of the human supply of any nation.

Even this is only the beginning of the obliterating power which now exists. There are the "G" gases, nerve gases, which can destroy anything they touch, in forty-five seconds, and they are invisible and unstoppable. One of our allies shunned possession of these gases after the last war ended and sank them in the middle of the Atlantic.

We have no alternative!

Perhaps the rules of physics which threaten our destruction may also teach us how to survive. In releasing the energy from atoms, we have progressed from fission to fusion. Atom bombs split the larger atoms. This process is fission.

Hydrogen bombs, which use the atom bomb as a detonator, force together the smaller atoms of hydrogen so that they join together to become larger and larger. This process is fusion.

Perhaps this foretells the destiny of the world. For centuries we have proceeded by fission, splitting the Adams of the world into different countries. The power released from this fission has been hatred and war.

Now, we must turn to fusion—the joining together of the Adams of the world, into a larger unity, into an international society. The power released from such fusion could be beneficial. If the United States could have rid itself of the burden of three hundred billion dollars spent in the last ten years for destructive and defensive armaments, and a current average expenditure of thirty-five billion dollars each year for the same purposes, what glories could be achieved.

We could build medical centers, the size of cities, to eradicate the scourges of mankind: cancer, heart disease and high blood pressure.

We could organize psychiatric clinics in all the cities of the nation, so that, instead of having one child psychologist for every forty-six thousand school children, as we have today in a few of our cities, we could provide adequate care for all emotionally disturbed children. We could wage war successfully against juvenile delinquency.

We could apply all the new techniques for healing the mind, so that we would no longer have one out of every ten Americans at some time or other occupying a bed in a mental hospital.

We could build geriatic institutions to study the aging process, and provide dignified and serene surroundings for the aged, so that they would live out their lives, rather than die out their lives.

We could construct an adequate and completely new educational system, both in bricks and mortar and in teaching personnel, adequate to the needs of a new society.

We could offer subsidies to all gifted children, so that they could follow careers in the arts, whether music, painting or writing and thus develop to the full potential the genius of our youth.

We could give subsidies to scientifically inclined children, so as to create a new class of physicists and engineers to usher in the new era of atomic energy and automation and, similarly, a new and adequate group of doctors, nurses and psychiatrists.

We could construct new housing for all classifications of income, with installations of the new miracles of science to control light, temperature and entertainment facilities.

We could do all this, and have billions left over to balance our budget.

Yes, we could create a veritable Paradise on earth.

We have no alternative!

I cannot believe that the destiny of mankind is international suicide.

If you will look at the map of the world, you will see that the bulge of Africa and the bulge of South America fit together. Apparently, they were once one continent. Perhaps what tore them apart millions of years ago was the same power which man has discovered today.

Shall nihilism be our unseen epitaph? Shall we look backward and say peace cannot be won because it has never been more than a temporary interlude? If we look backward, we will move backward. Nothing is inevitable that is resisted. Mankind faces the greatest of all dilemmas, the most fearful of all challenges, the most sublime of all choices. Will we end the story of man, in one final, suicidal holocaust which obliterates all living things and, perhaps, the planet itself? Or will we vindicate the evolution of reason and erect a peaceful society, blessed with the joys of noblest fulfillment?

It is a moment for religious evocation. Isaiah prophesied that "Nation shall not lift up sword against nation, neither shall they learn war any more."

Perhaps an allegory points the way:

The master of the library was asleep, and the books in the library took to quarreling with one another as to which was the most important in the library. The dictionary argued that he was the king of the library for, without him, there would be no language. The book of science said that he was the king of the library, because without him man could not have progressed to the heights he now enjoys. The book of poetry said he was the king, because he gave peace and surcease to people who read him. The novels claimed that they were the masters, because they had the most expensive gold backing, and described the foibles and joys of mankind.

And so, the din rose, and the fury of argument grew greater and the shouts and noise were deafening.

Then, from an old worn book on a table in the center of the room, there came a thin voice which said: "The Lord is my Shepherd; I shall not want." All the noise and fury ceased. There was silence in the library, for everyone knew who the real King of the library was.

We have reached the stage in international affairs where, despite all the din, contentiousness, confusion, and threats, we must resort to the one hope that there is a true Master of the world, and that He has decreed for us a fate of peace and existence.

CHAPTER 62

The Nuremberg Verdict—An Appraisal

OF THE MILLIONS of Germans who had a direct hand in the slaughter of thirty million human beings, only twenty-two were tried in Nuremberg. Only twelve of these were condemned to die. The words "guilty as charged" for these twelve defendants were an echo of a judgment rendered years ago by all mankind against all twenty-two defendants and against millions of other Germans. This was a verdict uttered by men in their hearts, wherever they happened to live, whether in a town in western United States or in a village in Korea, and whatever they toiled at, whether pressing pedals on a monotonous machine in some huge factory or coaxing oxen over a dried road in India. It was a verdict rendered by every rectangle of ground which contained a skeleton of a man who could still have been living, of a woman who could still have been enriching life, of a child who could have been maturing to fulfill its future.

The verdict at Nuremberg is an echo, long delayed. Radio waves rush around the globe seven times in one second, but man's moral pronouncements are still ground slowly through a mill. There is something leisurely about such a delayed verdict which is in itself infuriating. The crimes were too great to have permitted such protracted and calm procedure. Formalism became enthroned and we lost the most precious ingredient of law, righteous indignation. When one is so fair to men who have killed thirty million people, he is automatically unfair to their victims and survivors. The choice is not between law and lawlessness. It is between swift, inexorable punishment and slow, self-defeating formalism; it is between justice and procedure.

With maddening "correctness" we granted the Nazi leaders nine months of comfortable life. They were shaved and cleaned daily by soldier valets. Their food was good, much better than that of Jews in displaced persons' camps. The prisoners sat before a great tribunal enjoying the attention of mighty nations making speeches about them, drinking in with deep draughts of satisfaction the constant photographing and polite interviewing which they "granted." They thrilled to the ceremony which permitted them to address the world as though they were cosmic figures rather than depraved men. They variously proclaimed their innocence, their patriotism and their lack of responsibility, creating even for a moment the illusion of martyrdom in their own minds and perhaps in others. Those who were ill or dope-ridden, like Goering, were cured by good doctors. They chuckled and laughed joyously at humorous incidents during the trial. They constituted their own claque, applauding one another's testimony and ceremoniously congratulating one another upon some skilful evasion or retort while under cross-examination. They pretended to the last that they were only the victims of their conquerors, not criminals being punished by society.

Several of them were acquitted and given freedom. Even the opinion of the court which freed them pointed to their guilt. The judges wrote that Von Papen helped "Hitler to form the coalition cabinet and aided in his appointment as Chancellor. From January 30, 1933, as Vice Chancellor in that cabinet, he participated in the Nazi consolidation of control in 1933." The opinion goes on to condemn Von Papen before freeing him. It states that, after the assassination of Dollfuss, Von Papen was sent to Austria and Hitler assured him of his "complete and unlimited confidence. As

Minister to Austria, Von Papen was active in trying to strengthen the position of the Nazi party in Austria for the purpose of bringing about Anschluss."

The following passages from the opinion would lead one to expect that Von Papen was going to be found guilty: "Von Papen was involved in occasional Nazi political demonstrations, supported Nazi propaganda activities and submitted detailed reports on the activities of the Nazi party and routine reports relating to Austrian military defenses." The court found that it was Von Papen who had arranged the conference at Berchtesgaden between Schuschnigg and Hitler "and at its conclusion advised Schuschnigg to comply with Hitler's demands. . . . Von Papen was in the Chancellery on March 11 when the occupation of Austria was ordered." Yet he was acquitted!

Similarly incredible is the portion of the opinion of the court which condemns Schacht while acquitting him. For example, the court said, "Schacht was an active supporter of the Nazi party before its succession to power on January 13, 1933, and supported the appointment of Hitler to the post of Chancellor. After that date he played an important role in the vigorous rearmament program which was adopted, using the proceeds of the Reichsbank to the fullest extent in the German rearmament effort." He is also condemned for having been "active in organizing the Germans' economy for war. He made detailed plans for the coordination of the Army with industry in the event of war."

The court also found, "On May 3, 1935, he (Schacht) sent a memorandum to Hitler stating that the accomplishment of the armament program was the great problem of German politics, and that everything else would be subordinated to this." Nevertheless the court claims that the rearmament was not in Schacht's opinion "part of the Nazi plan to wage aggressive war." Is it conceivable that Schacht as president of the Reichsbank and a member of the cabinet associating with all the other conspirators did not know that Hitler was interested in offense, not defense? Can world opinion be expected to be so naive as to respect such refined conclusions about a man who made possible the launching of the war? What would the American boys who perished in this war say if they were alive and knew that Schacht was acquitted on such technicalities?

Even more offensive is the acquittal of Hitler's cabinet and general staff. If the cabinet as an organization was innocent of conspiring to wage war, then so was Hitler. Aside from the voluminous evidence at Nuremberg, anyone who knows anything about German military history knows that its general staff is composed of Junkers and pan-Germans who have constantly plotted the conquest of the world.

Swift and certain punishment is the surest deterrent to potential criminals. This rule of penology should have been applied in the international realm. Its impact would have been great upon any future dreams of world conquest. Also, the living are to be considered as well as the unborn. Our dislocated generation must know that its sacrifices are not regarded of less weight than the formalities of a trial. The conscience of mankind is instinctively true and it knows that not even death or, if we were capable of it, torture, would be adequate punishment for these men. Ought we not at least to have satisfied that conscience by a speedy disposition of the matter, as if to say that we could not waste more than a moment upon such base men? Many a lowly spy has been thus summarily blotted out. Were these evil men entitled to more?

There is a legal precedent for punishing "rulers" without trial. Napoleon was not tried. By treaty among the conquering nations he was declared an enemy of society and banished to St. Helena. Would it not have been better to have brought these twenty-two evil men before military tribunals for identification only and summarily executed them within twenty-four hours after they were apprehended? Later we could have issued an official report of the incriminating documents found in German archives, supplemented by affidavits and depositions, and we could have thus established a formal, authentic record of the greatest crime in all history.

The defendants violated the rules of warfare set up at the Hague and Geneva conventions. Consequently they were proper subjects for instantaneous military justice. The victorious nations chose instead the method of trial before an international tribunal. The yawning inattentiveness with which the people of all nations greeted the gruesome revelations is significant. It is a measure not of their boredom but of their impatience. It is as if the common man was saying, "We know what you are, so let's get this formality over with. Maybe it is necessary for history to go through this ritual, but we're sick and tired of you and don't care very much what your alibis are."

However, had the defendants been hung swiftly pursuant to orders of a military tribunal and thereafter had the evidence of their incredible iniquity been confirmed by German records, the revelations would have had enormous impact. In attempting to dramatize the event through an international trial, we undramatized the issue. For sincerity is an essential of emotionalism and we know how unreal was our alleged impartiality in determining whether these defendants were guilty or innocent. We were forced into the position of the judge who announced, "I will reserve decision for two weeks to give consideration to the briefs and arguments, and then will decide for the plaintiff." In adopting this procedure we have stirred up a divisive dispute as to whether the trial itself was legal; whether it wasn't an *ex post facto* proceeding, so that, in some quarters, the defendants were actually being defended on the theory that they were victims of a "lynching." So legalism begets legalism until the central moral core which is the basis of law disappears from consideration.

However, having adopted the method of formal trial by international tribunal, it becomes important to defend it from its detractors and sweep away the confusion which surrounds its achievements. Almost all who decry the trial do so, not because they would prefer more effective punishment, but because they can see no legal authority for punishment at all. It is therefore essential to examine the basis of the verdict. All but three of the defendants were found guilty of (1) preparing and waging wars of aggression, (2) violating the rules of warfare established in international law, and/or (3) committing crimes against humanity. It should be noted that the first charge was based on the Kellogg-Briand Treaty, the charter of the League of Nations, and numerous other international commitments which had outlawed aggressive war. The second of these charges was founded on the Hague and Geneva conventions and treaties among nations which constitute the acknowledged body of international law.

Even if the court had been limited to orthodox and traditional offenses, the verdict would be fully justified under existing law. For example, the defendants were convicted for "genocide," which is but another name for the oldest capital offense, murder. The fact that the murder was on a mass scale should not confuse us as to the nature of the crime. It was still simply murder. It differs from other vile murders only in quantity, not quality. Have we become so calloused to German atrocity that we fail to recognize genocide as common murder? Need we search for laws under which such crimes can be punished? I cannot recognize the quest for precedent or authority as anything but moral astigmatism.

Even if no treaty or convention had previously condemned these acts, the convictions would be valid. The *ex post facto* argument runs to the effect that one can not be found guilty of a crime which was not a crime at the time it was committed. This argument does not apply here, for there are laws by custom as well as by statute and treaty. Indeed, some of the most elementary crimes have never been reduced to formal international statement. Piracy was considered a crime long before there was a treaty on the subject. Preying on another's shipping was simply deemed larceny on the seas by universal custom just as thievery on land was considered a crime long before it was reduced to a statutory prohibition. For that matter, all major crimes in our penal

statutes were outlawed by custom long before they were outlawed by statute. The common law was based upon experience and tradition. Laws are the crystallization of customs.

Society need not go unprotected because a precedent is
lacking. At one time or other there was no precedent for any
punishment. Then society was guided by morality to establish precedent. There is a common-sense view of the use of
precedents which should prevail. It is wise to profit from the
experience of the past, but we must not be enslaved by
precedent when conditions have changed. Nor need we be
stymied by the lack of precedent, for similar situations may
not have confronted our ancestors. Law is dynamic. It grows
and changes as circumstances change. No other generation
has suffered two world wars within a period of twenty-five
years. Never before was it possible to strike over so wide an
area in surprise attack or to kill so many, destroying cities
as well as soldiers. Now we are confronted with new weapons
so terrible that they can annihilate in one fell swoop most of
mankind and all that it has built over the centuries. Should
we have paused in our efforts to prevent such a catastrophe
because there was no precedent? There was no other choice
but to pierce the veil of sovereign rights and to warn all
future aggressors that plotting and waging aggressive war
will be punished as common murder under international
law.

More than this, precedent has now been established (so
that none in the future will carp on the subject) for the
collective guilt of organizations which execute the illegal
orders of the leaders. There were millions in the Gestapo,
SD and SS. The Political Leadership Corps had a membership of one to two million. The Gestapo, SD and SS were
declared criminal. They were held to be guilty of conspiracy
against peace, waging aggressive warfare, committing war
crimes and crimes against humanity. This verdict does not
automatically establish the guilt of each member of the organizations. It merely creates a presumption of guilt which
must be overcome. The individual defendant cannot chal-

lenge the decision against the organization. The sole question is the extent of his participation in it, in order to determine the degree of his guilt. This leaves wide discretion in the courts.

The tendency to forgive and forget is growing stronger with each passing day. For one thing, our vigilance is decreasing. We are the victims of the bribery of boredom. For another, the duel between Russia and her western allies is preoccupying minds which might be used for better purpose. Already an "amnesty" has been declared for all in the Hitler youth movement and "small" Nazis. The great danger is that the Nuremberg convictions may draw the lightning away from hundreds of thousands of criminals who may never be tried.

At the end of the first World War there was the same hue and cry for the punishment of war criminals. After several years of procrastination, the original list of fifteen hundred war criminals, a trifling number, dwindled to fourteen. Of these only four were convicted and received inconsequential sentences. For all practical purposes it may be said that none of the hundreds of thousands of war criminals were punished. This time we have not left the matter to the courts of a German republic. But it is still a grave question whether the hundreds of thousands of young Nazis who killed millions of people illegally and who may constitute the nucleus for the next German aggression will not go scot free. Indeed, it is already doubtful that the leaders of the economic division of the German conspiracy to wage war will ever be tried. Surely the acquittal of Schacht is inconsistent with any charge of guilt against lesser fry.

The directors of I. G. Farben and other industrial combines of Germany were not merely business men. They worked hand in hand with the German militarists to plan economic attack as part of war and to collect the loot as an agency of the armed forces. I have detailed elsewhere * their nefarious activities, their continuing conspiracy to prepare

* Louis Nizer, *What to Do with Germany*, pps. 110-132.

Germany for war, their control of strategic materials, their financing of fifth columns throughout the world, their scientific looting through the WIRÜ, and their fraudulent acquisition of Europe's leading properties through disguised companies.

The German high command, in anticipation of defeat, prepared for its third attempt at world conquest. By waging a biological war the Germans decimated Europe and preserved their own superiority in manpower. All of Europe except Germany has been enervated by deliberate starvation and suffering over a period of five years. Only Germany, despite her recent food stringency, is still strong and unregenerate. Germany remains a great menace and the deterrent effect of the Nuremberg trials will be insignificant if the millions of rabid Nazis who executed the terroristic policy of their convicted leaders and the "economic" war criminals are not brought to trial.

The significance of the Nuremberg convictions may therefore be summarized in four statements:

(1) The protracted, formalistic nature of the trial should have been avoided in favor of summary executions. The deterrent effect of the latter method would have been greater, and this method would have accorded better with the conscience of mankind. The record of German guilt for historical purposes could have been gathered and published independently.

(2) The acquittal of Von Papen, Schacht and Fritzsche, the high command, the cabinet, and the inadequate punishment of the other defendants who received mere prison terms are a shocking obeisance to technicalities. They do not demonstrate a sense of justice but rather a callousness to the enormity of the crimes and a willingness to give the "benefit of the doubt" to fiendish criminals who did not extend one whit of compassion toward millions of their victims. Such moral strength as could be derived from the judicial procedure was reduced to a minimum by the generosity extended to the defendants.

(3) The trial, however, established the valuable precedent that "sovereignty" and "obedience to command" will not constitute a defense for those who have committed war crimes.

(4) Most significant was the conviction of German organizations such as the SS and the Gestapo. The salutary effect of these convictions will depend, however, upon the vigorous prosecution of the hundreds of thousands of individuals who participated in the barbarous activities of these organizations.

The Nuremberg trial was a step in the direction of international cooperation and justice. It has established the principle that aggressive warfare is "the supreme crime" and that in dealing with it national sovereignty is superseded by international law. The trial, like all experiments, was a tentative and somewhat groping step. It we can hold the ground gained and move forward with sequential trials and convictions we may still protect international society from the persistent criminal tendencies of German aggression. Above all, we have taken a historic step on the judicial side toward world government, the only ultimate guaranty against national trial by combat.

CHAPTER 63

Emil Gets Away with Murder

A REMARKABLE international auction is taking place. The Russians have bid for German military support. Molotov, forgetting how the Germans tore the vitals out of Russian provinces, made a speech offering the Germans a high price for their support. England and the United States were alarmed. They bid higher for German favor. Byrnes flew to Stuttgart and, in a radio address listened to avidly by seventy million Germans, proposed a unified central government for Germany as soon as possible and economic assistance so that she could get on her feet. Both Russia and the western powers scorned France's request that the Ruhr be cut off from Germany so that the source of her military power would be removed. No, the Ruhr, supply center of coal and iron, must remain in the Reich. Germany's victims are ignored. Consideration of their economic distress is not high on the agenda. Germany must be won over by friendship. The auction has not yet been concluded. Russia will undoubtedly raise the bid.

Thirty million people laid down their lives to fend off the mighty attack of Germany, but in less than two years their sacrifices have been subordinated to the "necessity" of courting the enemy we finally defeated. Are we mad? Did we not once before go through this very same process with the identical parties and come out with another world war?

Perhaps the issue can be seen most clearly in the art form. Last year an eloquent play dealing with the German problem became a motion picture. Its title was *Tomorrow the World*. This picture is the measure of our clarity and also, alas, of our confusion. I should like to analyze the German problem through criticism of this play and movie.

Tomorrow the World presents the story of the perfidy of German youth. The power of dramatic presentation is used to reveal universal truth through an individual case. Emil, a twelve-year-old Nazi, becomes the symbol of the German people, particularly those fanatically trained in unscrupulousness. This child comes to live in a typical American home and his debased standards clash with everything around him. Until the last moment of the film the analysis of his conduct is brilliantly etched. The Nazi child is a laboratory demonstration of incorruptible corruption. He is cruel, cunning, mature, humorless, obscene, persistent, merciless, energetic, vile, defiant, aggressive, unscrupulous and fanatically sincere.

Above all, the film gives insight to the amoral code which motivates Emil's conduct. Since, as he believes, kindness is

weakness, he is unmoved by generous treatment. Since forgiveness is Christian decadence, his grotesque convictions
are confirmed when he is forgiven. Since tolerance is stupidity, he utilizes it in others so that he may practice
intolerance. Since moral right is irrelevant, he clubs a child
almost to death to achieve his objective by force. Since honor
is a false concept to protect the weak, he revels in breaking
his word. Since the end justifies the meanness, he cunningly
plays on the weakness or generosity of every character who
surrounds him.

Nothing is beyond him. Emil resorts to insult, libel,
thievery, spying, incitation of race hatred, and attempted
murder. He pretends to be reformed in order to obtain a
better opportunity to steal certain war plans. He is viciousness incarnate. He is fearless in all his machinations because
he believes it his mission to be tortured and to die so that
tomorrow Germany may rule the world!

Here is a solid revelation of the German problem. It is
pictured in all its horror and magnitude. It is not pretty, but
it is true. To a lesser or greater degree, Germans have for
generations been miseducated to these depraved standards.
This is why they have waged five wars in the last 87 years
and in the last 34 years have twice drenched the world in
blood and caused more wretchedness than any other bar-
barians in history.

Now we face the most fanatically trained youth of all
time, determined to slaughter us if we relax for a moment
because of sentiment or misguided confidence in their speedy
reformation. Yes, the Germans are preparing World War III
right now with all of the demoniacal efficiency with which
they prepared the Second World War. Once again they will
hold forth a so-called German Republic which we will install
while, behind the scenes, the pan-Germans, fully supported
by unregenerate masses, plot another attempt at world conquest. Once more there will be tears by German "democrats"
and pleas for help as a substitute for punishment.

What in the last thirty years has given us reason to hope

for a more sincere conversion this time by the German people? Even before Nazi fanaticism the Weimar Republic, through a freely elected Reichstag, met in open session and, in violation of the Versailles Treaty, voted to protect its war criminals and refused to surrender them to the Allies for trial. Wilson distinguished between the German government and its people, but the German people themselves wiped out this distinction. They ultimately succeeded in seeing to it that no war criminals were punished and elected one of them, Hindenburg, as President. They prepared the Second World War for the pan-Germans who were always in control because the people shared their aspirations.

Are we again to be taken in by a "German Republic" which is a mere form without the support of the genuine democratic convictions of the people themselves? The movie's answer is "yes," although it believes it is saying "no." After Emil has done his evil and has been captured, disarmed and subdued by a little unarmed Polish lad whom he has stabbed, he sheds a tear and is forgiven! The police are sent away. Instead of punishment, a friendly arm is placed around his shoulder by his uncle (whose little daughter still has seven stitches in her scalp from Emil's poker blows). He is taken into the family. Only a few minutes before this "conversion," the Nazi had threatened to run screaming into the little girl's sickroom, thus to frighten her to death. He even threatened to tell the police that her father, and not he, had beaten her. This had so enraged the father that he had seized Emil and almost choked him to death. But his Jewish sweetheart had intervened and preached the Christian doctrine of turning the other cheek. And the sight of a wrist watch, given to Emil as a gift by the child he had almost killed, brings on a hysterical outburst of repentance. He is then absolved from all his sins.

The ending violates the entire moral of the story. Either Emil's ingrained viciousness depicted during the whole length of the film is false, or the ending is false. Both can't be true. A child capable of such emotional response to a watch given him by his victim would not have previously struck her with an iron rod, especially when he knew she had arranged a birthday party for him. A child capable of gratitude would not have written obscene things on the sidewalk about his Jewish teacher who had shielded him with her kindness. A child who could respond to reverent reminders about his father would not have previously condemned his father as a coward and traitor to the Third Reich nor would he have plotted to steal the war documents of his uncle.

The fanatical viciousness of this German child is a fact. His sudden repentance is a theory. When a fact collides with a theory, that is a tragedy. And the world has suffered many tragedies because of the Germans. We have put our arms around them and accepted their "repentance" only to be stabbed in the back again and again. Can't we recognize that their tears after defeat are no more significant than the glycerine which flowed down Skippy Homeier's cheek? Of course there are thousands upon thousands of sincere Germans who are as horrified as we are by German bestiality. But they have always been ineffectual. They have never been able to prevent German aggression. Many of them were quite neutral when the loot was flooding into Germany and the air was filled with the pride of military achievement. In any event, these good Germans are in mortal danger from the rest of the Germans and their hope for salvation, like ours, lies in curbing the German menace. The good Germans would only defeat their purpose if they succeeded in shielding the German nation.

If the solution in *Tomorrow the World* were merely a Hollywood "happy ending" one might ignore it. Unfortunnately it is a symptom of our confused times. We are so stunned by mass unscrupulousness as a national policy that we lose our sense of values. We know what to do with one criminal, no matter how debased and incorrigible he may be. But when we are faced by millions of criminals acting in concert, we confuse justice with revenge, and reform with forgiveness.

It would be a new crime against the millions slaughtered by the Germans if the murderers were to go virtually scot free for fear that otherwise we might be guilty of taking revenge! It would be a monstrous offense to the millions of dislocated families all over the world, impoverished and miserable, if we sought to reform Germans by waiving punishment except for a trifling few. Above all, we would have upon our hands and conscience the blood of the next generation which would be spilled again by Germans scoffing at our generosity as weakness and plotting to set fire to our homes and to butcher us in human slaughter camps in their next march to the throne of "supermen."

I would like to add a reel to the movie. I could draw my text from the previous scenes. Once before the uncle shook hands with Emil in a solemn pact that henceforth the child would change his ways. Emil had even promised to read a book about his father's valor. As the uncle walked out of the door, Emil threw the book aside and rushed to the desk to pry open a drawer containing a war secret. As the movie ends, the family walks off with Emil, forgiven, in its midst. My added sequence would show Emil the next day cunningly exploiting the new confidence in him. He ultimately obtains a copy of his uncle's war document, kills his little cousin who detects him, and plants suspicion upon his Jewish teacher, now his aunt. The uncle, stricken with grief, and convinced that his wife's preachments had turned him from his original intention to turn Emil over to the police, blames her for the child's death. She, overwhelmed by the accusations against her from all sides, commits suicide. These are some of the probable consequences of Emil's actions. They signify a third World War if we forgive the German Emils and take them to our hearts!

What then shall we do with Emil? If Emil were American and had cracked a child's skull, we would not even pose the question. We would put him into a reform school, the nearest equivalent of a jail for minors. But such is our confusion on the German question that the ordinary laws for dangerous juvenile delinquents are considered inapplicable. Since Emil is German and an extreme case, he winds up without so much as a slap on the wrist. Even the Johnston Code, which requires that villains be punished, is relaxed for Emil's sake. The heroine brings on this result through her philosophizing. To put Emil in jail, she contends, would be an admission of *our* failure toward the whole German youth. This reasoning is so profoundly perverse and symptomatic of the soft peace argument that I pause to analyze it.

The first duty of society is to protect itself against the marauder. Perhaps the criminal's murderous tendencies are due to illness rather than innate wickedness, but the dead victim can derive no comfort from this fact. None of us is ready to submit a wife or a daughter to his repeated assaults because only illness motivates him. Our prison system and execution chambers may be archaic but until we learn a more effective system, all of us are resolved that the criminal must at least be isolated so that we do not suffer from his abnormalities. It is he who is deformed in character, not we. It is he, not we, who must bear the consequences.

But in dealing with the German problem, these elementary principles are discarded. There is a curious tendency among us to assume responsibility for Germany's misconduct. The distinction between our failure to restrain German aggression and her criminal aggressive urge becomes blurred. The result is that we substitute our guilt for hers. We no longer see the difference in degree which makes our "crime" a misdemeanor through negligence and hers, wilful and deliberate murder on a mass scale.

That is why one hears so much about *our* responsibility for having made loans to German industry and so little about German use of these moneys to prepare a war machine. From the other side of the street, we hear so much about *our* responsibility for starving German children after the last armistice and so little about the fact that this starved German generation grew up sturdy enough to withstand the rigors of sub-zero Russian weather and the boiling temperature of North Africa, where they went to kill and steal. That is why one hears so much about England's responsibility for turning German aggression in Russia's direction and so little about Germany's avaricious appetite which required that one victim or another should be devoured. That is why the crime of Munich is considered England's and France's while Germany becomes a mere accessory after the fact. Many authors and lecturers are so busy finding "deep" causes for the German outburst that they barely notice that they are blaming everybody but the Germans! As to the future, we already hear that if we are stern with the Germans *we* shall be responsible for the next Hitler.

Perhaps there is a psychiatric explanation for our absurd assumption of guilt. Like the mother who, being cursed with a criminal son, shields him by blaming herself for his shortcomings, so the family of nations, ashamed of its murderous son, seeks some frailty in itself to explain his barbarism. But we do not heed the pleas of the mother that her son is really good at heart and should not be confined in jail. We recognize her bias and place our concern for other peaceful citizens above our sympathy for her. Thus we must shun the German apologist who argues that once the Scandinavians, the Dutch and the French were aggressors and now they are peaceful nations. When Germany has proved by her conduct that she too will be law-abiding, we shall welcome her into the circle of repentant and reformed sinners.

But the evolutionary process which has raised nations above their warrior castes has not touched Germany. On the contrary, hers has been a retrogression in standards which has dragged us all back several centuries. We have not recently sent our sons to fight the Scandinavians or Napoleon. It is the German menace that is current and must be restrained. No theory about the prior guilt of others can assuage the wounds we suffered yesterday from the Germans. The only citation of history which is pertinent is that the Germans consider no defeat final. They are determined to

try again and again until they dominate the world. Who
knows but that next time they may actually blow out the
light of civilization and trample us all to death? It is suicidal
to risk the next generation by relying upon the sudden
"repentance" of the Germans. Who has yet heard any prominent German say, *"Mea culpa"*?

Our philosophy must not be the kind which disarms us
and bares our breast to the assassin. It must be strong enough
to protect us and be a living inspiration to us. The Emils
of the world must be made absolutely and irrevocably harmless. They must be disarmed economically as well as mili-
tarily so that they cannot construct a military machine when
our wariness has been relaxed. They must make restitution
by labor, money and goods for the devastation they caused.
They must be trusted with no government behind whose
facade of sovereignty they can claim immunities not otherwise available. When Oliver Cromwell first coined his
money, an old cavalier looked on one side of the coin and
read, "God is with us." On the other side he read, "The
Commonwealth of England." "I see," he said, "that God and
the Commonwealth are on different sides." Only when the
Germans have learned that God and the Reich must be on
one side, only when they have been educated by the realities
of defeat and our determination not to have victory dissolved under our still bleeding hands, only when they have
given evidence by *conduct* that their pagan ideologies have
been genuinely abandoned and they no longer believe that
"war is beautiful because it permits you to kill without passion," only when democracy has become accepted by the
German masses as a minimum concession to each man's
nobility and is not scorned as decadence—only then can we
accept the Germans back into the concert of nations as safe
citizens of the world

How old will Emil be then? The late Dr. Nicholas Murray
Butler thought at least twenty-five years older. Others think
sixty years. That is up to the Germans. If we do not relax

the reins of victory, at least we shall have a chance to grow older, too, and to die natural deaths.

In the meantime, it is necessary to record that we are permitting the Germans to transform defeat into victory.

We are proceeding on the false theory that it is essential to the reconstruction of Europe that German economy should once more dominate the continent. German interests have convinced Allied officials that to achieve this purpose it is essential to rebuild or protect Germany's heavy industries. Thus in the British zone, which contains the heart of Germany's industries, only seven per cent of the tank, aircraft, artillery and other factories deemed dangerous by Allied experts have been dismantled. Similarly, German steel production and large machine, tool, synthetic and coal-tar-dye industries have been preserved. The international steel cartel of Luxemburg, established and dominated by the Germans since 1926, is active again.

The Germans are shrewdly limiting their coal production to obtain their objectives. Germany's coal mines were not destroyed. According to British reports, only fifteen of one hundred and twenty large mines in the Ruhr were damaged and all were repaired by 1945. In peacetime Germany exported 45,000,000 tons of coal per year. If she could do so again, she would have an income of at least $750,000,000 per year which she could use to pay for foods and other imports and relieve the American, English or French taxpayers of paying reparations to the Germans, instead of the reverse.

At present Germany retains seventy-nine per cent of the coal produced in the Ruhr and only twenty-one per cent is sent to all her neighbors against dollar payment. The present German consumption of coal per capita per year is greater than in France. It is well known that the democracies in Western Europe could be quickly rehabilitated if they only had coal, yet the Germans have more than their victims and are withholding further production as a political and economic weapon against Germany's neighbors.

An analysis made by United States experts shows that Germany could have a decent level of industry on the basis of approximately 5,000,000 tons of steel per year. In March, 1946, the Allied Control Council decided to permit Germany a production of 5,800,000 tons of steel per year. Before Hitler came to power in 1932, Germany's annual consumption of steel for peacetime needs was about 4,000,000 tons. One would think that the allowance made to her was therefore generous. Nevertheless, tremendous pressure is being exerted to raise this figure to 10,000,000 or 12,000,000 tons per year.

We are sending to the Germans 300,000 tons of foodstuffs a month. Huge quantities of this food disappear into the German black market. We permit the Germans to sabotage food production and food deliveries. If we would adopt a policy of ordinary common sense and rebuild the liberated nations by delivering coal and other raw materials to them as Germany's reparations, there would be no need to rebuild Germany as a dominant power in Europe. By helping Germany first, we will make the war-torn countries of Europe economic satellites of Germany and we will lose the peace.

The most shocking phase of our distorted policy in Germany is the fact that we have placed many Nazi leaders in important economic posts. I mention some of them:

(1) Alfred Hugenberg was a member of Hitler's first cabinet and a heavy contributor to the Nazi party's funds. He remains active in the German steel cartel, is chairman of the board of Vereinigte Stahlwerke, the second largest steel combine in the world. When the British authorities were asked, on December 4, 1946, why they did not remove Hugenberg, they replied: "It takes a vote of the shareholders of the company to remove him as board chairman." Hugenberg remains at his post and is active in the rehabilitation of the German steel industry in the Ruhr.

(2) Dr. Ernst Poensgen is now seventy-seven years old and has been the spokesman for German heavy industry for more than thirty years. He was decorated by Hitler personally with

the title of Wehrwirtschaftsfuehrer. Although Poensgen was a member of the Nazi party, he was never punished, is now the head of the Vereinigte Stahlwerke and heads the reconstruction of Germany's war potential.

(3) Heinrich Dinkelbach is a notorious Nazi. He is now director of the iron and steel industry in the British zone. By virtue of his position, he succeeded in freeing twenty-seven of the thirty-one high officials of the Vereinigte Stahlwerke who were arrested as Nazis.

(4) Robert Pferdmenges was a notorious Nazi and collaborated with Baron von Schroeder, one of the most important Nazi economic leaders under Hitler. He is today a member of the new Germany Bi-Zonal Economic Council.

(5) Dr. Wolf Witzleben was a high official of the Siemens Electrical Trust, the largest in Germany. The Siemens company was instrumental in installing gas chambers and electrical devices in the Auschwitz and Buchenwald extermination camps. Witzelben is a prominent Nazi and was found guilty of war crimes by German denazification courts. Nevertheless, he is now active in the operation of the Siemens company in the four occupied zones of Germany.

(6) Johan Benkert is an engineer who assisted Witzleben in devising instruments of extermination in the German concentration camps. He, too, was convicted by the denazification courts but has been reinstated to his former post by the British authorities.

Many similar cases could be cited. This is sufficient to illustrate the way in which we have lost the path so dearly opened for us by hundreds of thousands of young men who vowed that this would be the last time the Germans would enslave other peoples. There can be only one explanation for our confusion. We wish to build a bulwark against expanding Russian tyranny. As one who does not underestimate the new Russian threat to liberty (I have analyzed it elsewhere in this book), I must point out that this motivation is no justification on grounds of principle or expediency.

Rather than argue the point, I shall be content with a simple question: Have we any assurance that if we build up Germany, she will not join with Russia against democratic nations everywhere?

PART V

Closing the Door

CHAPTER 64

The Fire

THE BEGINNING IS LIFE . . .

THE AIR was sharp as if it remembered its contact with ice on the Canadian Rockies. My shoulders were hunched to protect my neck from its shriveling impact. In the room was a brick fireplace which bore the honorable black scars of past activity. I decided to build a fire. I tore several sheets of newspaper into various sizes and shapes, crumpled them into spongy balls and set them carefully between the two iron posts which stood like soldier guards in front of a vacant square. Then from the handy bin I took several heavy pieces of bark wood and criss-crossed them over the paper. With hands sticky from the sap on the bark, I lit a match which, like a miniature log, turned blue and then spluttered into a tiny flame. I touched a protruding piece of paper. It hesitated and became black at the edge. Then, as though its eyes had opened, two little lights fluttered upward. The thin yellow spread suddenly to the center of the ball and a gay, almost whitish flame jumped upward. Its size was out of all proportion to the bit of thin pulp which it represented. For all its childish energy, the flame was weak and destined to be of short duration. The heavy wood above it seemed impervious to the attack. Disdainfully it remained thick and black while the flashy, feeble lights jumped toward it and, when repelled, turned sideways around it.

For several moments it was impossible to tell whether the paper's flame would suddenly shrink and expire, leaving the bark unharmed, or whether the bright yellow messengers

[285]

would find re-enforcements in the outer surface of the bark. There were wheezes, coughs and other infantile sounds. I slapped the back of the fire with a poker. The air rushed in with a desperate gasp. Then the doubt was resolved. The bark suddenly revealed tiny blue flames which flickered irregularly in all directions. The hushing sound of the paper's flames gave way to small crackling noises like ineffective firecrackers exploding weakly, while puffs of gray smoke floated upward and disappeared against the blackened brick background.

Then, as if to signal its first triumph, the stiff log emitted a flaming dagger of its own. Its light was deep yellow and it announced its ascension with a breath-sucking roar. The paper's flames danced happily underneath and gradually joined the stronger flame above, leaving behind, black with mourning, the charred, shriveled ball of paper from which they had sprung. Flames were beginning to swirl horizontally underneath the logs and their motion caused the flaky, burnt-out paper to quiver.

One end of the log was now enveloped in fire. Many tiny blue and orange flames ran busily back and forth across the log as though they were searching for a door into its center. The ridges on the bark made it look like a relief map and the burning added bright color to the map.

The noises kept pace with the growing activity. Sporadically a flame would break through a crevice with a windy snarl. Here and there little explosions added to the tumult and a tiny piece of wood would be shot into the iron screen which guarded the hearth. Flickering lights ran across a still resistant surface and then disappeared, only to venture out again and again with a soft licking sound. Occasionally a tiny blue flame would meet a sharp rebuff, turn suddenly into a wisp of smoke and bleed across the bark in gray streams. The sounds, colors and smells seemed to melt into one another, creating an indistinguishable impression of prancing sun-rays, gurgling breezes and fresh smoke perfumed with pine.

Soon the flames were raising their heads in every dark area of the arena. They joined hands beneath the logs and grew in strength from the common effort. Now they were vying with each other in height, first one and then the other jumping high. The logs became clothed with a shimmering coat of flowing fire. Sometimes the coat was transparent and the white surface of the wood could be seen, stained black where the sap was running over it to herald the approach of the fierce, consuming aggressor. Sometimes the coat was opaque, offering no window into the scene within.

The flames swerved in whirlpool circles at the bottom, as though recoiling for the upward spring, and turned blue with the effort. They assumed a consistent deep yellow color as they swept upward furiously, then curved, changing their shape from daggers into scythes and back again. Then they branched out prong-like in reindeer horns of fire.

The noises grew deeper and fiercer, like a howling wind. Then, accompanied by climactic roars, the flames leaped upward with orgiastic frenzy, higher and higher, gasping for breath—geysers of fire-spitting cinders blinding the eyes with heat and hysterical lights. Rocket-like, an arrow of fire sprang to the very top of the fireplace with such wild abandon that it dismembered itself from the main body and disappeared up the chimney with a savage crackle.

I threw a heavy log into the blaze. Ordinarily its weight would have crushed the fire. But now the flames, in the full strength of maturity, seized the huge obstacle in their eager arms, lit it with fiery kisses and made it the center of a new outburst of violent energy. The yellow waves danced wildly in reckless patterns, hissing, murmuring and then exploding with pistol-shot noises. They reached new dimensions, flowing swiftly into the chimney like a volcanic golden river rushing upwards in reverse motion. They turned invisible as they reached the screen and slid through in heat waves which undulated in accordance with the intensity of their visible comrades within. The entire fireplace became feverish with light. The room swayed and bent in its reflections.

The fire was contorting itself, now looking proudly beautiful in its vivid colors, now comical in grotesque designs, now patriotic, like a flag blowing in a strong breeze. But its brilliance, power and motion were hypnotic. I could not take my eyes from it. Here were tenderness, warmth and beauty vying in one cauldron with destruction, insatiable appetite and sheer ferocity.

Then, almost imperceptibly, the flames began to subside. They became more even in height, substituting the beauty of symmetry for the valor of abandon. The noises, too, diminished in scale. The basic sound was like that of a good motor, purring so evenly and softly that the ear had to make a special effort to detect it.

The fire seemed more steady and reliable now that its flames were not leaping recklessly to impossible heights. The tips of the flames were no longer thinned out to disappearing points. The flames were heavier on top as they huddled more conservatively at the base. But at the edge a protruding log would lose its light and seem to go to sleep, only to awake, yawning, a new flame implanted on it by the adjoining heat. Then for a moment this flame would leap higher than the others as though to demonstrate its revitalized vigor, but always it would curl up tired from the effort and the log would doze off again.

Stranger still was the behavior of the center of the fire. The straight spine of a sturdy log was curving and pieces of wood softly collapsed into the pit with swishing gasps of resignation. Proud, erect logs were shrinking and bending over.

But beneath them a new phenomenon was taking place. A new and celestial glow appeared. It gave forth no flames. It did not flicker or even move. Its color was a dazzling golden orange like that of a brilliant setting sun when it is low on the horizon. The embers formed an almost solid base of intense heat. The shavings, bark and disintegrating wood melted into it in a new unity and form, as though all the preceding processes had been designed for this ultimate achievement.

As the fiery lining of the logs dropped onto the embers, the orange light became blindingly golden. The yellow flames above flickered like protruding wicks. They seemed trivial and ineffectual as they shimmered above the embers. The remaining portion of the logs became black and corrugated silhouettes against the powerful light below. These surviving husks seemed pitiful for they no longer had their original strength nor had they achieved the magnificence and regal maturity of the embers.

The glowing base seemed to take on additional dimensions. Powerful rays were emerging from it mysteriously in fascinating combinations of color and light. Gone were the panicky flames. There were austerity and dignity in the quiet glow. But there was also reminiscence for a few of the still lingering flames above cast shadows on the wall and these cold and dark reflections were exaggerated in size and activity. They resembled the vigorous dancing flames which had prevailed when the fire was young.

Then suddenly the embers began to gray at the temples. The edges of the fire lost their color and turned ashen, as though the orange tints could not circulate to the extremities. Now there were no flames to multiply in number. Each recession of light and heat was final. The magical beauty of the embers' radiance disappeared and there was revealed a powdery mass of ashes, wrinkled with crevices. Soon the sickly gray ashes formed a semi-circle around the still incandescent center.

Darkness had crept downward from the top of the fireplace until it pervaded all but the last heart-throb of light. The blackness melted into the surviving orange tints to create mournful purple hues. The ashes lay in thin inanimate heaps. They were cold and gray. The last ember was turning pale pink. Then without warning it fluttered, turned blue for an instant, and expired. There was complete silence.

THE END IS DEATH . . .

Not till the fire is dying do we look for any kinship with the stars. I pondered what millions of others do when they pray, "What more is there between You and me?"